AF863410

edge Studies in Nineteenth-Century Philosophy

Scotch Metaphysics
ntury of Enlightenment
ge E. Davie

kegaard's Upbuilding ourses
sophy, Literature, and logy
ge Pattison

3 **Dialectics, Politics, and the Contemporary Value of Hegel's Practical Philosophy**
Andrew Buchwalter

4 **Hegel and Psychoanalysis**
A New Interpretation of Phenomenology of Spirit
Molly Macdonald

Hegel and Psychoanalysis

Both Hegel's philosophy and psychoanalytic theor
enced contemporary thought, but they are tradit
separate rather than intersecting universes. This bo
tation of Hegel's *Phenomenology of Spirit* and br
with the work of two of the best-known conter
Christopher Bolas and André Green. *Hegel and*
consideration of the *Phenomenology* on the figur
sciousness and the concept of Force, two areas that
studies which focus on the master/slave dialectic.
for why now, more than ever, we need to recogniz
subjectivity, Force, the third, and binding are essen
of our modern world. Such concepts can allow for
can be seen as the profoundly false and construct
and friendship created by social networking sites,
"global community," which thrives at the expense
tive relations.

Molly Macdonald is Lecturer in Literary Theory at
of London, United Kingdom.

Rou

1 Th
A (
Ge

2 Ki
Di
Ph
Th
Ge

Hegel and Psychoanalysis

A New Interpretation of Phenomenology of Spirit

Molly Macdonald

Routledge
Taylor & Francis Group
NEW YORK AND LONDON

First published 2014
by Routledge
605 Third Avenue, New York, NY 10017

Simultaneously published in the UK
by Routledge
2 Park Square, Milton Park, Abingdon, Oxon OX14 4RN

*Routledge is an imprint of the Taylor & Francis Group,
an informa business*

Library of Congress Cataloging-in-Publication Data

Macdonald, Molly.
Hegel and psychoanalysis : a new interpretation of "Phenomenology of spirit" / Molly Macdonald. — 1 [edition].
pages cm. — (Routledge studies in nineteenth-century philosophy ; 4)
1. Hegel, Georg Wilhelm Friedrich, 1770-1831. Phänomenologie des Geistes. 2. Psychoanalysis. I. Title.
B2929.M25 2013
193—dc23
2013010212

ISBN: 978-0-415-85426-9 (hbk)
ISBN: 978-0-203-74445-1 (ebk)

Typeset in Sabon
by Apex CoVantage, LLC

I dedicate this book to my brothers, Ian and Lucas.

Contents

Abbreviations Used in the Text and Notes

CHRISTOPHER BOLLAS

FA	Free Association
BC	Being a Character
FD	Forces of Destiny
SO	The Shadow of the Object
CU	Cracking Up
MT	The Mystery of Things
FM	The Freudian Moment

ANDRÉ GREEN

WN	The Work of the Negative
CE	The Chains of Eros
OPM	On Private Madness
TP	Time in Psychoanalysis
DP	Diachrony in Psychoanalysis
KI	Key Ideas for a Contemporary Psychoanalysis: Misrecognition and Recognition of the Unconscious
Squiggle	André Green at the Squiggle Foundation

G.W.F. HEGEL

PS	Phenomenology of Spirit
JS	The Jena System (1804–05)
PP	The Philosophical Propaedeutic
PM	Philosophy of Mind
SL	Science of Logic

Abbreviations Used in the Text and Notes

Acknowledgements

I would like to thank Queen Mary, University of London, and the Overseas Research Scheme from Universities UK for awarding me the funding that allowed me to undertake the research for this book. I was fortunate enough to be guided from beginning to end by Paul Hamilton and to be the recipient of his wisdom, humour, and kindness. I am grateful to Jacqueline Rose for the invaluable support and encouragement she provided throughout, and particularly with the last two chapters. Thanks to Howard Caygill and Peter Dews for their insightful reading and commentary on an earlier draft of this book.

I am privileged to be part of the community in the School of English and Drama at Queen Mary and to have found people who have enriched and inspired me through this project and beyond; in particular, thanks to Rowan Boyson, Suzanne Hobson, and Anurag Jain.

I thank my mother, Caroline, my father, Torbert, and the rest of my family, especially my aunts Laurie Macdonald and Catharine R. Stimpson, for their unconditional love and care. The beautiful friendships of Lauren Antler, Laura Rosenfield, Daphne Walker, and Katherine Wolkoff have sustained me since our undergraduate days. Thanks to Bobby, Paula, and Kate for welcoming me to the Hershkowitz fold. I am grateful for Jesse Hershkowitz, who has brought love, levity, and joy, and for our Annie, who came into the world just as this book was going out into it.

Portions of the Introduction were published in an article for *Philosophy Compass:*

Hegel, Psychoanalysis and Intersubjectivity, Philosophy Compass, 6 (2011), 448–58. doi: 10.1111/j.1747-9991.2011.00407.x.

HEGEL: PHENOMENOLOGY OF SPIRIT translated by Miller (1979) 3500w. By permission of Oxford University Press.

Acknowledgements

Introduction

> But perhaps the most substantial legacy of the formal operations synthesized by Hegel [. . .] consists in the foundation of the psychoanalytical subject, the subject of psychoanalysis, in the phenomenological subject, the subject implied by the Hegelian *Phenomenology*.[1]

SETTING THE STAGE

In 1955 Jean Hyppolite delivered a lecture to the French Society for Psychoanalysis titled 'Hegel's Phenomenology and Psychoanalysis.' Years later, Hyppolite described, to the editor of a collection in which his lecture was to be published, a discussion he had with Jacques Lacan directly following the lecture. The exchange was transcribed into a footnote included at the end of Hyppolite's article. Hyppolite recounts that Lacan asked him what he meant by his use of the "we," "not only as an encounter of two consciousnesses, but as making the encounter possible." Hyppolite responded by asking Lacan "what psychoanalysis in its practice may contribute to the third term which appears in the interaction of two consciousnesses." The discussion continued:

> The question was raised again and again concerning the duality of consciousness and the significance that this going beyond could have both on the positive level where the field of consciousness appears as a kind of impersonal multiplicity, and on the ontological level where original speech, a primordial 'logos' might be revealed. The problematical nature of this revelation, both in Freud's psychoanalysis and Hegel's phenomenology, is at the centre of the issue. Naturally the question of the philosopher or of the analyst being beyond such discussion was inevitably raised.[2]

At the heart of my book lies a set of questions about the nature of intersubjectivity, raised when regarding the notion of the "we" and inspired by this exchange between Hyppolite and Lacan. What is it that is revealed and created in the encounter between two consciousnesses? What is it that can be connected to, yet moves beyond, speech and that simultaneously creates and lays bare this "we"? What is it that is responsible for binding two consciousnesses together? What is responsible for binding together the two consciousnesses that comprise the analytic pair of analyst and analysand? What happens when the intersubjective relation breaks down? What, finally, is this "third" term? In order to find a way of answering these questions, and the set of questions they in turn raise, my book aims to create a speculative dialectic, a conversation between Hegel's *Phenomenology of Spirit* and two particular strands of psychoanalytic theory, represented by the work of André Green and Christopher Bollas.

The interactions between Lacan and Hyppolite, in Lacan's seminars and elsewhere, are the key points of departure for any discussion regarding Hegel and psychoanalysis, as they were, in André Green's words, "taking place at the highest point of Hegel-Freud relations."[3] Indeed, a history of the engagement between the philosophy of Hegel and psychoanalytic theory can be traced back to the first part of the twentieth century, and its roots can be found in the figures of Lacan and Hyppolite. Lacan, as a psychoanalyst, used Hegel's thought in his own theory, as is well-known,[4] while Hyppolite was arguably one of the first to write from a philosophical angle about the links between the two seemingly opposed systems of thinking.[5] *Hegel and Psychoanalysis*, however, does not aim to be a comprehensive history that traces these links but will, as needed, mark the importance of certain developments along the way. Although there are many works of theory and philosophy that have been produced since that apex which gesture towards the resonance between the two fields, there are very few book-length studies that are dedicated to exploring the rich possibilities of what an examination of Hegel's philosophy alongside strands of Freudian (and now post-Freudian/post-Lacanian) theory offers.

It can be argued that the most limited, standard approach that psychoanalytic literature takes when making links between Hegel and psychoanalytic theory is to stay within the well-known confines of the master/slave paradigm as a model for intersubjective relations and, if the theory is Lacanian, to work through Hegel's concepts of recognition and desire. While there is clearly merit in these lines of theorizing, and due attention has been paid to them, my book will engage with them in order to illuminate the limitations they pose and to illustrate alternative routes for the way in which resonance between Hegel and psychoanalytic theory can be explored. Part of doing this is to locate a certain base level "economics" of Force in the *Phenomenology of Spirit*, introduced by Hegel in the third chapter "Force and the Understanding," so that I can begin to form a model of the economy of intersubjective relations worked through in the "Self-Consciousness" section. While I read Force as a model for the subsequent movements of recognition and desire, I do not entirely dismiss the idea that there could be something very real about the physical nature of Force that Hegel likely saw as existing and in the way in which consciousness responds to the external world and instead read this as part of his metaphysical view of the world. Related to this, I locate the importance of the concept of Life in the *Phenomenology* and think a re-consideration of the concept of Force alongside the concept of Life crucial to understanding the movement of the work as a whole. I argue that this concept of Life in the *Phenomenology* can be thought of as a form of Eros, a drive towards life that Hegel sees at work in the process of becoming of consciousness. This drive towards life, this Eros at play, counterbalances the vision of Hegel that most are familiar with, the Hegel who is focussed on 'negation,' death, and annihilation. I will further trace the way in which understanding a kind of Eros in Hegel allows us to read him alongside psychoanalysis and will further allow for my formulation of a theory of both intra- and intersubjective binding.

Jacques Derrida, in his essay 'Force and Signification,' suggests that, "In the future, [structuralism] will be interpreted, perhaps, as a relaxation, if not a lapse, of the attention given to *force,* which is the tension of force itself. *Form* fascinates when one no longer has the forces to understand force from within itself."[6] In a sense, I am locating us at the point in this "future" that Derrida was pointing towards, and I aim to understand Hegel's concept of Force from within itself. I am sympathetic to a line of thought offered by Arkady Plotnitsky, particularly when considering what a speculative model of an "energetics" might look like in Hegel. On one hand, Plotnitsky sees economy as implying notions of exchange in the historical, political, or material realm and, on the other hand, as implying an energetics that does not operate strictly within a system of exchange. He writes:

> 'Economy' suggests a metaphor of energy and, more thermodynamically, of the expenditure of energy. Thus economy-energy is the play of forces. The metaphorics of the play of forces and of differences of forces is suggestive of the general economic *dissemination* of descriptions; and as such it operates against metaphors of exchange and interest.[7]

I suggest that Hegel's concept of Force can be read for the potential it holds not only within Hegel's own system but also, as I will argue, as a way in which we can understand the notions of Force and the economy/energetics which arise out of Freudian theory. Although Plotnitsky and a select few others argue for the metaphorical potential of the concept of Force, as noted above I would like to suggest that it be considered more along the lines of a particular Hegelian metaphysics. As Hegel himself writes in his *Introductory Lectures on the History of Philosophy*:[8]

> Everyone possesses and uses the wholly abstract category of *being*. The sun *is* in the sky; these grapes *are* ripe, and so on *ad infinitum*. Or, in a higher sphere of education, we proceed to the relation of cause and effect, force and its manifestation, etc. All our knowledge and ideas are entwined with metaphysics like this and governed by it; it is the net

> which holds together all the concrete material which occupies us in our action and endeavour. But this net and its knots are sunk in our ordinary consciousness beneath numerous layers of stuff. This stuff comprises our known interests and the objects that are before our minds, while the universal threads of the net remain out of sight and are not explicitly made the subjects of our reflection.

Hegel's defence here of metaphysics is striking. That he posits that all of our knowledge and ideas are entwined and governed by metaphysical thinking can shed light on how we read the role of Force in the *Phenomenology*. The way in which Hegel describes 'metaphysics like this' (and of course his particular mention of Force) as the net, sunk beneath the layers of our daily life of action, thought, interests—that it is not part of our ordinary consciousness or made subject to our reflection—hints towards a kind of realm akin to that of the unconscious. In other words, the world cannot simply just be as it *appears* to us but must take into account those things that are underneath the so-called surface of existence. These metaphysical elements we can only know when they manifest themselves, but that does not make them any less real for Hegel.

Of course, Hegel's relationship to metaphysics (and clearly his responses to Kant in this sense) is one of the longest running points of inquiry and one of the most obvious dividing lines in the history of his reception. My purpose is not to open up that particular battleground here, nor even to chart it, but to stake a claim about the nature of Force in the *Phenomenology*. Most recently, Robert Stern's *Hegelian Metaphysics* offers a robust set of arguments for a new (or rather renewed) appreciation of this aspect of Hegel's thinking and bolsters my own position. Stern fully acknowledges that metaphysics is a disputed branch of philosophical thinking and that his own position is contra many readings of Hegel. Yet, he wants to argue that Hegel was invested in thinking through metaphysics and that to undervalue this aspect of his philosophy is to do damage to the potential this kind of reading brings to contemporary thought. Stern writes:

> Put very briefly, I take Hegel's response to the demand that metaphysics should be set aside, to be that in a very real sense, metaphysics is unavoidable: that is, we cannot escape making metaphysical assumptions in everything we believe, in how we act, in how we live our lives and relate to the things around us. Thus, if we take metaphysics to be concerned with our fundamental view of ourselves and of the world of which we are part, of its basic nature and structure, we cannot help subscribing to some such metaphysics, so that speculation on this matter is inescapable, and anyone who thinks he does not have a metaphysical position, or can opt out of having one, is deluding himself.[9]

Stern points to the *Phenomenology of Spirit* as the crucial text where Hegel works through the difficulties of how to incorporate our understanding of metaphysics, an understanding and an articulation of which cannot be taken for granted because it both complicates and illuminates how we are able think about and know ourselves and our relation to the world.

I would like to suggest that if I am reading Force via the lens of Hegelian metaphysics, then the move I make in reading him alongside psychoanalytic thinking is to put his metaphysics in conversation not only with Freudian metapsychology but also, importantly, with what André Green will come to consider "metabiology." Green places the subheadings of Force, Binding and Unbinding, the Work of the Negative, and Energy under this category. How this comes to pass is the subject of my third chapter, circling around the idea of energy, a particularly slippery notion in Freud's work. It is one of my aims to examine Hegel's notions of Force alongside the notions of energy and economy that Freud began to formulate in his *Project for Scientific Psychology* of 1895 and continued to elaborate upon, in various forms, throughout his work. The suggestion is not that Hegel described "psychic energy" as such but that we must look at the building blocks of his system of consciousness as having economic aspects that often remain on the fringes of discussion. I will by no means treat the concept of energy in any comprehensive manner but will be investigating it as the foundation of the binding process. In other words, such an investigation offers possible ways of thinking about a kind of erotic process of binding both in psychoanalysis and in the *Phenomenology*. Such a reading of Hegel's work can allow for a non-metaphorical interpretation of Hegel's concept of Force.[10] With that in mind, I believe a way of understanding Hegel's ontology of becoming as based on a dynamics of Force will open up.

Plotnitsky sees Hegel's notion of Force as undermining the famously Derridian "restricted" economy of *Aufhebung*.[11] Keeping this in mind, I locate the foundations for an alternative economy at work in the *Phenomenology*, denying it closure in the "End of History" and "Absolute Knowing" and arguing instead that both are simply *moments* in the process of becoming. The designation of "moments" as found in the *Phenomenology* is used throughout my book to refer to particular points that exist within the dynamic movement of the process of becoming of consciousness that the work traces. This is a process by which, like psychoanalysis, the *Phenomenology* educates consciousness and the reader to understand and to use but does not complete for them.

For my first premise, I propose that Hegel used the concept of Force as a model for the subsequent, far more examined concepts of recognition and desire. Often ignored in arguments that locate in Hegel an intersubjectivity based on recognition is the very presence of Force and the play of Forces. A close reading of "Force and the Understanding" will not only illuminate this idea but will also allow us to understand better the dynamic "process of becoming" that is the labour of consciousness as Hegel sets it forth in the *Phenomenology*. This process of becoming is the movement behind the creation of the subject. My purpose is to show that one can interpret Hegel as building a model of the subject, and its intrapsychic and intersubjective relations, through his exploration of the dynamic concept of the play of Forces, thus anticipating the formulation of the "play of forces" most commonly credited to Nietzsche.[12] Following on from this, I argue that Force is a universally binding, generative substance and that it is through the play of Forces that we can understand subjects, consciousnesses, becoming bound to one another. Furthermore, recognition modelled on Force provides an alternative way of looking at the ontology and epistemology that the *Phenomenology* offers.

Herbert Marcuse writes of Hegel's "process of becoming" that it "sustains itself through knowledge of what has become, while at the same time relating itself to it." It is, furthermore, "a process of becoming which returns from each individual shape of existence back to the unified subject of this movement which sustains them all, and which comprehendingly 'mediates' each form with the preceding one."[13] I will come to designate the object created between two consciousnesses as "the third" and will see, through my examination of the concept in psychoanalytic theory, that this third is essential to all transitions between and transformations of moments of knowledge and thought (of knowing and thinking). It is not simply that the subject is the product of its own self-reflection and wholly responsible for its own self-development. My claim is that the subject (as a Force) can only truly find freedom in being bound to the other (another Force). Moreover, I argue that not only is self-sufficiency not enough, but also the recognition and utilisation of that which is created out of the intersubjective relation is essential. Through what is found in psychoanalytic language as a tripartite process of binding, unbinding, and rebinding, I argue that the process of becoming is a dynamic, living process that brings to the subject new levels of knowledge about its self and its own process, what I will find designated by Hegel as "shapes of knowing" (*Gestalten des Wissens*).

The tendency to focus on the master/slave dialectic and the totalizing aspects of "Absolute Knowing" and the "End of History" neglects those elements of the *Phenomenology* that threaten to disturb such a concentration. Arguably, Force is one such element and the figure of the unhappy consciousness is another. The different sort of economy I am exploring proposes a re-centring of the movement of "Self-Consciousness" around the figure of the unhappy consciousness.

FRENCH HEGEL AND THE NECESSITY FOR THE UNHAPPY CONSCIOUSNESS

In her work *The Psychic Life of Power*, Judith Butler writes that the transition from the "Lordship and Bondage" section to "The Freedom of Self-Consciousness: Stoicism, Scepticism, and the Unhappy Consciousness" section "is one of the least interrogated of Hegel's philosophical movements."[14] This for the most part still holds true. In the main, this is due to the overemphasis on a reading of the "Lordship and Bondage" episode that still cannot escape the impact that first Marx's reading and then the reading and interpretation of this episode by Alexandre Kojève has had on the wider understanding of this particular section of Hegel's work.[15] Robert Williams argues that Kojève's narrow focus, which equates recognition with the struggle between master and slave, "distorted" Hegel's original concept of intersubjectivity. Williams further claims, as do I, that the scope of the concept of intersubjectivity in the *Phenomenology* is "wider than master and slave," and while the categories of master and slave are an important "first phase of unequal recognition," they "*must* and *can* be transcended."[16]

A compelling reason for the seductive nature of Kojève's reading is offered by Butler when she notes, "Perhaps because the chapter on lordship and bondage secured a liberationist narrative for various progressive political visions, most readers have neglected to pay attention to the resolution of freedom into self-enslavement at the end of the chapter."[17] While agreeing with Butler wholeheartedly, I can also say that she does not go far enough in her reading. She stops just short of the tremendous resolution into freedom from the state of self-enslavement that the unhappy consciousness (*das unglückliche Bewußtsein*) secures. This is equally one of the least interrogated moments of the *Phenomenology*, and it is to that moment my book will give great weight and argue that it has much to offer to our understanding of Hegel's thinking on the complex nature of intersubjectivity. As I will explore, this resolution lies in Hegel's introduction of the "Third," "the mediator as counsellor."[18] In most of the Kojève-inspired readings of this chapter, both of the resolutions and the original ontological and epistemological possibilities they embody have been neglected or purposely glossed over.

The manner in which I read the figure of the unhappy consciousness, and the line of thought from which I draw my general approach to Hegel's philosophy, follows the thread of a tradition whose origins are predominately found in another strain of twentieth-century French philosophy that arose almost simultaneously with Kojève's reading. This tradition understood the unhappy consciousness as a moment in the *Phenomenology* which not only represented a key stage in the movement of consciousness but that could also be used paradigmatically in the reading of the work as a whole. It is widely acknowledged that the publication in 1929 of Jean Wahl's *Le Malheur de la conscience dans la philosophie de Hegel* not only set the stage for a new kind of reading of Hegel's text that was not steeped in Marx's thought but also gave a particular importance to the figure of the unhappy consciousness as the prime figure of the *Phenomenology* (as opposed to the lord and bondsman).[19]

Bruce Baugh describes how Wahl wrote in *Le Malheur* about his belief that the unhappy consciousness "represents every sort of experience of a self divided against itself, and the motor of the dialectic."[20] Baugh's work traces

Hegel's influence on twentieth-century French thought and philosophy; it argues for a re-centring of Hegel's notion of the unhappy consciousness and charts the importance of the concept in considerations of the *Phenomenology*, beginning with Jean Wahl's publication of *Le Malheur*. Baugh's work is rare in contemporary Hegelian scholarship in that it performs the task of giving central importance to the unhappy consciousness and focuses more on the "existential" Hegel rather than the Hegel of "the system." Indeed, my book aims to position itself amongst studies that emerge from this tradition, which does not entirely discount Hegel's importance as a systematic thinker but chooses to read against that grain in order to explore the more existential aspects of his thought. Prominent amongst these studies is Judith Butler's well-known and influential work *Subjects of Desire: Hegelian Reflections in Twentieth-Century France*, which charts the rise of French Hegelianism and the centrality of the unhappy consciousness as one line of its development. Butler emphasises the impact of Hegel's concept of desire and recognition on thinkers such as Lacan and Sartre and acknowledges the great importance of Wahl and Hyppolite in this history.[21] As part of Michael Roth's larger project of illuminating the history of French Hegelianism in his *Knowing and History: Appropriations of Hegel in Twentieth Century France*, he includes a lucid and compelling discussion of Wahl and a lengthy discussion of Hyppolite's impact. Importantly for my own study, following Hyppolite, Roth argues against the "End of History" as a "final resting place."[22] A third text that deals with Wahl's interpretation explicitly and is essential for a cobbling together of Wahl's thought is Barry Cooper's *The End of History: An Essay on Modern Hegelianism*, although Cooper is ultimately and unwaveringly focussed on the importance of the Kojèvian legacy for political theory and notions of history. He argues that what the Kojèvian line "accounts for is modern self-consciousness" or the "self-understanding of modernity."[23] What I eventually agree upon with Cooper, however, is that reaching the "End of History" or the state of "Absolute Knowing" in the *Phenomenology* is simply to then be sufficiently equipped to return to the beginning. Finally, Robert Sinnerbrink's work *Understanding Hegelianism* also locates the importance of Wahl's influence on French Hegelianism and discusses the significant contribution that Baugh's work has made in the effort of re-establishing the importance of Wahl's place in twentieth-century French theory and philosophy. Sinnerbrink additionally emphasizes Hyppolite's focus on the unhappy consciousness, while admitting that there are links with psychoanalytic theory and Hegel's philosophy that he did not have the scope to make.[24]

Building on the work of Wahl, Hyppolite believed that "unhappy consciousness is the fundamental theme of the *Phenomenology*. Consciousness, as such is in principle always unhappy consciousness, for it has not yet reached the concrete identity of certainty and truth, and therefore it aims at something beyond itself."[25] Similarly, I wish to re-centre this concept not only within the framework of the *Phenomenology* but also within the framework of a theoretical subjectivity and intersubjectivity that I am drawing out of the *Phenomenology*. Michael Roth comments that, "Hyppolite meant his emphasis on the unhappy consciousness to keep the Hegelian dialectic open, to undermine the totalizing aspects of Hegelian systematization."[26] I aim to join this effort to "undermine the totalizing aspects" of traditional readings of Hegel, and following Hyppolite's line on the unhappy consciousness, in combination with my reading of Force, is one of the ways in which this will be done.

My own take on the figure of the unhappy consciousness is that it can be used, perhaps more effectively than can the master/slave paradigm, as a model for the necessity of the other in the movement of self-consciousness. This necessity as presented by Hegel is not really in dispute, but what is often overlooked in readings of this episode is how this necessity is fulfilled by the "the Third" (*das Dritte*). As I will argue, the unhappy consciousness is the paradigm of the split, suffering consciousness for the very reason that it has almost completely unbound itself from its relations with the external world and has bound itself only to its own self and the pain of its existence. Most importantly, it does not know how to free itself. I am thus using this paradigm as an illustration of the dangers of the movement of becoming (as a play of Forces) when it is internalised and stops involving the external world. In other words, when it is purely confined to the intrapsychic realm. It is here I locate the importance and the therapeutic effect of the third consciousness. In order to understand and elaborate upon this model, I turn to psychoanalytic theory.

HEGEL AND PSYCHOANALYSIS

Although the history of the confluence between Hegel and psychoanalysis stretches over the twentieth and early twenty-first centuries, the studies that are heavily engaged with it are few and far between. After Hyppolite's articles, Paul Ricoeur's *Freud and Philosophy* examines the potential resonance between the two fields. While it is not devoted entirely to Hegel's philosophy (and I am certainly not claiming in my book to trace the history of the resonance between psychoanalysis and philosophy in general, but only where Hegel is concerned), Ricoeur does centrally place Hegel's philosophy as key to helping illuminate Freud's thought.[27] Ricoeur offers for psychoanalysis the model of an "energetics" that I use in my reading of the *Phenomenology*. He sees psychoanalysis as "an explanation of psychical phenomena through conflicts of forces, hence as an energetics," as well as a hermeneutics.[28] He has a particular investment in pursuing the question of how the energetic (and thus economic) explanations are inextricably connected to the notion of meaning and in proving the certain impossibility of totally integrating Force into language. For Ricoeur, a philosophical critique of psychoanalysis necessarily involves an "energy discourse" that is to be found at the intersection of language and desire. My aim is to take this formulation and go even a step further back in Hegel to see that for him Force lies as a model for desire. The approach I am taking to matters of language is in some senses to say, along with Malcolm Bowie, that in the particular strains of psychoanalytic thinking I am pursuing, represented by André Green and Christopher Bollas, "language matters, but is not alone in mattering."[29] That is to say, I am interested in looking at that which exists along with language as a binding entity but that resists complete incorporation into systems of language. This position will become more perceptible as my book progresses.

More recently, the work of Slavoj Žižek has brought to wide attention his particular version of Lacanian-Hegelian theory.[30] Although Žižek's name might be the first to spring to mind these days when the words Hegel and psychoanalysis are uttered in the same sentence, and although I engage with his thought throughout my book, most predominately in Chapter Three, I will not trace his reading of Lacan and Hegel in this present study. Let me say something about this decision, as many readers may turn to a book titled *Hegel and Psychoanalysis* expecting to see Žižek's presence in a more sustained manner. This is an expectation that would be due to Žižek's high-profile status and considerable stake in thinking through connections between Hegel and Lacanian psychoanalytic theory; Žižek's own body of work is vast and the amount of scholarship about him is ever-increasing.[31]

It is not because I am not interested in the Lacanian/Hegelian connection, or Lacan's thought in general, or indeed in Žižek's own work, that I will not engage with his thought in depth. I do not believe that I am alone in thinking that it is incredibly difficult to synthesize, in any concrete manner, Žižek's lines of argumentation, although I concede that he is often at his most grounded when he is engaging with Hegel and on the interconnections with Lacan. His most recent work, *Less Than Nothing: Hegel and the Shadow of Dialectic Materialism*, offers many brilliant insights into this line of thinking, and I engage with this work at various points.[32]

In addition to Žižek, the work of Alenka Zupančič, who, along with Žižek, Mladen Dolar and others, is part of the Ljubljana School of Psychoanalysis, deserves particular mention here, as her project of reading German Idealism alongside Lacanian theory has much to offer. Her book *Why Psychoanalysis?: Three Interventions* contains a striking discussion of the work of psychoanalysis as the work of de-interpretation, which she phrases as a kind of unbinding.[33]

Yet by not strictly engaging with those elements of thought that trace the Hegelian/Lacanian nexus, I am attempting to draw out the alternative reading that is by no means a critique of Lacan but instead offers other ways of looking at what Hegel has to offer to psychoanalytic theory. With my present study, this is perhaps particularly but certainly not exclusively to make links to Object Relation theory, a branch of psychoanalytic theory with which Hegel is rarely put into conversation. That being said, Lacan's thought will necessarily be engaged with at particular points in my argument, predominately in Chapter Three, as Lacan's thinking is essential to André Green's development.

A move away from a Lacanian-focussed reading can create some breathing room for the consideration of perhaps quieter but nevertheless significant recent studies that re-centre discussions of Hegel alongside psychoanalysis and along with which I aim to locate my own work. Jon Mills's lucid and original work *The Unconscious Abyss: Hegel's Anticipation of Psychoanalysis* represents one of the only full-length studies devoted entirely to the connections between Hegel and psychoanalysis. Mills traces the concept of the unconscious in Hegel's thinking, locating its presence predominantly in the *Philosophy of Mind* as well as the *Phenomenology of Spirit*.[34] As both a philosopher and practicing psychoanalyst, Mills's treatment of Hegel's thought as having anticipated many elements of psychoanalysis is of high importance. His work finds its place amongst the few contemporary psychoanalysts and theorists who aim to effect a change in the field of psychoanalysis by translating multiple aspects of Hegelian philosophy into psychoanalytic theory. Mills stands apart, however, with his emphasis on psychoanalysis as "process" and his comprehensive and detailed analysis of Hegel's philosophy from this angle. While a different project than Mills's, in that he is interested less in an anticipation of Freud and more in situating the concept of madness (albeit a reading informed by psychoanalytic theory) amongst Hegel's wider philosophical concerns, Daniel Berthold-Bond's work *Hegel's Theory of Madness* also serves to create a rich and nuanced dialogue between Hegel and psychoanalytic theory.[35] Berthold-Bond illuminates Hegel's writings on psychology, medicine, and the ontology of sanity and insanity. He argues that, for Hegel, the line between a healthy mind and a "diseased" mind is actually quite thin and that both share the same basic structures. In addition, Wilfried Ver Eecke's work *Denial, Negation, and the Forces of the Negative: Freud, Hegel, Lacan, Spitz, and Sophocles* uses Hegel's philosophy as a way of interrogating the Freudian concepts of denial and negation, the second of which I will explore in Chapter Three, and he argues for the usefulness of Hegel's philosophy for helping to "clarify the logical structure of Freudian insights."[36] Richard D. Chessick's work *The Future of Psychoanalysis* includes a chapter devoted not only to what Hegel can offer to psychoanalytic theory but also to what in Hegelian philosophy is important to the "phenomenology of the history and development of psychoanalysis."[37] Although Chessick's approach is not entirely pertinent to my project in that it is centred on the use of Hegel as the thinker of a "system" in order to critique what he sees as the "confusing plurality" that is the state of psychoanalytic development today, I highlight his contribution in order to show further evidence of current interest in Hegel's relationship with psychoanalytic theory. Rebecca Comay's *Mourning Sickness: Hegel and the French Revolution* is not a psychoanalytic work, but she uses psychoanalytic theory in her reading of Hegel in a thought-provoking manner, and her book is a prime contemporary example of how such work has purchase even outside the confines of the psychoanalytic discipline.[38] The area of scholarship that combines a philosophical, as opposed to a clinical, approach regarding the use of Hegel's philosophy for psychoanalysis remains underdeveloped. It is my aim to add to this growing yet undernourished body of work by exploring aspects, especially the concepts of Force and the unhappy consciousness, that have not been given due consideration.

HEGEL, PSYCHOANALYSIS, AND THE CONCEPT OF INTERSUBJECTIVITY

I have so far made the claim that we are to read Force as a model for Recognition and thus for desire and that at the heart of the consideration of this model lies a set of questions about the nature of intersubjectivity. Although I cannot do justice to the complexities of the concept of intersubjectivity here, and by no means can I chart the complete history of the use of the term, it is important to gesture towards the way in which I am positioning my reading of Hegel.

It has been argued, by Hyppolite and a select few others, that Hegel is the inaugural thinker of the intersubjective relation. Hyppolite writes:

> All conditions of human existence, or, as Hegel puts it, of self-consciousness of life, are contained in the need of desire for recognition in another desire, or in *intersubjectivity* which is the sole means by which consciousness of life may become something other than a reflection of this life. It is through this necessary intersubjectivity and the relation with nature or universal life that Humanity and History, or, in Hegel's terminology, Spirit, are founded.[39]

Taking Hyppolite's line of thinking as my foundation, it is odd to find that although nearly all of the scholarly texts on the *Phenomenology* discuss the concept of recognition, few translate it into terms of intersubjectivity. In part, this is because Hegel himself did not use the term and so clearly any reading of intersubjectivity into his philosophy is possible only because of twentieth-century theoretical and philosophical formulations. Strangely, not having noted Hyppolite's acknowledgement of intersubjectivity in Hegel, Robert Williams's *Recognition: Fichte, Hegel and the Other* also claims that recognition (*Annerkennung*) is the ground of intersubjectivity but that the concept of intersubjectivity "in German idealism is all but unnoticed."[40] Williams credits Fichte and Hegel with having brought the concept to philosophy and spends his work detailing the inception and progression of the concept of intersubjectivity. His aim is to recover this original ground for what he identifies as a burgeoning interest in the philosophy of intersubjectivity and the "problem of the Other" taking place in twentieth-century intellectual thought.[41]

There are those in the field of Hegel scholarship, however, and we can take philosophers such as John McDowell as a prime example, who do not see the self-consciousness chapter as an exploration of intersubjectivity at all but see it rather as an illustration of only one biological consciousness educating itself. McDowell believes that the master/slave episode is the illustration of this single consciousness and that "the real topic is two aspects of the consciousness of a single individual, although at a stage at which that is not clear to the individual in question."[42] I am sympathetic to this reading to the extent that my own study attempts to explore the intrapsychic realm as represented by the figures of the stoic/sceptic and unhappy consciousness, where each represent a particular stage of a single consciousness that is learning to negotiate the intersubjective world. However, I argue that it is the illustration of the transition from the intersubjective state, represented by the lord and bondsman's "struggle to the death," to the intrapsychic (McDowell's single biological consciousness), represented ultimately by the unhappy consciousness, that is of crucial importance. It does not have to be an either/or between intra- and intersubjective positions. My interest, then, is in locating the ways in which Hegel can be seen as the precursor to theories of intersubjectivity in the twentieth century and in exploring fruitful intersections with psychoanalytic theory.

While the Lacanian model of intersubjectivity is taken as essential background, I also explore a model of intersubjectivity based on the play of Forces and ask what a model could look like that takes both a dynamic model and a linguistic model into account. We can locate the concept in Lacan and his indebtedness to Hegel in his first seminar. Lacan argues, "Speech is the founding medium of the intersubjective relation" and locates hate as one pole (as the opposite of love) of the "very structure of the intersubjective relation." He remarks that this is "what Hegel recognises as the impasse for the coexistence of two consciousnesses, from whence he deduces his myth of the struggle for pure prestige."[43] Again, we can note the confines of the master/slave dialectic in this formulation. Roger Frie charts the impact of Hegel on Lacan and follows its trajectory through to Sartre, Ludwig Binswanger, and Jurgen Habermas in his cogently argued study of the concept, *Subjectivity and Intersubjectivity in Modern Philosophy and Psychoanalysis*.[44] This work is of key importance for understanding the evolution of thought regarding the concept and the ways in which an emphasis on language and communication, especially in the work of Habermas and Lacan, altered theories of intersubjectivity.[45] Frie helpfully highlights the main tensions that have arisen in relatively recent theories of intersubjectivity in both philosophy and psychoanalysis between such categories as "subjectivity and objectivity, internal and external, private and public, separateness and togetherness."[46] I explore the tension between the internal and external, of togetherness and separateness in the forms of binding and unbinding, and argue that it is when this tension dissolves that the movement that is becoming runs into considerable difficulties.

In recent years there has been a movement towards intersubjective theory on the side of psychoanalytic theory written from a more clinical perspective. Although I am implicitly engaging with these schools of thought and practice, I cannot fully address the complexities of the contested nature of such developments in psychoanalytic theory. I can only suggest the way in which my own argument can be situated. Arnold H. Modell doubts "whether our present psychology of intersubjectivity could have developed without Hegel. For Hegel appeared to have intuitively grasped the fundamental aspects of the psychology of self and other." Indeed, Modell continues, "Hegel can justifiably be termed the first intersubjective or relational psychologist."[47] The predominately American "intersubjective" and "relational" schools of analysis had their origins in late 1970s American psychoanalytic movements. The best-known representatives of the intersubjective school for one line of theory are Robert Stolorow, James Atwood, and Donna Orange. They define intersubjectivity as a "sensibility that continually takes into account the inescapable interplay of the two subjects in any psychoanalysis. It radically rejects the notion that psychoanalysis is something one isolated mind does to another, or that development is something one person does or does not do."[48] A second strain of the intersubjective school is of note for the use of Hegel and the master/slave paradigm as a model for recognition and intersubjective relations. The work of Jessica Benjamin and Thomas Ogden is representative of this line and is of the most interest to me in this respect. I will engage with both Benjamin and Ogden in Chapters Three and Four.[49] The relational school is mainly associated with the work of Stephen Mitchell and Jay Greenberg and of the two schools is of less interest to me.[50] According to Jon Mills, both lines, in regards to theory, "converge with each other, emphasizing the nature of contextuality, emotional transmutation, meaning construction, mutual yet asymmetrical connectedness, and recognition."[51] Mills cautions, however, that both movements hold many nuanced distinctions that call for varied critiques.

With this context in place, I must note that although I am considering the concept of intersubjectivity in their work, neither of the two psychoanalysts that are the focus of my book would align themselves with either the relational or intersubjective schools. Both are, however, and Bollas more so than Green, invested in the idea of the analyst as an active, and not entirely neutral, subject. My own implicit critique of those of the intersubjective and relational schools will come in Chapters Three and Four via the work of Green and Bollas, where I acknowledge that although they give Hegel a place of due importance in the history of the concept of intersubjectivity, there is a certain limitation to their readings. This limitation arises because there is more to the movement of intersubjectivity than simply the "struggle for recognition" as based in the master/slave dialectic. A further critique of this movement lies in the idea that they champion the intersubjective relations, and the emphasis on subjectivity arising only in intersubjectivity, at the expense of an idea of a subject having any autonomous, inner kernel, illustrated by Christopher Bollas's idea of the "idiom," which finds its elaboration, but not its entire sense of meaning, in the intersubjective relation. In order to see the way in which I am drawing my own concept of intersubjectivity as a play of Forces out of Hegel, I will situate my reading of the concept of Force.

THE CONCEPT OF FORCE AND ITS ROLE IN THE *PHENOMENOLOGY*

Although there is general consensus that the *Phenomenology* can be read in terms of the notions of "process" and "movement of becoming," very rarely is the concept of Force understood to play a fundamental role in this movement.[52] The standard reading of the "Force and the Understanding" chapter, which, of course, is still valid, holds that through his examination of Force, Hegel is critiquing standard methods of scientific enquiry as he saw them, predominantly in the work of Newton, Leibniz, and Kant. Rather than trace this critique, I aim to see how Hegel uses the concept of Force as a way of prefiguring the subsequent movements of consciousness, reworking and translating the play of Forces into the realm of self-consciousness. Although I locate Hegel's consideration of Force in some of his other works, I do not aim to treat the concept exhaustively and will predominantly focus on its role in the project of the *Phenomenology*. The chapter "Force and the Understanding" is a crucial transitional point in the *Phenomenology*. It is out of this section that self-consciousness is born, and it is also here that, in giving us the movement that is behind the notion of the Understanding, Hegel is arming us with the methodology that we will use to read his work and thus to come away with an understanding of our own process of consciousness.

Although of course I acknowledge the presence the weighty philosophical tradition that lies behind Hegel's work, I have chosen to take an approach that reads Hegel for what he might have anticipated rather than for what he was critiquing. In other words, methodologically I read Hegel "forward," rather than "back" into the history out of which he emerged. This decision was made partly because one of my aims is an attempt to take the *Phenomenology of Spirit* on its own terms by approaching the contents anew to see how they might relate to one another. That being said, I fully acknowledge that each concept I am unpacking arrives freighted with the history of its reception, a history which I cannot do justice to in the scope of my project. This is a position that Heidegger took when reading the concept of Force in Hegel, and it is very much along these lines that my decision was made. Heidegger writes:

> Therefore, it is not at all an adequate understanding to say that Hegel took from Kant in a certain way the categorial determination of the essence of the thing as force. This statement is correct; but as long as it remains only correct, it does not say anything [. . .]. It would not say any more even if we would try to explain the meaning of the concept of force for the substantiality of the substance by looking back to Leibniz or

> looking ahead to the effect on Hegel of Schelling's philosophy of nature and his *System of Transcendental Idealism* of 1800. What matters is to see how Hegel took up and penetrated all these issues and transformed them *into his* problematic—'*his*' understood not in terms of personal intellectual production, but *his* as the material completion and unfolding of what came earlier.[53]

I read this to mean that what we are offered in the *Phenomenology* holds "what came earlier" within it, but we must take Hegel's transformations as they are and try to understand them on their own terms.

There is too vast an amount of literature on Hegel, both works that are introductions to the *Phenomenology of Spirit* and those that treat the *Phenomenology* as a part of a larger argument about Hegel or philosophy in general, to discuss. For my purposes, I can chart three ways in which the concept of Force and the chapter in which it is found are dealt with in studies on Hegel. I do not aim to be exhaustive but to indicate that the way in which the treatment of Force I embark upon is rooted in Hegelian studies. The manner in which I read it, however, is a response to the general lack in the existing scholarship of such a reading, a lack I seek to rectify with my own reading.

The first approach is taken by those who focus on the historical/philosophical background to Hegel's engagement with the concept. That is to say, Hegel's response to or critique of Newton's theories of attractive and repulsive forces and to the formulations of Leibniz or Kant are recounted and explored in varying degrees of detail. For more recent scientifically and historically grounded discussion of Hegel's relationship to the concept of Force on the strictly Newtonian side of things, one could turn to Wolfgang Neuser's 'The Concept of Force in Eighteenth-Century Mechanics' and Karl-Norbert Ihmig's 'Hegel's Rejection of the Concept of Force.'[54] Along those same lines, Peter Kalkavage's accessible work gives great importance to the concept of Force and devotes two chapters to working through the "Force and the Understanding" chapter which provides considerable insight into Hegel's text, especially regarding the Newtonian influences.[55] Although there is no direct engagement with Kant's writings on Force in my own work, I do acknowledge that Hegel is not only responding to Newton and Leibniz in "Force and the Understanding" but that he is also addressing Kant's writing on attractive and repulsive forces. Implicitly then, Hegel is responding to what the relationship between force and epistemology might be.[56]

The second approach taken is to perform this standard reading and perhaps infuse it with a brief interpretation that goes beyond these confines. Michael Forster performs such a reading in *Hegel's Idea of a Phenomenology of Spirit*.[57] In short, Forster argues that Hegel admits there are forces existing in the world that are supersensuous but that we cannot understand in the ways that science/philosophy attempts to understand them. Similarly, Robert Solomon posits that not only is Hegel critiquing scientific methods but that he is also implicitly accepting that there is something more beneath the surface of things. Ultimately for Hegel, Solomon argues, it is the appearance of that thing that matters, for that is all we can actually know.[58] Once that which is internal is articulated, it is not simply part of the inner world but takes on life in the external world. So, in other words, the mystery is not in what lies beneath (whether or not, for instance, Force is internal to the object) but in how we translate, understand, and utilise that which appears, comes to the surface. Hans-Georg Gadamer's treatment of the concept locates the central importance of the "Inverted World" section of the "Force and the Understanding" chapter as "one of the most central in the structure of the *Phenomenology of Spirit*" and thus emphasises the importance of the chapter for the whole of the text. Gadamer also comments that the "dialectic of force is one of those sections of Hegel's work on which he himself has most thoroughly commented [. . .]. It has something so immediately compelling and illuminating about it that Hegel could be said to see what everybody would see if all sophism were dispensed with."[59] Gadamer points to the *Logic* and the *Encyclopedia* as the places where Hegel deals most significantly with Force, but, as I will shortly show in Chapter One, it is crucial to an understanding of Force in the *Phenomenology* to locate the concept in the *Jena System*, as the treatment given to Force there is longer and clearer than in the *Phenomenology* and serves to bolster the claims I am making about the connecting/binding nature of Force. It is in the *Jena System* that I find the grounds for my discussion of Force as a category of "relation." By building my argument on these grounds, I posit that one can better understand the "relation" between consciousnesses as a play of Forces.

The third, and by far the most rare, treatment of Force in Hegel is to read Hegel as working through the concept of Force as part of his metaphysically oriented vision of the world, the shape of which I gestured towards above.

This method of reading allows for the argument that Hegel anticipated claims regarding the activity of Force that are commonly attributed to both Nietzsche and Freud, where the shift in Freud is to a metapsychological realm, as will be touched upon on Chapter Three. Alongside the metaphysical readings, there are those that attempt to read Force metaphorically. Akin to Arkady Plotnitsky's text mentioned above, another of the texts that situates Hegel along these lines is Henry Sussman's *The Hegelian Aftermath: Readings in Hegel, Kierkegaard, Freud, Proust, and James*. Sussman's work is of note for thinking about the concept of Force in Hegel on both a metaphorical and literal level (via physics). Sussman's attempts to read Force in light of this dual approach are instrumental in opening up the *Phenomenology* to alternative readings and to giving Force a place of importance beyond the simply structural. Particularly because he thinks of the *Phenomenology* as an "organic text," his work is of great use when I pursue notions of Life and process in the *Phenomenology*.[60] Finally, Judith Butler, in *Subjects of Desire*, allows for the concept of Force to take on a more prominent role and illuminates my own reading.[61]

For my own contribution, then, I am not only reading the concept of Force as a model for recognition and desire but am also reading it as representing a binding, generative entity in the *Phenomenology* that allows us to read an intersubjective theory based on a theory of "relation." Taking these as my most basic claims, I will now turn to the way in which I am setting about my exploration of the links amongst Force, binding, and intersubjectivity.

WHAT FOLLOWS

The chapters that follow are, on one level, set up in dialectical tension with one another. The first two chapters are devoted to close readings of Hegel's philosophy, and the second two chapters are devoted to elaborating on this reading via psychoanalytic theory. The psychoanalysts focussed on here are not being used as representative of psychoanalysis as a universal practice but have been chosen because they allow for the most fruitful work with the formulations of my Hegelian model. To be more precise, I will be using the two bodies of psychoanalytic writing as "case studies" of sorts for scrutinising our notions of the subject that I take out of my reading of the *Phenomenology*. I believe that Green and Bollas, along with other strands of psychoanalytic thinking, offer a fresh approach to thinking about the connections between Hegel and psychoanalysis.

My first chapter, as a close reading of the concept of Force, sets out the framework for the exploration of the predominantly intrapsychic realm that will be examined in Chapter Three via psychoanalytic theory. My second chapter reads the concept of the play of Forces into the movement of self-consciousness and locates the introduction of intersubjectivity in the *Phenomenology*. I thus build the framework for the move to the intersubjective realm of the psychoanalytic sphere that is entered in Chapter Four. Clearly, however, each chapter builds upon its predecessor, and in this way my book cumulatively gathers the language in which all four chapters can speak to one another.

This investigation is not to be built upon a simple procedure of comparison, where a Hegelian concept will be neatly applied to a psychoanalytic concept or vice versa, but the work of each psychoanalyst will be used to cast light back on the Hegelian concepts that I will be using to move into their texts. Correspondingly, I will develop my reading of these psychoanalytic texts out of my understanding of the key concepts drawn from Hegel. When moving between the two fields of Hegel's philosophy and of psychoanalytic theory, there is a potential danger for confusion of terminology, and I aim to be careful to designate the origin of the concept as I am using it. In other words, it is important when using the word *binding*, for example, to recognise that this is a concept that Hegel does not explicitly articulate with his writing on Force but one I am reading *into* him by locating its origins in psychoanalysis and reading backwards. Likewise, my discussion of the Hegelian concept of Force will be used to read *into* the concept of binding and into Freud's notions of energy and force, and thus my reading of Hegel in a forward trajectory. However, it can be argued that it is precisely in the blurring of lines, the mixing of the two disciplines, that the true illumination as to the depth and texture of the concept will be found. With this in mind, my general outline is as follows.

Chapter One builds a conceptual and theoretical framework out of which to argue that Hegel's notion of Force, alongside his notion of the negative, can be read as a binding and generative dynamic entity that helps us to understand the binding nature of both intra- and intersubjective states. Furthermore, in understanding the mechanisms of Force as a category of "relation," I lay the foundations for showing how Hegel used it as a model for both recognition and desire. Thus I recognize in Force an epistemological and ontological weight that it is rarely given and create an alternative economy through which the *Phenomenology* can be understood. I interrogate a handful of key concepts such as vanishing (*Verschwinden*), solicitation (*Sollizitieren*), preservation (*Aufbewahren*), explanation (*Erklären*), expression (*Aussprechen* or *das Auberung*), and suppression/repression (*Unterdrückung/ Zurückhalten*) and discuss the formulation of the activity of the play of Forces (*Spiel der Kräfte*). The ground is then prepared for Chapter Two, wherein I perform a reading of the "Self-Consciousness" chapter of the *Phenomenology* as a re-running of the play of Forces in the intersubjective realm.

The key concepts scrutinised in Chapter One are now located and expanded upon in Chapter Two in light of the new presence of desire (*Begierde*) and as they are found in the "Lordship and Bondage" and "Stoicism, Scepticism, and the Unhappy Consciousness" episodes. How each episode enacts its own play of Forces is examined, and my primary concern is to see the unhappy consciousness as a paradigm for what happens when the play of Forces becomes internalised and the process of becoming is threatened with stasis. Furthermore, the concept of Life is introduced and discussed. I suggest that alongside negation there is a drive towards life, a form of Eros at work in the *Phenomenology*. The concept of vanishing is a point of focus in order to make way for the introduction of the figure of the "vanishing mediator" seen in the figure of the Third (*das Dritte*) that is brought in by Hegel to rescue the unhappy consciousness from itself. This move into the intersubjective realm sets the stage for the investigation of the concepts of binding, the third, and thirdness in psychoanalytic theory.

Chapter Three marks a transition into the realm of psychoanalysis where primary attention will be paid to the work of French psychoanalyst André Green. As a starting point for a discussion of negation and the emergence of the psychoanalytic concept of the third, I will use Green's text *The Work of the Negative*, wherein he highlights the importance of considering comparisons between Hegel and Freud via the concept of the negative. I continue my work by anchoring my reading in a second exchange between Hyppolite and Lacan. This exchange, on Freud's paper 'Negation' (*Verneinung*),[62] in Lacan's seminar (1953–54) marks a crucial moment in the history of the relationship between Hegel's philosophy and psychoanalysis. Elisabeth Roudinesco notes the significance of this moment in her biography of Lacan. It was, she remarks, a critical turning point in Lacan's intellectual development that saw him begin to "liquidate" the discourse of philosophy as a "direct result of the advent of structuralism." The philosophical approach, according to Lacan, could not deal properly with the Freudian idea of the unconscious and thus, according to Roudinesco, it was structuralism that prevailed.[63]

In my return to this original exchange on the concept of negation, I will be exploring what Hyppolite's reading offers as a philosophically centred alternative and what such an interpretation offers back to a reading of Hegel via the lens of psychoanalysis. One main reason for focussing on this exchange between Lacan and Hyppolite is that it, in some senses, demarcates the dominant way in which Hegel was to be utilised (or not) by psychoanalytic theory from that point on. What I am also locating via Hyppolite's reading is a way of thinking about the origins of the "process of thought" and "judgement" and of the "drives" in the activity of negation itself. Much as I will find that the crucial moment in the "Force and the Understanding" chapter is that consciousness locates the difference between the internal and external world, I will find in 'negation' that judgement is the intellectual act concerning what comes in (internal) and what stays out (external).

I further anchor my study in Freud's posthumously published paper 'Project for a Scientific Psychology' (1895) and the famous paper 'Beyond the Pleasure Principle' (1920) for my exploration of the concept of binding in Green's work and as it applies to notions of energy and binding that I read into the *Phenomenology*.[64] Green's model of binding involves a three-part process of binding, unbinding, and then a final rebinding and takes into account two modes of binding, intrapsychic and intersubjective. Green, heavily invested in Freud's "metabiology" and "metapsychology," reads binding and unbinding as alternative terms for Eros and the destructive drive, the potential origins of which I discuss. With these models in place, I re-examine the transitions of self-consciousness in the *Phenomenology* and argue that consciousness, as a process, repeatedly undergoes a series of these binds. Here my designation of Force as a model for recognition will come to fruition, and I underscore the presence of Eros and the destructive drive in Hegel's work. My final move in Chapter Three is to discuss Green's concepts of the third and thirdness in order to understand his designation of the "analytic third" as an object that is created out of the intersubjective work of the analytic pair.

The fourth and final chapter picks up the threads of binding and the third from Green and moves them, via the work of Christopher Bollas, into an even more considered study of what it is that is created in the analytic setting. The way in which Green's tripartite process of binding can be found in Bollas's work is investigated, and I trace the theoretical oscillations regarding the formation and utilisation of the third throughout his body of work. I find that Bollas's designation for that which I have been exploring as the third is "analytic genera," and I explore the complexities of both how this third is created and what happens to it after the analytic session ends. I ultimately argue that what the third creates, as a transformative and transitional object, are new moments of knowing and understanding that are then incorporated by the patient and analyst and made part of their psychic life. These new psychic structures can be seen in the light of Hegel's designation of new "shapes of knowing" or "shapes of consciousness," and I discuss the notion of the process of becoming as composed of these shapes.

Before turning to Chapter One, I ask for a brief consideration of what manner of "bound" relationship we have as readers, as the philosophical travelling partners, as the other part of Hegel's "we," with the text of the *Phenomenology*. I am in many ways picking up a line of argument that considers the reading of the text as work, as an active, interactive process, and that asks of us a form of reading, commitment, that other texts do not necessarily ask. My book asks that we consider ways in which we are bound to the text, to the language, to the process of reading, to the processes of thought and consciousness that it is describing. Karen Feldman discusses the concept of binding and the binding effect of Hegel's text in a compelling manner. She writes, "The *Phenomenology* claims for itself a certain binding force on the existence of the Spirit whose unfolding it narrates." Feldman further notes that, we, the readers, are Spirit, in Hegel's understanding. As forms of Spirit, we are also "topics of the text" and "what is true for Spirit should be at various levels true for us." This is why, she writes, "The text of the *Phenomenology* is thus peculiarly binding upon us, its readers; for it is [. . .] not only an abstract analysis of the unfolding of theorized Spirit but also an analysis of that which we ourselves are."[65] The moments of the text will only work together if we recognise that they have been bound by their movement and by our reading of them.

1 Hegel's Concept of Force in the *Phenomenology of Spirit*

> It is indeed remarkable to find investigations of the question whether attractive force may not be an entirely universal force of nature, perhaps even of spiritual nature. This is in fact the case, for attractive force is connection as such, and there is, to be sure, no force more universal than the force of connection.[1]

> What appears as an 'other' and solicits Force, both to expression and to a return into itself, directly proves to be *itself Force*; for the 'other' shows itself to be as much a universal medium as a One, and in such a way that each of these forms at the same time appears only as a vanishing moment. (*PS*, 83)

INTRODUCTION

The intention of this first chapter is to build a speculative model of the economy of Force at play in the *Phenomenology* and to consider the way in which Hegel is using the concept of Force as an ontological and epistemological category. My emphasis is on the role that Force plays in the dynamic process of becoming that consciousness embarks upon. The first aim, and the main premise with which I am operating, is to show, through a reading of the mechanisms of Force as Hegel describes them, that both desire and the process of recognition are prefigured by and modelled on the concept of Force. In so doing I am preparing the way for my argument that Hegel's formulation of self-consciousness as a play of Forces (*Spiel der Kräfte*) allows for a reading of the *Phenomenology* informed by psychoanalytic theory, wherein the movement of self-consciousness can be discussed as a tripartite process of binding-unbinding-rebinding. Thus, I am laying a conceptual foundation for a way of understanding how the Hegelian subject is bound to itself, to its own process of consciousness, and to the external world. I am also preparing the ground for the larger claim that true freedom only comes from recognition and acceptance of this bound state.

In the third chapter of the *Phenomenology*, "Force and the Understanding: Appearance and the Supersensible World," we can locate the first link between the inner world of consciousness and the external world. There we witness the birth of self-consciousness. As Judith Butler remarks, "Force is essential to the transition from consciousness to self-consciousness because it posits the externality of the world of sensuous and perceptual reality as one that is essentially related to consciousness itself; in effect, Force posits externalization as a necessary moment of thought."[2] Hegel's discussion of this link between the interior and the exterior, between the inner life of consciousness and the external world of objects and others, is one of the threads that is shot through the fabric of my book because it allows me to flesh out my model of binding.

The second aim of this chapter, therefore, is to prepare for an exploration of the shift from the *inter*subjective to the *intra*subjective realm and back again in the "Self-Consciousness" chapter. It is important to understand the activity of Force itself in order to understand the move that Hegel makes in "Self-Consciousness" and his formulation of the famous master/slave dialectic as a play of Forces. As stated in the Introduction, my aim is to remove the master/slave dialectic from the box into which readings of Hegel have put it and reread it alongside the other, more neglected moments that constitute the birth of self-consciousness. My reading of "Force and the Understanding" provides the tools for doing so. Referring to the master and slave episode, John Burbidge writes, "'Spirit,' as Hegel carefully explains in the *Phenomenology,* is the play of forces that develops where a number of players mutually recognize each other. So even absolute spirit is not a singular entity but a dynamic interplay, as many agents reciprocally interact." It is, Burbidge argues, crucial for Hegel's project that Spirit is understood as "the life of self-conscious individuals interacting within a play of forces that produces communities, of varying degrees and complexities. In principle it can cover the whole spectrum of human life."[3] It is precisely this "dynamic interplay" that is often overlooked in Hegel, and we find the model for this interplay in the concept of Force.

The third aim of this chapter is to investigate, at the level of the universal, the root of Spirit's emergence as based in the play of Forces. I will address the birth of Spirit again most significantly in Chapter Four after I have worked through the stages necessary for understanding its arrival. I will locate in this play of Forces an illustration of a precursor to the key, afflicted figure of the unhappy consciousness (*das unglückliche Bewußtsein*). The initial and generative movement of Force is that of self-diremption into two different Forces, and the aim is that of reunification. However, similar to the experience of the unhappy consciousness, the split Forces do not realise that they are, indeed, the same. We will also find an inner being that gazes (*Schauen*) into its inner world and feels the agony of contradiction much as we will find in the unhappy consciousness "the gazing of one self-consciousness into another" without the realization that it *is* both sides of this split (*PS*, 126).

That being said, the movement of Force is not yet formulated as the moment of potential crisis that is found in the unhappy consciousness.

Significantly, the unhappy consciousness requires "a Third, a mediator as counsellor" to emerge in order to reunify its split, and with this reunification we find the birth of Reason (*PS*, 138). The "Force and the Understanding" chapter presents a model that illustrates the act of splitting and then reunification in which a new, more advanced moment of being (a new appearance of Force) is created. We will soon see this as a model for the activity of unbinding and rebinding. In the Force chapter, the splitting of two Forces and their reunification is a moment out of which self-consciousness is born and consciousness gains the ability to see that, in its new form of self-consciousness, it is consciousness of itself in relation to its inner world.

In short, the third aim of this chapter is to argue that, for Hegel, one of the purposes of the "Force and the Understanding" section is to lay the groundwork for an understanding of how moments such as "The Unhappy Consciousness" episode eventually unfold, thus indicating that consciousness, from the moment it becomes self-consciousness, acknowledges the nascent roots of the unhappiness that it will forever carry within itself. It realises at this moment that the other is essential for its becoming but that this other is constantly just beyond full possession, and thus it is always striving towards this beyond. I conceive of the *Phenomenology* in much the same way that Jean Wahl did when he wrote, "This book is the story of consciousness' efforts to forget the distance and separation which it feels within itself."[4] This effort is what Wahl terms the "motor of the dialectic" and therefore is indispensable in the process of becoming. Most importantly, Wahl sees the translation of the play of Forces into the world of self-consciousness as the shift from a "logical dialectic" to a "historical and emotional dialectic."[5] I will return to the figure of the unhappy consciousness and to the importance of Wahl's reading in Chapter Two when I perform my own translation of the play of Forces.

Hegel proffers in the "Force and the Understanding" chapter a handful of wonderfully rich concepts from which I have selected those most important for my purposes. Keeping my three primary aims in mind, I will examine each of these concepts in turn, illustrating how they function in the "Force and the Understanding" chapter and in so doing situate, more solidly, the text as a whole. I will treat these concepts as the foundation for my forthcoming discussion of what is created out of the play of Forces and is designated as the third or thirdness. These concepts will be translated into a model that describes the move from the intrapsychic realm to intersubjective relations, first in Hegel and subsequently in the psychoanalytic setting. These concepts do not function in isolation, so both here and in the next chapter subsidiary terms will be discussed depending on the role they play.

The first amongst them is the concept of vanishing (*Verschwinden*). In the next chapter I will expand upon this concept and introduce the figure of the vanishing mediator, a move that will link to the idea of Force as a universal medium and to my discussion via psychoanalytic theory of, amongst other things, the various forms the vanishing mediator can take, including the form of the third. Hegel also offers the space of the inner world of consciousness as a void (*Leeren*) and the concept of Explanation (*Erklären*) as an action that the Understanding uses to describe self-consciousness and one that affords a large amount of self-satisfaction, a rare and fleeting moment in the *Phenomenology*. Furthermore, in the action of the Force splitting into two separate Forces, we see the interaction between expression (*Aussprechen* or *Äußerung*) and suppression/repression (*Unterdrückung/Zurückhalten*). This raises implications as to the positive functioning of the notion of repression in Hegel's system. In Chapter Four I will parallel this with the generative notion of repression as found in the work of Christopher Bollas.

A PRELIMINARY DEFINITION OF FORCE

Before delving into the aforementioned concepts and into my speculative endeavour in detail, I will describe Force in the *Phenomenology* in the simplest of terms. However, it is only in working through the chapter, in pulling apart the nuances and making our way through the difficult transitions that Hegel offers, that Force as a concept comes alive. This is, in many ways, the Hegelian method of using the form of his argument to embody its material content. As noted in my Introduction, on the most basic level, and the level on which the chapter on Force is most often read, Hegel is attempting to work through the problems that an empiricism based on perception causes for consciousness. However, the aim of this present chapter is not to examine his critiques on this level. As we will find, Force is a unique entity within the system of the *Phenomenology*. In order for it to "*be*, it must be completely set free from thought," it must be allowed to exist and function without meddling from any process other than its own (*PS*, 82). It is not enough simply to *think* Force; we must understand it in its embodied state, in action. This embodiment, this appearance of Force is, in many ways, the only way in which we can *know* Force. Peter Kalkavage comments, "Force [. . .] must not be a mere idea in the mind. It must be substantial or real – something actual or *at work* in the perceptual world."[6] In light of this, we can begin to understand how investigations of the notion of Force and the aspects of consciousness contained therein can create a useful paradigm for exploring the concepts of binding and of energy as they are found in psychoanalytic models. Importantly, it is in the appearance or manifestation of these elements that their existence is located.

Apart from the *Phenomenology*, Hegel's early thinking on the concept of Force can be located in the *Jena System: Logic and Metaphysics* (1804–05) and in the *Philosophical Propaedeutic* (1808–11). Although I cannot discuss these texts in any comprehensive manner due to the scope of my book, I can briefly draw out two key elements of the way in which Hegel was writing about the concept of Force both prior to the *Phenomenology* and in his later teaching. I agree with H. S. Harris when he writes of the *Jena System* that its contents are "especially interesting for the light that they throw upon the parallel discussions in the third chapter of the *Phenomenology* (Force and the Understanding)" (*JS*, 46).[7] Aside from the relief of an easier read that the *Jena System* offers, this light for our purposes is the way in which Hegel discusses Force as a relationship (*Verhältnis*), moving out of a simple connection (*Beziehung*), and the way in which it prefigures a form of recognition. Hegel writes, "Force thus expresses the idea of relationship itself" (*JS*, 55–56). My decision to use the term *relationship* throughout this book is, then, made on the basis that it is more true to Hegel's own categories, especially in the *Jena System*, than a term such as *modality*.[8] It is in the section on Relationship in the Logic portion of this text that the most fruitful discussion of the concept of Force takes place. H. S. Harris points out that what Hegel is dealing with here is the "prevailing scientific conception of force" and with conceptions of "causal explanation." Harris also notes that it is in Relationship that substances are "realized," linking the idea of relationship with recognition: "In order to express its own self-sufficient permanence permanently, the substance itself (as permanent) must be recognized by another substance."[9] These are all aspects of Force that I read as existing implicitly in the *Phenomenology*.

Between the 1804–05 manuscript and the 1807 *Phenomenology*, Hegel makes a move from a discussion of the mechanisms of *a* Force towards understanding the idea of a play of Forces. Such a transition allows Hegel to explore the workings of two different Forces, rather than just the properties of one Force. Robert Solomon discusses the "conflict of forces" in the *Phenomenology* as having their origins in Hegel's earlier work but rests his argument mostly on the shifts between the *Encyclopaedia Logic*, rather than the *Jena* material, although the move that I am making here is very much along the same lines.[10] Solomon also sees the link that I aim to make between the concept of Force in Hegel and psychoanalytic theory. He writes of this shift to the exploration of the conflict between forces: "It is clear enough what Hegel has in mind: we know it best in Freud, but Hegel takes it from Heraclitus and Empedocles—the view that all change is to be explained by a *conflict of forces* (life against death, sex against ego, love against strife, force against inertia)."[11] Because Hegel describes this conflict as *spiel* or play, I will also do so. This sense of play necessarily incorporates notions of struggle (as with the master/slave dialectic) as such conflict is an intrinsic element in the development of consciousness. In Chapter Three, when I elaborate upon the potential for reading life and death drives into Hegel via the lens of psychoanalysis, this parallel will come to fruition.

The language of binding that I am reading implicitly into the *Phenomenology* finds its roots in the *Jena Logic*. Terms such as *bind up*, *bond* (*Verbinden*), and *bonding*, as well as *combination* (*Verbindung*) come out of Hegel's writing on Relationship. The task that Hegel sets for himself in this section is to work out the nature of the relationship between substances and how the internal dividedness of substance "is held together throughout." Essentially, he is interested in moving beyond a simple understanding of cause and effect. Furthermore, "the only thing to be done is to determine more closely this oneness of what is divided" (*JS*, 40). It is in pursuit of this determination that I find the language of binding, for Hegel writes of the "bound" state of these substances. The substances are "bonded by something quite other than what they are themselves" (*JS*, 51). Hegel finds that above and beyond "causal linkage," it is Force that "unites within itself both of the essential sides of the relation, identity and separateness, and unites the former precisely as identity of separateness or of infinity" (*JS*, 54).

Hegel clearly affords Force a position of importance that goes beyond its place in the physical sciences: "In that force thus expresses relationship in truth, it is no wonder that the so-called discovery of attractive force [. . .] or of the force of chemical affinity has been accounted such an enrichment of knowledge in general" (*JS*, 56). I take this to mean that Hegel saw the potential in the concept of Force to expand the ways in which we know. In so doing, as readers we can begin to better understand his own expansion and formulation of the interaction of two consciousnesses as a play of Forces that is found in the *Phenomenology.*

As one would hope for, Hegel's own introduction to philosophy for students, the *Propaedeutic*, is remarkably clear and accessible. There are three points that I draw from these lessons, which, although written after the *Phenomenology*, help cast light on the concept of Force. In "Phenomenology for the Middle Class" (1809), we find the "Inner of Things" as a "simple Force which passes over in Determinate Being [Dasein] into its Expression [or manifestation]" and Force as brokering the relations between consciousness and "difference." Ultimately, this leads to a way of thinking about the relation between consciousness and the concept of the other:

> This concept, applied to Consciousness itself, gives another stage thereof. Hitherto it was in relation to its object as something alien and indifferent. Since now the difference in general has become a difference which at the same time is no difference, the previous mode of the difference of Consciousness from its object falls away. It has an object and is related to an Other, which, however, is at the same time no 'Other'; *in fine*, it has itself for object.[12]

Firstly, we find the potential to read Force as a model for how consciousness holds the properties of difference within it and for helping consciousness to realise itself as an object in relation to this Other and move to a new shape of consciousness (*Gestalt des Bewußtseins*) and thus a new shape of knowing (*Gestalt des Wissens*). This we will see fully developed in the *Phenomenology*, as consciousness locates the distinction between its internal and external world. The significance of these shapes of consciousness will be touched upon at various points in the first half of my study, but the way in which Hegel's formulation anticipates the manner in which the concept the third (*das Dritte*) can be formulated comes to fruition most fully in Chapter Four.

Secondly, we again find Force under the category of Relations and find simple language for understanding the role of Force in the discussion of form and content that Hegel will offer us in the *Phenomenology*. On the matter of form, we find that "the Whole, as the inner active Form, is Force [*Kraft*]. It has no external Matter as its condition but is in Matter itself. Its condition is only an external impetus which solicits it. The latter is itself the expression of a Force and requires to be solicited in order to be manifested" (*PP*, 86).[13] Thirdly, what is key, Hegel posits, is that each side of the activity of solicitation is the "ground of the activity, or the Expression of the other" (*PP*, 132).[14] Crucially, therefore, and I will discuss this in greater detail as the chapter progresses, there is no activity of Force without another Force to call it into action. On the matter of content, we find that "Force in its expression exhibits what it is in-itself since as Form it contains within itself its determinations and there is nothing in its expression which is not in its Inner" (*PP*, 86).[15] In other words, Force is its expression. To have briefly located the way in which Hegel was thinking about and teaching the concept of Force before and directly after the publication of the *Phenomenology* gives me accessible ground for Force from which to begin my examination. So I move now to the *Phenomenology of Spirit* to continue my preliminary definition of Force.

Having established the relationship between consciousness and the outer world through the explications of sense-certainty and perception, Hegel uses the "Force and the Understanding" section to trace a turn to the relationship between the inner and outer worlds for consciousness and the unification of these worlds through the movement that is Force and the concept of the Understanding. It is a turn where consciousness, having arrived at thought via perception, has taken the "unconditioned universal" for its object. However, because consciousness is not yet *for itself*, it does not yet see itself in the object; it does not yet see itself in the notion of the universal. The problem posed, then, is how to get from one pole to the other, how to move from a split consciousness, and the universal as object of this consciousness, to knowledge of the self as self and *as* this universal. It thus becomes a matter of form and content and how to negotiate the space between the two. Hegel writes:

> But, in general, to be for itself and to be in relation to an other constitutes the nature and essence of the content, whose truth consists in its being unconditionally universal; and the result is simply and solely universal [. . .]. But because this unconditioned universal is an object for consciousness, there emerges in it the distinction of form and content. (*PS*, 80–81)

He introduces the idea of Force to broker this negotiation and to act as what I am designating the binding material between consciousness and its objects, between the form and the content. Jean Hyppolite writes:

> It is crucial to note that what is now given to consciousness, which has become understanding, is the transition itself—the connection—which

> previously occurred in it without its knowledge and which was, therefore, external to its movements. Nonetheless, this transition first appears to understanding as having an objective form; for understanding, the transition will be *force.*[16]

It is in this way that I ground my understanding of Force for the purposes of my work. I will read the idea of Force as transition and connection to explore the concept of Force as universal medium and binding substance. Henry Sussman writes of this element of binding, "Force demonstrates the hitherto unprecedented capability to either 'consciousness' or its objects, to bond this particular level of functioning to its general existence as a whole."[17] When I interrogate the movement of self-consciousness in the next chapter, I will be building on the model found in Force with an exploration of the intersubjective binding process, which includes the activity of unbinding. My turn to psychoanalytic theories of the binding process in Chapters Three and Four will illuminate the rich potential of this concept for an understanding of how to read this model in the *Phenomenology*. This is a model that has both epistemological and ontological strains running through it, so that we can also begin to conceive of a binding process as it relates to the binding of knowledge and thought that helps to constitute our becoming.

Hegel considers Force to be the movement that occurs when "'matters' posited as independent directly pass over into their unity and their unity directly unfolds its diversity, and this once again reduces itself to unity" (*PS*, 81). Force is thus the movement of "matters," of moments, of objects, that causes them to leave their individuality behind, becoming one with the other(s), only to break this unity back up into its particularity and then start the whole process again. Furthermore, Force is the "unconditioned universal which is equally in its own self what it is *for an other;* or which contains the difference in its own self—for difference is nothing else than being-for-*another*" (*PS*, 82). This sets forth Force as a neutral, but by no means static, property, one that belongs to the concept of the Understanding. However, even in this belonging Force is not something that is owned but is, rather, an entity that exists to serve as a medium, as this connection and transitional quantity between consciousness and its object(s), between individual matters and the unity of the unconditional universal.

The penultimate basic point is that there are two moments of Force: the "expression" of Force and Force "proper." The expression of Force is that moment which holds the "dispersal of independent 'matters,'" and the second moment, Force proper, is the moment into which the independent matters have disappeared, or "Force which has been *driven back* into itself from its expression" (*PS*, 81). I will further investigate the idea of expression and what it means to be driven back into itself in due course. For now it is sufficient to understand that Force itself, even as a moment of transition and connection, also requires a moment of mediation between its own two moments. In this case, it is its own mediator.

Let me begin my close reading of the "Force and the Understanding" chapter with the concept of vanishing (*Verschwinden*). This is perhaps one of the most slippery, overlooked, yet fundamental notions with which Hegel's system operates and one that is given an extremely active role in the "Force and the Understanding" section. Of interest here is the relationship that the idea of vanishing has with the idea of negation. Furthermore, I am interested in what the activity of vanishing means to the notion of Force and to the play of Forces insofar as it holds a potential to generate what could be looked at in dynamic/economic terms as a connecting and transitional energy. Arkady Plotnitsky writes: "Hegel's analysis of force anticipates both Freud and Lacan, by way of an interplay of the exchange and reserve economy and the economy of energy and play of forces, specifically in the economy of desire."[18] I will read this Hegelian model alongside a metapsychological framework built by Freud, which I will then trace in Green and Bollas. Here I endeavour to find the theoretical and conceptual roots in "Force and the Understanding." My discussion of vanishing is essential for the way in which I am considering notions of transition and transformation, process and movement throughout my study.

THE CONCEPT OF VANISHING

Prior to the "Force and the Understanding" chapter, the action of vanishing occurs only a handful of times in the *Phenomenology*. The use is predominantly concentrated in one particular section of the "Sense-Certainty" chapter. So although the concept is introduced and utilised earlier, it is not until it reaches the stages of the Understanding that it becomes a fully blown, necessary activity for Hegel. In "Sense-Certainty," Hegel writes: "If I turn round, this truth has vanished and is converted into its opposite: 'No tree is here, but a house instead.' 'Here' itself does not vanish; on the contrary, it abides constant in the vanishing of the house, the tree, etc., and it is indifferently house or tree" (*PS*, 60–61). The physical action of the "I," the turning round, and thus a shift of focus, causes truths to vanish and convert. What we are grappling with is not an actual material vanishing of a substance (e.g. tree or house) but rather a vanishing of the external that takes place on some level within the "I" due to its perspective and sensory, in this case visual, relationship with the external world of objects, a relationship that Hegel calls the "immediacy of seeing" (*PS*, 61). There follows a passage wherein, "the vanishing of the single Now and Here that we mean is prevented by the fact that *I* hold them fast." A bit further on we find that "the one truth vanishes in the other" (*PS*, 60). What we have here, then, is a secondary action of the "I," this time one of *prevention* of vanishing by the intervention of the "I," and one in which truths are not simply converted but can vanish in other truths. The seeing, sensing "I" is firmly in place as an agent of at least one form of vanishing. We have seen the potential power of the "I" in its ability not only to convert a truth into its opposite via an act of vanishing but also to prevent such a vanishing from occurring. It must be noted that we have yet to discover if by vanishing Hegel means "lost," completely disappeared, never to return, or if some other form (of knowing, of being) is born of this vanishing. We are made to wonder if there is something unalterable about a conversion or whether a conversion as a result of vanishing is simply another way to illustrate the transformation of a relationship between consciousness and itself or consciousness and the external world. The aim of my book is to show that the latter is true; that in the activity of vanishing a transformation occurs that alters the shape of consciousness by giving it a new moment of being, a new form of knowing. In Hegel's system, vanishing is not alone in holding this transformational quality, but it is a wonderful and under-explored example of that potential.

On the subject of disappearance, it might be helpful to recall just one example from Hegel's Preface to the *Phenomenology*, where he writes that the "bud disappears in the bursting-forth of the blossom" and goes on to discuss how the fruit's supplanting of the blossom, and so on, means that these forms are "mutually incompatible." However, crucially, he states: "Yet at the same time their fluid nature makes them moments of an organic unity in which they not only do not conflict, but in which each is as necessary as the other; and this mutual necessity alone constitutes the life of the whole" (*PS*, 2). It is in this way that I am trying to think about vanishing moments and moments of disappearance; the whole as such is dependent upon these vanishings, and they subsist, even in a new shape (of knowing) or a new form (of being) as part of the whole. Thus we begin to understand both the ontological and epistemological importance of the activity of vanishing. At this point, what must be noted is that the power that remains after this series of vanishings is this "I," for Hegel then states that it is the "I" as a *universal* that "does not disappear" (*PS*, 62).

The final use of vanishing in the "Sense-Certainty" section is worth noting for its links with the idea of remainder, of potential excess that is a result and survives the movement of the becoming of consciousness. Hegel writes:

> The Here, which was supposed to have been pointed out, vanishes into other Heres, but these likewise vanish. What is pointed out, held fast, and abides, is a *negative* This, which *is* negative only when the Heres are taken as they should be, but in being so taken, they supersede themselves; what abides is a simple complex of many Heres. (*PS*, 64)

Hegel can be seen as simply building upon the earlier use of vanishing, wherein the truth vanished and was converted into its opposite. "Here," as a truth that has been pointed out, vanishes into a multiplicity of truths that also, in their turn, then vanish. What is left is the *negative* "This," which only exists because of the action of the "Heres," which have, in themselves, vanished.

At stake is the question of remainder, of what it is that can "abide," of what can literally put up with, tolerate, this vanishing. What seems ultimately to survive in this instance of vanishing is the simple complex of many "Heres," a movement carving its way, with the help of the act of vanishing, through multiplicity, gathering itself into a simply unity, into a universality. This concept of remainder is of importance to the understanding of the notion of vanishing in general. I conceive of the notion of remainder in light of the idea of subsistence (*Bestehen*), as that which survives. I will formulate this idea of subsistence as I proceed.

Vanishing appears next in the "Perception or the Thing and Deception" chapter of the *Phenomenology*. Interestingly, it emerges directly after consciousness "enters the realm of the Understanding" for the very first time. Hegel writes: "Thus the singular being of sense does indeed vanish in the dialectical movement of immediate certainty and becomes universality, but it is only a *sensuous universality*. *My* 'meaning' has vanished and perception takes the object as it is *in itself*, or as a universal as such" (*PS*, 77). Here we are told that it is "dialectical movement" that causes the vanishing to occur, a point that is of interest for our understanding of the agency/agencies, if indeed there are any, behind this action. Whether or not this agency is always at play or whether vanishing is an act unto itself is also a question at stake. In any case, we are beginning to see vanishing as a form of transition, of the space or the object created between self and other (the object, the external world in its many forms) that belongs to neither but is essential for their relating. This is a crucial designation of vanishing that anticipates the complex nature of ownership we find in psychoanalytic theory, which I will discuss in terms of the third thing that is created in the intersubjective analytic encounter between the analyst and analysand. That which is created can be seen as that which subsists, remains, survives this encounter.

There are varying degrees and tenses of vanishing in this section, indicating the distinction between the action of a verb, "to vanish," which would include a present and past tense as well as implicating an agency behind the vanishing; the simple presence of "a vanishing," which implies a state of being; and the idea of a "vanishing moment," which is perhaps the combination of the prior two. It is of interest to my present discussion to first look at these vanishing moments as moments of transition, as connections, and furthermore, as moments that by their movement (action) and their existence seem to simultaneously represent, are, difference and the disappearance of difference.

In the only piece of Hegel scholarship I have come across that directly addresses the concept of vanishing, Stephen Houlgate discusses it as "one of the most difficult dialectical moves in the *Logic*."[19] It is important to note that Houlgate's work concentrates on the activity of vanishing in the *Logic* and does not examine its presence in the *Phenomenology*. Nevertheless, his argument is extremely helpful to our understanding of the purpose of vanishing in Hegel's thinking. He writes that it is not enough simply to acknowledge that "becoming depends on the absolute difference between being and nothing" (*OHL*, 289). What is key, Houlgate argues, is to recognise that for Hegel, the vanishing of each into the other is the "collapse of pure difference between being and nothing." Vanishing can only occur based on this absolute difference, but, paradoxically, the "vanishing into its other proves that it is *not* different from that other after all." Importantly, when difference vanishes, becoming ceases. What this means, Houlgate explains, is not that "vanishing and becoming never occur. It is to say that becoming necessarily entails its own cessation" (*OHL*, 290). On a structural level, this will become key to our understanding of the moments of stasis that occur in the process of becoming and that we will see illustrated in the unhappy consciousness.

The very idea that being and nothing are indistinguishable from one another (and thus a unity, entirely bound to one another) is the collapse of becoming into itself and for Hegel is the process of becoming. Yet unity does not mean that they exist "side by side" but, rather, that both are moments in the same process that vanish into one another (*OHL*, 287). Houlgate emphasises Hegel's point from the *Logic* ("Sublation of Becoming") that becoming is "the vanishing of its own vanishing" (*OHL*, 292).[20] However, this vanishing is a sort of fusion; it is not a passing *into* but an absolute *inseparability* in which the "purity of being and nothing disappears," and they are "logically bound up with the other" (*OHL*, 291). Crucial to the notion of vanishing, for Houlgate, is that we recognise that simply because being and nothing vanish it does not mean they exist outside of thought. What Hegel describes in the *Logic* is that what they are is nothing but this vanishing. Houlgate writes: "The fact that they vanish the moment they are thought does not demonstrate that their immediacy somehow eludes our grasp. Rather, it reveals that logically the immediacy of the one *is* its own vanishing into the equally vanishing immediacy of the other" (*OHL*, 272). Further, Houlgate argues, "'Nothing' is simply the name we give to the complete and utter *vanishedness* of being" (*OHL*, 279). When each vanishes into the other, they revive one another and are thus dependent upon one another for a certain level of vitality (*OHL*, 284).

My present concern with vanishing is not focussed so much on the relationship between "being" and "nothing" but is more focussed on the collapse of difference as such. Additionally, I am interested in the notion that for Hegel "becoming" is the vanishing of being into nothing (and, significantly, nothing back into being) and the way in which, in this vanishing, they are bound to one another. To that end, I will not pursue Houlgate's line of discussion any further. What I take from it is the dialectical/structural importance of vanishing in the *Logic* as a way of bolstering my own claims for its vital role in the *Phenomenology*. In Chapter Two I will briefly touch upon the designation of vanishing magnitudes from the *Logic* as it pertains to the same in the figure of Scepticism. Here, however, I take from Houlgate's reading an understanding of vanishing as not only a form of transition but also as aiding in the activity of binding that I am attempting to locate, the mechanisms of which I must here continue to flesh out.

As noted earlier, Force is "equally for its own self what it is for another" and thus "contains its difference in its own self" (*PS*, 85). In its dual form as the "expression" of Force and of Force "proper" (as driven back into itself), Force exists as both a dispersal of multiple facets of difference (itself) and as a unifying property. Yet we must take these moments for what they are. In Hegel's first use of the idea of vanishing moments with relation to Force, he writes: "But Force is also the whole, i.e. it remains what it is according to its Notion; that is to say, these *differences* remain pure forms, superficial *vanishing* moments" (*PS*, 82). It is made clear here that whatever difference exists within Force is purely transitional and possesses a form unto itself. Nevertheless, difference is an intrinsic and essential moment in the movement. It is the existence and the subsequent vanishing of these differences that gives rise to the properties of Force. The difference is fleeting, impermanent, and does not penetrate or cause change in Force itself.

Hegel uses the category of a vanishing moment, as distinct from the various other forms of vanishing, only three other times in this section. Each time it is used, it serves to reinforce that what appears as a difference, as an other, as an extreme, is really only a momentary designation and never a permanently fixed form in the movement that is Force. He posits: "What appears as an 'other' and solicits Force, both to expression and to a return into itself, directly proves to be *itself Force*; for the 'other' shows itself to be as much a universal medium as a One, and in such a way that each of these forms at the same time appears only as a vanishing moment" (*PS*, 83). Recall here that Force contains its difference within itself and that what is "other" for it is only Force itself. The moment of vanishing occurs to provide a motor to the movement of Force. Without this appearance of the other and its subsequent and inevitable vanishing, Force would remain a static notion and not at all the universal, binding medium that we can recognise it as being. Hegel graciously hands us this notion of vanishing moments as transition when he writes:

> The fact that the extremes, from the standpoint of both these sides, are thus nothing *in themselves,* that these sides in which their different essences were supposed to consist are only vanishing moments, are an immediate transition of each into its opposite, this truth becomes apparent to consciousness in its perception of the movement of Force. (*PS*, 85)

As he does often in the text, Hegel then differentiates between consciousness' self-understanding and our own understanding, as readers, of the process at this point. How he addresses the reader with the inclusive "we" and "for us" is a topic for an entirely different investigation than this present one and one that is commented upon in many works of Hegel scholarship.[21] It is sufficient to note that he writes that what was more apparent "for us"

(Hegel and the reader) here is that the differences in content and form vanished, whereas what consciousness became aware of were only the vanishing moments themselves. Of course, as observers of the process, we have a more concrete understanding of the movement than simply a perception, and our role as philosopher-partner to Hegel is fortified.

We must also briefly consider the act of vanishing as it pertains to the act of reading and engaging with Hegel's text, thus binding ourselves to the text and the process of consciousness set forth in the *Phenomenology*. As we make our way through the work, a trail of vanishing concepts follows, re-emerging and then vanishing again, perpetually, constituting our growing consciousness and knowledge. In a sense, we turn our back to the conceptual "Thises and Heres" in order to engage with another moment, yet they can always be rediscovered with a shift of focus. Let us hold onto this role of vanishing in our experience of reading the text when I turn later to a discussion of the shapes of knowing. For now, I must simply acknowledge the link we can make between vanishing and ourselves as readers, as universal mediums, for the movement that is Hegel's text. So, returning to the discussion at hand we find that consciousness is only able, at this point, to *perceive* these moments, and truth becomes "apparent" but is not yet fully known.

All vanishing, whether designated as a "moment" or simply as a result of the movement of Force, is the vanishing of these distinctions, these extremes, in order that we may return to the Force before its self-splitting, to Force as a whole. Just as this return is necessary, we will also return to the moment of splitting, for such is the nature of Force. In one of the most important designations of Force as a vanishing, Hegel writes:

> From this we see that the Notion of Force becomes *actual* through its duplication into two Forces, and how it comes to be so. These two Forces exist as independent essences; but their existence is a movement of each towards the other, such that their being is rather a pure *positedness* or a being that is *posited by an other*, i.e. their being has really the significance of a sheer *vanishing*. (*PS*, 85)

As we have just seen, prior to this passage Hegel has broken down the idea of difference into its twofold meaning, one being a matter of form and the other of content, but has subsequently vanished these distinctions. Force is only Force in that it is two essences moving towards each other. Since the distinctions have already vanished, their existence in themselves and with the other is given meaning in the vanishing. As the distinctions are Force itself, Force thus comes to be through this vanishing; Force, as we have already seen, is transition. It is of note that Hegel qualifies this vanishing with the word *sheer*, thus emphasizing how complete and total this vanishing of distinctions that constitutes the being of Force actually is and must be.

I have already established that Force belongs to the Understanding. While the primary point of focus of this chapter is the concept of Force and not, in as much detail, that of the Understanding, I will just briefly introduce how the Understanding comes into play in relationship to Force, rather than the other way around. At this point, we can look at how it finds itself in relation to the idea of vanishing. As noted, when, in the stage of perception, consciousness enters the realm of the Understanding for the first time, we see one of the first instances of active vanishing. The realm of the Understanding has been entered with the introduction to consciousness of "unconditioned absolute universality," when there is a unity acknowledged between being-for-self and the being-for-another with which it is "burdened." We then move directly into the passage that was referred to above, where the "singular sense of being" vanished in the "dialectical movement." The universality achieved is simply sensuous. Hegel writes, "*My* 'meaning' has vanished" and we are led to the idea that through such a vanishing, when self-meaning is removed, perception is paired with the Understanding and the object can then be taken "as it is *in itself*" (*PS*, 77). So here, it is not that the difference between the self and the object has (been) vanished, for that is yet to come. Instead, it is a moment of growth for consciousness in the realm of perception, and one where we can see a link between the realm of the Understanding and the power of the vanishing. By this I mean that we can begin to see that the introduction of the Understanding moves consciousness beyond pure perception, beyond a purely sensuous relationship with objects, with the external world, and begins to draw the object into a relationship with the internal space, the inner world, via the power of Force and the activity of vanishing.

Let us return, however, to the "Force and the Understanding" section. Once he has established the basic structure and movement of Force in relation to consciousness, Hegel turns to the matter of the relationship between consciousness and its inner being. It is a mediated relationship and one that is contingent upon the "mediating play of Forces." The Understanding utilizes this play of Forces to look into the "true background of Things." Hegel writes: "The middle term which unites the two extremes, the Understanding and the inner world, is the developed *being* of Force which, for the Understanding itself, is henceforth only a vanishing" (*PS*, 86–87). A meaningful shift in the action of Force is indicated here.

In its being, it is not a vanishing moment, it has not been vanished. It is a vanishing but is still a uniting force, a mediator. Force, the neutral, generative point of transition, soon finds itself, in its being, to be simultaneously a "reflection of the inner to itself" and this vanishing. This inner is a world of rapid and immediate motion, where the things of perception "without rest or stay turn into their opposite" and consciousness are involved in the conversion of the truth of its movement into an "objective inner." Consciousness is able to distinguish the reflection of itself from the reflection of things and has the ability to possess the knowledge of the inner (as the in-itself) as an extreme in relation to itself (as a moment of being-for-self) and is able to recognise this inner world as the True and Notion but does not yet know what this means. Somehow this knowledge is still "*objective* vanishing appearance" and not yet its own (*PS*, 87). What consciousness is after, and now realises exists, is a world that lies beneath the vanishing, that exists because the activity of vanishing exposes it and, in some senses, creates it. This world seems to be solid and true. Hegel writes,

> There now opens up above the sensuous world, which is the world of *appearance*, a *supersensible* world which henceforth is the true world, above the vanishing *present* world there opens up a permanent *beyond*; an in-itself which is the first, and therefore imperfect, appearance of Reason, or only the pure element in which the truth has its *essence*. (*PS*, 87–88)

We have encountered a new angle of the concept of vanishing. Not only does it act as a mediator or is a moment, but we can also conceive of entire worlds as vanishing when the knowledge of another world is gained. By "world" I understand Hegel to mean a way of knowing, a way of experiencing, that consciousness holds to be its truth at a particular point. The world that has vanished and that itself came about because of a play of Forces, and is a product of multiple vanishings, is the world of appearance. This "supersensible world," this world of the "beyond," is really the "inner world," and this inner world holds as its essence, as its "filling," the world of appearance. So, even though the world of appearance has vanished, leaving us only the supersensible world, we see that appearance has not truly disappeared but has only vanished, has given itself over, so that the inner world might be viewed. Again, we have a moment when Hegel is writing about the philosopher's relationship with the inner world and how to access it, for at this point self-consciousness has not yet come into being and thus consciousness has yet to fully gain this truth.

There is, as we have seen, a multiplicity of Forces created by Force itself in the process of its own movement and its relationship with the world of appearance and now with the *supersensible* world. Yet Hegel again uses the notion of vanishing to do away with these distinctions of Force, these potential contrasts. He posits that the relations between the Forces, whether it is Force as solicited or solicitor, as a "passive medium" or as an "active negative unity" are really just "one in the same." He writes:

> In this way there vanishes completely all distinction of *separate,* mutually contrasted *Forces* which were supposed to be present in this movement, for they rested solely on those distinctions; and the distinction between the Forces, along with both those distinctions, likewise collapses into only one. (*PS*, 90)

It is important to note in this designation of an act of vanishing the introduction of absolute flux (*die absolut wechselnde*) as a result of the collapse. In absolute flux "there is neither Force, nor the act of soliciting or being solicited nor the determinateness of being a stable medium and a unity reflected into itself, there is neither something existing singly by itself, nor are there diverse antitheses." In collapsing itself, Force has negated its purpose as "stable medium," as transitional point and active agent, and has simply become part of the movement that is appearance. In this movement, difference is simply universal difference and is "the *simple element in the play of Force itself* and what is true in it. It is the *law of Force*" (*PS*, 90). I would argue, however, that this negation is never a permanent state and is, instead, a generative entity. In this case, what is generated is this law of Force. I will not be exploring this concept of the law of Force any further on its own but only as it may relate to the notion of Explanation that I will examine shortly.

Once the notion of flux, of the law of Force, has been introduced, the notion of vanishing all but vanishes itself until Hegel weaves a compelling conclusion to the end of the "Force and the Understanding" episode. There is only one brief use, when Hegel sees "determinateness" as a "vanishing moment." Here he is speaking of the determinateness between specific laws wherein the Notion of law not only "transcends specific law" but also "law as such" (*PS*, 92). The action of consciousness shifts as it moves closer to the introduction of self-consciousness, becoming that of an emphasis on cancellation, attraction, and then repulsion, splitting, sundering, self-destruction and self-supersession. It must be noted that of all of the above, supersession has been most at play since the beginning of the "Force and the Understanding" section. Hegel writes that the two moments of Force, the "expression" of Force and Force "proper," exist independently but that the existence of Force is contingent upon both their independence, their "enduring" being, and in the fact that they in turn supersede themselves, thus setting a movement into motion, a movement which is perceiving. What is key to keep in mind about the movement of attraction is that at this stage it falls under the law of universal attraction that "merely asserts that *everything has a constant difference in relation to other things*." The role of Force comes into play in that it is at this point an "abstraction which absorbs the differences themselves of what attracts and what is attracted" (*PS*, 91–92).[22] In Chapters Two and Three, where it takes a more prominent role in my discussion, I will show how the notion of attraction (and its counterpart repulsion) translates into the intersubjective realm in Hegel and then further into the psychoanalytic sphere.

It is possible that the shift described above is related to the fact that one of the discussions that Hegel embarks on after introducing the law of Force regards the second supersensible world, that of the "inverted world." One of the trickier sections of this already difficult chapter, the discussion of the inverted world would take us on another path than the present one so I can address it only briefly.[23] The inverted world does not seem to be a world that profits by vanishing any of its elements. Indeed, the whole point of the inverted world is that there are extreme opposites that exist within it; the inverted world is a stark illustration that a thing would not exist without its opposite. However, it transpires that the properties hold their inversions within them. For a time, then, we are not in the realm of Force, via the vanishing, as purely transition or connection.

It is key to note that the concept of desire (*Begierde*) has yet to be introduced; this will come almost immediately in the "Truth of Self-Certainty" portion of "Self-Consciousness" when Hegel states, "Self-consciousness is Desire in general" (*PS*, 105). Thus, the language of "Force and the Understanding" can only begin to hint at the unrest that awaits it. At this stage, it is sufficient to remark that the root of this desire is the essentiality that self-consciousness must recognise for the unity of itself with itself. As I have been discussing, in the "Force and the Understanding" chapter, consciousness does not yet recognise that it is a split self, a split that it experienced the moment self-consciousness was born and thus does not yet possess the ability to recognise that its unity is of the utmost importance to its survival. With the introduction of desire, consciousness, in its new form of self-consciousness, enters a realm wherein violence and extreme unrest are recognised as being intrinsic and inescapable aspects of the process of becoming, but in "Force and the Understanding" we are clearly not yet there. Self-consciousness, as we shall soon see, is only introduced at the tail end of this section. The shift into self-consciousness as desire, and the implications it has for our understanding of the language of Force, is something that I will investigate in Chapter Two. There I examine whether desire is one version of a vanishing mediator, a mediator brought in to unify the split self. If I am taking the line that Force is a model for the concept of desire and subsequently for the concept of recognition, then I can posit that desire is a unifying principle much like Force that operates by combining the activities of attraction and repulsion, binding, and unbinding.

In returning to the concept of vanishing, I assume, however, that the notion of vanishing does not leave us, for it has been established as one of the main activities at work in the movement of Force. And indeed, there is one last, crucial double occurrence of vanishing yet to come, the acts of which help to give birth to self-consciousness. Although this section serves to reiterate the new birth of self-consciousness, which, as we will later see, initially comes about via Explanation, it is necessary to witness the moment that self-consciousness takes its first full breath as a result of these vanishings and truly looks at what it now is:

> Raised above perception, consciousness exhibits itself closed in a unity with the supersensible world through the mediating term of appearance, through which it gazes into this background [lying behind appearance]. The two extremes [of this syllogism], the one, of the pure inner world, the other, that of the inner being gazing into this pure inner world, have now coincided, and just as they, *qua* extremes, have vanished, so too the middle term, as something other than these extremes, has also vanished. This curtain [of appearance] hanging before the inner world

> is therefore drawn away, and we have the inner being [the 'I'] gazing into the inner world—the vision of the undifferentiated selfsame being, which repels itself from itself, posits itself as an inner being containing different moments, but for which equally these moments are immediately *not* different—*self-consciousness*. (*PS*, 103)

We not only have here the key vanishing of extremes but also the vanishing of the middle term, the mediator of these extremes, bringing together the inner world and the inner being and vanishing their mediator: appearance. Hegel offers us an image of a curtain being drawn as if the whole world were, indeed, a stage, as if the "I" has now been granted backstage privilege. The "I" is clearly not yet a participant but instead gazes (*Schauen*) into this inner world and in so doing has found its first moment of self-consciousness. This notion of gazing will arise again most prominently in the episode of "The Unhappy Consciousness," to which I referred briefly above. A fuller comparison of the two episodes of gazing will be profitable for my study at that stage. Just prior to this moment of gazing there is another instance of "repelling" that is a key moment of self-consciousness. As we will soon see with its birth out of "explanation," self-consciousness is the new shape of consciousness that holds the knowledge that "what is distinguished from myself is not different [from me]." This comes about because "I," the "selfsame being, repel myself from myself," and that which is distinct from me no longer is distinct. Self-consciousness ultimately is "consciousness of itself in its otherness" (*PS*, 102). "I," we could say, is a Force that attracts and repulses itself and attracts and repulses the other, "objects in general," and knows itself in this movement and in this other. We will see how Hegel elaborates on this activity in the next chapter, when one self-consciousness meets another self-consciousness.[24]

At this stage we can note that it is only for us, the external reader, that this new truth of self-consciousness exists and not yet for consciousness itself. To remind us of this fact, Hegel makes another pointed address to the reader, his fellow traveller. As though it should be obvious, he refers to the curtain as "so-called" and its purpose as "supposed" and states that the curtain is not going to magically open itself. He thus insists that "*we* go behind it ourselves, as much in order that we may see, as that there may be something behind there which can be seen" (*PS*, 103). He is urging us forward, to push beyond the simple recognition of the birth of self-consciousness and in so doing to discover as well as create that which will be behind the curtain, that which is in the inner world. We must keep the movement going, and where we are going will "require still a more complex movement" than the one in which we both just took part and witnessed. He acknowledges that the "knowledge of what is the truth of appearance" and "its inner being" were "a result of a complex movement whereby the modes of consciousness 'meaning,' perceiving, and the Understanding, vanish." We are rapidly moving towards a "cognition of *what consciousness knows in knowing itself* [. . .] the exposition of which is contained in what follows" (*PS*, 103).

FORCE AS A UNIVERSAL MEDIUM

I will return to this concept of vanishing, but with a basic foundation of its properties in place I turn to the notion of Force as universal medium. This will help to expand my conception of Force as a binding, transitional, connecting movement. In so doing, I am further preparing the ground for the exploration, which will take place in Chapter Three, of the origins of the binding process in Freudian theory as taken up by André Green. Again, in the discussion of Force as this universal medium, the distinctions between form and content are rather slippery. By this I mean that we can begin to understand the idea of a universal medium as one that can conceptually be broken down in much the same manner in which I discussed the idea of vanishing. It is, in itself, a cohesive, emulsifying, formless essence of sorts, "in which the moments subsist as 'matters.'" The idea of "subsistence" (*Bestehen*) or moments subsisting is of great interest to one of the threads that I am following: the idea of survival touched upon above. Indeed, at one point Hegel formulates Force as the "subsistence of unfolded 'matters'" (*PS*, 83).

If we are looking at the idea of subsistence in the most simplistic terms, then we must consider Force (both the existence of and the employment of) as a sort of mechanism of survival, as an agent of continuation, as a life-giving property. Hegel wants to make perfectly clear that Force is not simply a unity that is acted upon when he states: "We must retract the assertion that Force is posited as *a One*, and that its essence is to express itself as an 'other' which approaches it externally" (*PS*, 83). For what solicits Force, what lies behind its continued motion, is Force itself. It is thus the medium in which the moments subsist as matters, that in which the moments are carried forward, that in which they manage to survive. Without Force, the moments would have no connection, no binding material, and no cause for momentum.

It is profitable, before moving forward with the idea of universal medium in the "Force and the Understanding" section, to move briefly backward in the text in order to ground an idea of what it is that Hegel means by "universal" and to locate the moment in which the idea of universal medium is introduced. As acknowledged in the Introduction, one of the aims of my book is to attempt to take the *Phenomenology* on its own terms and approach the contents anew to see how they might relate to one another, while always acknowledging that each concept I am unpacking is freighted with the history of its reception, a history which I cannot do justice to in the scope of this project. Of course, Force is not the only universal medium that Hegel employs in his system, although it is amongst the most vital and is less an "abstract universal medium" as concept and more of a medium without which the movement of consciousness, and indeed of the *Phenomenology* itself, would cease.

Because it is not in my interest to explore fully the notion of universal, it is sufficient to give Hegel's earliest definition that comes in "Sense-Certainty." He writes: "A simple thing of this kind which *is* through negation, which is neither This nor That, a *not-This*, and is with equal indifference This as well as That—such a thing we call a *universal*" (*PS*, 60). We can thus understand Force as a universal along these lines if we recall that it is "equally for its own self what it is *for an other*" and that it is in this sense a neutral property even in its belonging, as it does, to the Understanding. Since I have already stated that Force is the unconditioned universal we have thus advanced beyond the conditioned realms of Sense-Certainty and "Perception," wherein, it seems, the idea of universal medium was still rather abstract. Hegel introduces the concept in his discussion of Perception:

> It is pure relating of self to self, or the *medium* in which all these determinacies are, and in which as a *simple* unity they therefore interpenetrate, but without *coming into contact* with one another; for it is precisely through participating in this universality that they exist indifferently on their own account [. . .]. This abstract universal medium, which can be called simply 'thinghood' or 'pure essence,' is nothing else than what Here and Now have proved themselves to be, viz. a *simple togetherness* of plurality; but the many are, *in their determinateness,* simple universals themselves. (*PS*, 68)

Note the formulation of a medium as a relationship in which determinacies, the differences, interpenetrate but make no contact. To make contact would presumably be to transform them and what is necessary at this stage is the recognition of their difference, their independence from one another, precisely their lack of transformation. Their existence as these differentiated properties is, however, fundamentally dependent upon this interpenetration and thus to somehow being bound to the other determinacies, as determinacies, within the medium. I have already established that Force, too, is a "togetherness of plurality" in that within the double movement of Force, in both its expression and in its proper state, a multiplicity of differences exist. The contrast, of course, is that in Force, unlike in the abstract universal, these differences are then made to vanish when Force is driven back into itself. So what is established here is the nature of what a universal medium can be: a pure relating of self to self that holds within it a multiplicity of differences.

As his discussion of Perception advances, Hegel builds upon the morphing definition of universal medium and posits that perception is, in some senses, a purely subjective, individual process. In it the diverse aspects of a Thing do not come from the Thing itself "but from ourselves," and they depend upon our perception, tied as it is to our sense-certainty. He then states: "We are thus the *universal medium* in which such moments are kept apart and exist each on its own. Through the fact, then, that we regard the characteristic of being a universal medium as *our* reflection, we preserve the self-identity and truth of the Thing, its being a One" (*PS*, 72). Two things are of significance here to consider. Firstly is the introduction of the idea that "we," the possessors of consciousness and purveyors of our own perception, "we" the observers of Hegel's process, are designated as this universal medium. We are thus a point, a method of connection between the Thing, the external world, and the internal world within which we are the agents of our perception. We keep within us, as mediums, the distinctions found within the Thing, the object, the external world, and yet preserve the Thing as a One. Secondly, in so doing we create the Oneness of the Thing in our capacity as that which holds its diversity, preserving each of its moments as separate, interpenetrating us without contact with each other. However, we are not at a stage yet when the Oneness is as a result of the disappearance of differences, as we have found occurs through the vanishing of differences as part of the action of Force.

Rather, Hegel is extremely invested, in his discussion of Perception, in positing that it is exactly this preservation of, the survival of, the distinctions that is of the utmost importance. He reiterates that the "Thing is the *Also*," is the universal medium in which, at this stage in Consciousness, the diverse properties of the Thing "subsist apart from one another, without touching or cancelling one another; and when so taken, the Thing is perceived as what is true" (*PS*, 73). So, if in the movement of Perception these distinctions can survive, if a Thing can be perceived in all of its diverse aspects, then what we perceive is what is true. In this way, "we" are equated to the "Thing," the *Also*, as a universal medium responsible for the subsistence of distinction. In this sense, we, as readers, are a universal medium, in that not only must we keep the multiplicity of moments that comprise the *Phenomenology* held within the activity of our reading, and do so without interpenetration so that we recognise them for what they are, but we must also somehow, simultaneously, create a "One" of the text by allowing the moments their movement. Regardless, for the purposes of the present discussion, what interests us most is the status of and investment in the idea, prior to the introduction of Force, that distinctions are kept preserved within the universal medium, whatever this universal medium might be at the particular moment under scrutiny. This helps us to understand better both the heightened role that vanishing then takes in the "Force and the Understanding" chapter and the nature of Force itself.

With that said, and the origins of the concept of the universal medium in place, I return to the discussion of Force as universal medium. In moving towards his explanation of what the movement of Force actually is, Hegel expands upon the earlier formation of the universal medium as that in which matters "mutually interpenetrate, but without coming into contact" because although they exist in the unity of the medium, they are still independent matters. But this time, in "Force and the Understanding," as well as reiterating that formulation, he takes us a step further. He states: "This also means that they are absolutely porous, or are sublated. This sublation, in its turn, this reduction of the diversity to a pure *being-for-self*, is nothing other than the medium itself, and this is the *independence* of the different 'matters'" (*PS*, 81). Here then, we get the true movement beyond the states of Perception and Sense-Certainty. As we noted previously, Force is then designated as the movement of independent "matters" into unity, an unfolding into diversity, and then a reduction back into unity. It is thus here that we see the transformative, transitional power of Force.

Recall that Force splits itself into two moments, that of the expression of Force and that of Force being driven back into itself, or Force proper, and also that Force is found to be that which "solicits" itself, that which calls itself forth, and is thus not dependent upon an "other" or an external "something else."[25] Julian Roberts discusses solicitation in a manner akin to my discussion of binding when he writes that for Hegel "the principle of solicitation makes the two elements inseparable from one another."[26] I am moving towards a formulation that Force soliciting itself is a form of desire prior to the introduction of desire proper and thus of recognition prior to the introduction of recognition in the "Self-Consciousness" chapter. H. S. Harris also acknowledges Force as a precursor to recognition and, further, the activity of solicitation as a method of recognition: "The two forces soliciting one another (or consciousness recognizing one another) are the two sides of one substantial reality" (*JS*, 46).[27] Desire, as we have noted, is desire for unification, a potential filling of a lack. In soliciting itself, in calling forth its own movement, Force desires the unification of its split self. The movement is born out of, and is dependent upon, the meeting of the expression of Force and Force proper. The relationship between this act of solicitation and the dependency that Force as a universal medium has on the interaction of the two moments of Force is described by Hegel:

> The soliciting Force, e.g., is posited as a universal medium, and the one solicited, on the other hand, as Force driven back into itself; but the former is a universal medium only through the other being Force that is driven back into itself; or, it is really the latter that is the soliciting Force for the other and is what makes it a medium. (*PS*, 84)

This passage is particularly vital to an understanding of Force as a universal medium based on the initial split of Force and on the perpetual process of this splitting and reunification. It can only be something in which other matters subsist if it simultaneously holds its own differences within it, allowing them to subsist, while also allowing for them to act upon each other. Only in this way will Force be able to survive.

The last relationship regarding Force as a universal medium is that of the interconnection between solicitation and negative unity. I have only lightly considered the idea of negation, of the negative, in the present discussion, but it can always be found in the shadows that my formulations cast, especially when we note that Hegel equates the idea of "universal medium" with "negative unity" (*PS*, 89–90). In Chapter Three I will approach the concept of the negative through the work of André Green and in so doing locate the negative as the "energy of thought" (*PS*, 19). The work I am doing to puzzle through the mechanisms of Force is necessary in order to understand that crucial formulation and thus the potential for an economy, a way of thinking about an energetics in Hegel. Hegel had previously defined Force as both a universal medium and a negative unity in that "it is likewise the universal medium *only through being solicited to be such;* and similarly, too, it is a negative unity, i.e. it solicits the retraction of Force [into itself], *only through being solicited to do so*" (*PS*, 84). Since my main interest is not to interrogate the concept of the negative at present, I will puzzle briefly on what the idea of a negative unity might actually be.

Having already established that what solicits Force is simply Force itself, we can note that not only does Force solicit itself into expression, but it also solicits a retraction, a withdrawal, and, if we are taking it a step further into the realm of language, a renunciation of itself or into itself. The negative of expression would be this retraction, or, as I will discuss, an active repression. Thus Force, in holding its two moments within it, held in perfect, active tension, soliciting itself, is its own negative unity. The designations of Force as universal medium and Force as an "active, negative unity" (*PS*, 90) pertain to its two moments individually (the solicited Force as passive medium and the soliciting Force as the negative unity). Since the two moments are simply Force itself, then Force is thus both a medium and a negative unity. Here we again enter the discussion of form and content and re-encounter one of the examples of vanishing, wherein the distinction of separate Forces collapses into one. Conceiving of Force as a universal medium allows us to understand how it acts not only as a medium in which matters subsist, thus allowing us to see its fundamental role as a connecting, transitional, and binding power in the movement of consciousness, but also as a medium between its own moments, being the same for itself as it is for an "other."

EXPRESSION AND REPRESSION/SUPPRESSION

I now turn to a brief examination of the ideas of expression (*Aussprechen* or *Äußerung*) and suppression/repression (*Unterdrückung/ Zurückhalten*) as they pertain to Force. I have already laid significant groundwork for the notion of expression in the discussion of the two moments of Force. The notion of repression warrants a closer look. Clearly, there would be no notion of repression without that of expression, but what exactly is Force holding back when it represses itself? In addition, is there something created in the act of repression, or is it only in the act of expression that we see the generative nature of Force? Is the movement of Force the only potential by-product of the double act of expression and repression? Furthermore, what would the implications be for our grasp of the notion of Force if we move from an examination of the expression/repression of Force on a physical level to one that looks at expression/repression in the realm of language? This present work comes to fruition in Chapter Four with the work of Christopher Bollas, who sees a generative potential for repression and who forms a theory of "reception." I find resonance with his theory that repressed ideas hold the energy for expression. So too does repressed Force hold within it the potential energy for its expression.

To begin with, in order better to conceive of repression in the *Phenomenology*, we must bring ourselves back to the notion of solicitation. Recall the moment of "sheer" vanishing of the two moments of Force as independent essences, wherein the result is the knowledge that the two extremes simply find their existence in their contact with one another, in their mediation. We can then move into the moment that directly follows when Hegel states: "In this, there is immediately present both the repression within itself of Force, or its *being-for-self,* as well as its expression: Force that solicits and Force that is solicited" (*PS*, 85–86). Thus we see that repression is the being-for-self of Force and can understand repression not as something that is buried and thus lifeless but as an action that is an intrinsic part of the movement of consciousness; it is the moment of grounding that gives power to expression. Expression is formulated as that which is solicited, and repression is given this power of solicitation. We must then begin to flesh out an understanding of repression as an active agent. If we try to extricate ourselves from the standard idea of repression as an act of inhibiting, containing, or suppressing and take it, as Hegel is asking, a step further and equate the act of repression with that of Force driving back into itself in order to call forth its expression, we can begin to infuse repression with generative power. Instead of suppression, we find "supersession" (*Aufgehoben*).

Returning to the idea of supersession, then, we find that, similar to the activity of solicitation, wherein that which solicits Force turns out to be Force itself, Force in its expression is simply superseding itself. Hegel states: "The *Notion* of Force rather preserves itself as the *essence* in its very *actuality;* Force, as *actual,* exists simply and solely in its *expression,* which at the same time is nothing else than a supersession of itself" (*PS*, 86). Knowing that supersession is a simultaneous act of negation and preservation, it is interesting to conceive of expression in the same manner, for one might think that expression is simply the release, the externalising of the internal. This formulation makes sense, however, when we recall that repression is intrinsically part of expression and that repression can be seen as holding properties of preservation. More than that, if Force exists solely in its expression and if this expression is only the supersession of itself, then Force, as actual, can also be seen as surviving due to its own negation and preservation. Hegel writes: "In other words, Force supersedes its expression. But in fact Force is *itself* this reflectedness-into-self, or this supersession of the expression" (*PS*, 83). The supersession of the expression must be the Force driven back into itself and must in some ways be seen as part of the repression. Thus we can see another facet of repression as a key component of a generative act.

The only significant use of the act of expression found prior to "Force and the Understanding" comes directly following the introduction of the concept of the Universal, used by Hegel when he is discussing language. It is here that the theoretical link can be drawn between "expression" in Force, which up until this point has been predominately an exploration of the (meta)physical nature of Force, and the notion of expression in terms of language. Hegel writes:

> It is as a universal too that we *utter* what the sensuous [content] is [. . .]. Of course we do not *envisage* the universal This or Being in general, but we *utter* the universal; in other words we do not strictly say what in this sense-certainty we *mean* to say. But language, as we see, is the more truthful; in it, we ourselves directly refute what we *mean* to say, and since the universal is the true [content] of sense-certainty and language expresses this true [content] alone, it is just not possible for us ever to say, or express in words, a sensuous being that we *mean*. (*PS*, 60)

At stake is the use of language to draw forth the internal response to sensuous contact, which is an act that turns language into the universal, whereas the experience language is attempting to capture is clearly that of the individual. Hegel is asserting that language will never do justice to the true meaning of the sensuous content but that in uttering, in putting into language the experience of sensuous being, we are somehow attempting to articulate what is ours alone.

It is becoming apparent that we cannot escape the presentation of the gap between meaning and expression, which is created by the utterances of the self. In addition, we are offered the potentially paradoxical formulation of language as the "more truthful," due to the fact that it has the power to refute meaning through our own use of it. Whether this refutation is a conscious act, or rather, whether such agency belongs solely to the nature of language itself, is a consideration that I cannot undertake here. I will continue to elaborate on this topic when I discuss the notion of the inner world. Before doing so, it will be profitable at this point to turn to the concept of Explanation.

EXPLANATION

Hegel offers us an illustration of the link between language, consciousness, and Force, and of the power, the force inherent, in the use of language itself, which can be seen not only as a unifying, binding medium but also as a property that holds destructive capabilities. That language holds within it the capacity to destroy as well as to create (to unbind as well as to bind) will be become increasingly important to my study when I approach the subject of unbinding as a destructive force, explored in the work of the negative through Green (via Hyppolite and Lacan) and in the work of free association and interpretation with Bollas.[28] My focus is on how Hegel conceives of the notion of Explanation, and clearly I cannot, in the scope of this investigation, take on the subject of his relationship with language in general in the *Phenomenology of Spirit*.[29] That being said, it is necessary briefly to sketch the way in which Hegel approaches the subject of language prior to his designation of Explanation in "Force and the Understanding" in order to help strengthen an understanding of Explanation itself and to lay the groundwork for the way in which I will consider the fashioning of an object out of language in the latter sections of this book.

In "Sense-Certainty," Hegel begins to grapple with the matter of description and the inability of language to actually convey what is meant. Again we are tracing the aforementioned gap between what is uttered and what is meant. Hegel writes:

> If they actually wanted to *say* 'this' bit of paper which they mean, if they wanted to *say* it, then this is impossible, because the sensuous This that is meant *cannot be reached* by language, which belongs to consciousness, i.e. to that which is inherently universal. In the actual attempt to say it, it would therefore crumble away; those who started to describe it would not be able to complete the description, but would be compelled to leave it to others, who would themselves finally have to admit to speaking about something which *is not*. (*PS*, 66)

The "they" to whom Hegel is referring are those who believe that "the reality or being of external things taken as Thises or sense-objects has absolute truth for consciousness" (*PS*, 65). I focus here on the idea that Hegel sees language as existing at a remove from the "this," from the object. It cannot reach the actual object, and when language is used to describe the object, the "this," the object itself, does not survive the description; it falls apart. Hegel clearly does see language as representative of the true, although we have seen that he does think of language as the more truthful, and goes on from here to build his case that the truth of the thing arises in the perception of it and not in the description.

I cannot help but get the sense that on some level he does not trust language when he writes, "Language [. . .] has the divine nature of directly reversing the meaning of what is said, of making it into something else, and thus not letting what is meant *get into words at all*" (*PS*, 66). Therefore, we must sometimes "help language out" through perceiving and sensing. Hegel has given ownership of language to consciousness, and thus it is a universal. Yet he simultaneously posits language as an incredibly powerful entity capable of acting of its own accord and one that is also, at times, in need of assistance. I highlight these moments in "Sense-Certainty" to not only pinpoint the building blocks of Hegel's relationship with language, and in particular so that we acknowledge Hegel's conflicted, paradoxical, and, at times, contradictory views on language itself, but also to illustrate the difference between the use of language via uttering or via description and the place that Hegel will soon afford to Explanation, yet a third example of language use.

Of interest to my present line of analysis is Hegel's formulation of Explanation as a process. He writes:

> This necessity, which is merely verbal, is thus a recital of the moments constituting the cycle of the necessity. The moments are indeed distinguished, but, at the same time, their difference is expressly said to be *not* a difference of the thing itself, and consequently is itself immediately cancelled again. This process is called '*explanation*.' A *law* is enunciated; from this, its implicitly universal element or ground is distinguished as *Force* [. . .]. The 'explanation' then condenses the *law* into *Force* as the essence of the law. (*PS*, 94)

Explanation, then, is set up as a tautological movement, where difference is introduced and then cancelled again, thus not actually existing as set difference but rather as part of the movement. This necessity belongs to the Understanding, and we can view Explanation as a process that the Understanding, belonging to consciousness, sets in motion. It is a necessary tool that the Understanding utilises to effect change, to move the process ever forward. Judith Butler sees Explanation "as the necessary *alterity* of consciousness itself ," a formulation that will come to fruition when I touch upon the "flowering of alterity" afforded by the psychoanalytic sphere and its dependency on forms of explanation.[30]

Whereas, prior to this moment, language seemed always to be chasing after experience, somehow just catching its tail before it moved off again, the "merely verbal" necessity that is Explanation is now illustrated as having a particular power; it can take a law and condense it into "Force as the essence of the law." Two things are of particular importance here. The first is that the process of Explanation has the ability to capture external realities and turn them into internal laws, essences of governance. The second is that Force is the essence of the law, meaning that we can conceive of law in the same manner in which we have been conceptualising Force. "Law" takes on the possibility, then, of vanishing, of being both expressed and repressed and as acting as a binding, universal medium. The full ramifications of Hegel's further assertion that "*Force is constituted exactly the same as law*" cannot be explored fully, but I take this to mean that Force can be known in the explanation, in the law of it. However, the effect that the process of Explanation has on Consciousness, via the Understanding, in changing and/or creating the "law of the inner world" is important to locate.

At this stage, we can position ourselves in the moment(s) where consciousness, in the realm of the Understanding, and its object are still two separate entities but only because consciousness sees the object as a unity that exists as separate from itself. Consciousness has neither yet realised that it is, simultaneously, both the object and itself nor that the differences do not concretely exist. However, this gap is beginning to close via the process of Explanation, and consciousness is beginning to experience the change, in the shifting of the object from "inner being as object" to the "other side," into the Understanding. We find:

> In the process, then, of explaining, the to and fro of change which before was outside of the inner world and present only in the appearance, has penetrated into the supersensible world itself. Our consciousness, however, has passed over from the inner being as object to the other side, into the *Understanding*, and it experiences change there. (*PS*, 95)

Here we see the potential strength that the process of explaining has for consciousness. It has the ability to facilitate the transition of the movement (of change), which was present only in the external world, into the inner world and thus to penetrate the supersensible world. In so doing, consciousness changes its own form and makes the move from experiencing its inner being as an object, but feeling no unity with this object, into the realm of the Understanding, where it will begin the arduous and perpetual process that is the reconciliation of this split.

Judith Butler writes: "As an 'Explanation,' the Understanding comes to be determinately manifest in material form; there is consciousness itself sprawled on the page, formed in letters and words, existing materially, outside itself. In recognizing authorship of that explanation, consciousness becomes aware of itself for the first time."[31] Because Hegel has allowed for a formulation wherein explanation also has the power to condense law into Force and Force into law, we can begin to understand this penetrative power much in the same way. We can observe that explaining has the potential to express, which we can see as a form of penetration, as well as it has to repress, which we can see as a manner of condensing. The role of language, of enunciation via explaining, has taken on an elevated position, and one in which Hegel has placed more confidence than he had done up to this point. Furthermore, it is not so much what the explanation is that seems to matter to Hegel most but more that the act of explanation itself, this "cycle of necessity," this "recital of moments," propels the movement of consciousness onward, effects this change.

At this juncture, this change means a move into the realm of the Understanding. Most importantly, "this change becomes for the Understanding the law of the inner world." This to-ing and fro-ing that Hegel refers to could also be understood as the "flux" to which I referred earlier. In a slightly rare gesture of helping us to follow his shifting use of terminology,

Hegel offers that this flux, which is again present, is the "same flux which presented itself as the play of Forces" (*PS*, 95). So this play, this motion of solicitation, expression, and repression, is also present in the process of explaining and in its by-products. As "this change becomes for the Understanding the law of the inner world," through the play of Forces we are in the realm of "absolute transition" and "pure change." Still, and always, difference is no difference at all and is simply a moment in the self-movement of becoming.

INFINITY AND FORCE

To elaborate on the continuing and invaluable place that Explanation holds in Hegel's system at this point, and its relationship to this self-movement, it is important to touch upon Hegel's introduction of the concept of infinity (*Unendlichkeit*), but without straying too far from a focus on Force. I do not intend, nor could I execute, a comprehensive treatment of infinity here.[32] Hegel writes in the *Phenomenology* that "simple infinity, or the absolute Notion" is the "simple essence of life, the soul of the world, the universal blood" (*PS*, 100). In returning to the *Jena Logic*, we can note the link between infinity, Force, and the designation of Force as relation that prefigures the *Phenomenology*. Not only does Force express "relationship itself," but it also expresses "the necessity to be within itself even in its being-outside-itself, or to be self-equal; in other words, it expresses infinity." Force is, in fact, the "cause of infinity." It is in this realm that simple connection becomes relation (*JS*, 47).

In the following we can understand the crux of the role of Explanation as a way of expressing, in the linguistic realm, what Force is and how with the help of explanation it can express infinity:

> Infinity, or this absolute unrest of pure self-movement, in which whatever is determined in one way or another, e.g. as being, is rather the opposite of this determinateness, this no doubt has been from the start the soul of all that has gone before; but it is in the *inner* world that it has first freely and clearly shown itself. Appearance, or the play of Forces, already displays it, but it is as '*explanation*' that it first freely stands forth; and in being finally an object for consciousness, as *that which it is*, consciousness is thus *self-consciousness*. The Understanding's 'explanation' is primarily only the description of what self-consciousness is. It supersedes the differences present in the law, differences which have already become pure differences but are still indifferent, and posits them in a single unity, in Force. But this unifying of them is equally and immediately a sundering, for it supersedes the differences and posits the oneness of Force only by creating a new difference, that of Law and Force, which, however, at the same time is no difference. (*PS*, 101)

There are three main points to make here. The first concerns the freedom that the process of Explanation affords infinity. Via Explanation, this "absolute unrest of pure self-movement" is able to stand forth unimpeded. We are told that this self-movement is the "soul" of everything that we have already witnessed up to this point and most freely lives in the inner world. Yet until Explanation, rather as Explanation, it has not been given a proper role. The play of Forces exhibited infinity as a facet of the movement, but the change effected here is monumental. The second major consideration, the outcome of this significant change, is that through this process infinity is made an object for consciousness. Subsequently, consciousness abolishes difference from its consideration of itself and its relation with the world and thus becomes self-consciousness. The third and last point is that self-consciousness has arrived because consciousness is now a "reflectedness-into-itself." Recall that we witness Force as this very "reflectedness-into-itself" and thus can see a perfect example of self-consciousness as holding the properties of Force. The unrest of self-movement, consciousness itself, has become its own object. For the Understanding, this becomes a description of this change, the description of its new form as self-consciousness.

We might be slightly apprehensive as to the reliability of this description (considering our prior discussion) if it were not for the idea that this description is purely for the sake of consciousness alone via the Understanding and not an attempt to describe a sensuous experience to an external entity. As Hegel writes: "The reason why 'explaining' affords so much self-satisfaction is just because in it consciousness is, so to speak, communing directly with itself, enjoying only itself; although it seems to be busy with something else, it is in fact occupied only with itself" (*PS*, 101). In this sense, then, there is no attempt to create meaning through language, but instead we have Explanation helping to give birth to the new state of self-consciousness. There is not the presence of a gap felt here but more that of an awareness of a process of unification, of differences posited into Force as a unity. Therefore, Force incorporates the energy and the power generated by Explanation and transforms itself. As Butler states, "Explanation becomes a curious kind of agent that turns on its user and shakes his identity."[33] There is, however, a rare moment present here, that of the self's enjoyment of self through explanation. Again we can speculate that this is because we are still in a stage of pre-desire, so the self's enjoyment of its own self-consciousness has a purity that will soon be complicated by the activities of self-consciousness as desire.

As we have come to expect, we should not rest too long with the notion of unification for we soon find that this unification is also, equally and simultaneously, a sundering. So, already mixed with this enjoyment is the destructive element. This unification via explanation, thus via language, which is at the same time a sundering, brings us back to an idea of utterance as we found it in the "Sense-Certainty" portion and reminds us of the falling apart of meaning. In Chapters Three and Four I will consider in more detail the implications of making meaning out of energy and, furthermore, what power language has to create but also to potentially transform the intrinsic energy and force of consciousness in its articulation.

For Hegel, this movement, this absolute unrest, is a necessity and is the movement of the Understanding. It is not, however, an "object" that belongs to the Understanding. What became an object for consciousness was consciousness itself in the realm of the Understanding. In light of this, we can better understand how the properties of Explanation relate to our present discussion of Force. If we recall that in a consideration of Force as a universal medium, matters (and moments) mutually interpenetrate, subsist, but do not come into contact with one another, then we can see that the objects that do belong to the Understanding, the "thousand other things that constitute the content of the moments of the movement" act likewise (*PS*, 101). Essentially, moments of the movement can belong as objects, but the movement itself, this pure self-movement, cannot be an object and must remain a movement. Without maintaining this movement *as* movement, consciousness would not reach self-consciousness. Explanation is one of the integral stages that allows for the movement to effect change because it, like Force, has the dual power of unification and sundering. This is by no means an attempt to posit that Force *is* Infinity but is to suggest that in unearthing the absolute Notion that is Infinity, we can pinpoint the conceptual location of the unrest that is behind the movement of consciousness in general. It should be noted that all of these changes and locations are only apparent at this stage to us, the phenomenological observer, and not yet to consciousness itself.

Much in the same manner as we are called upon to act as universal mediums in that we attempt to keep the multiplicity of moments comprising the *Phenomenology* held together without interpenetration, while also creating a unity within the text by allowing the moments their movement, we must also allow for the expression of these moments to push us ever onward. Simultaneously, however, we must recognise the repression inherent in such expression by holding, condensing, preserving the moments within our understanding and allow this repression its release back into expression. As we witness consciousness move through the stages of its becoming, we witness the very movement of it reaching its next moment through the repression of the previous moment and then through the incorporation of this new knowledge into our own understanding.[34]

This is not to equate the movements of expression and repression with the act of sublation (*Aufhebung*), although we could understand the activity of reading the text as structured like this negating, preserving, superseding movement. It is rather to suggest that there might be more at stake in the activity of the play of language here and in the structure of the *Phenomenology* itself. All of this we witness through Hegel's use of language, with his assiduous articulation of the process. Never are we more aware of the gap between language and the immediate "truth" of existence and the process of becoming than when we are involved in the process of reading about the composition of this very truth itself. We could argue that a fundamental aspect of the entire work of the *Phenomenology* is the attempt to put into language, to articulate, a way of filling this gap.

THE INNER WORLD, THE "VOID," AND THE PLAY OF FORCES

I have been talking around and through the concept of the inner world for nearly the length of this investigation thus far, as its discovery is clearly what lies very much at the heart of the "Force and the Understanding" section. Indeed, it is the realm that is sought by consciousness, the stage in the process into which consciousness now moves, and it is through the play of Forces and the work of the Understanding that, as we witnessed above, the inner world comes to be gazed upon by the inner being. But what is this inner world, of what is it comprised, and by what agency, if any? Furthermore, is this inner world something that *can* be articulated, or is there a portion of it that remains beyond language? Additionally, what is the difference between the notions of inner being and inner world, and what are the potential readings one might make of Hegel's differentiation and final vanishing of the difference between the two?

To begin, the concept of the inner world comes about for the very first time in the "Force and the Understanding" section. Whereas many of the concepts we have been discussing here had minimal, if any, usage in the first two sections of the *Phenomenology*, it is precisely the culmination of the work of Force, of the play of Forces, that brings about the knowledge and true presence of the inner world. Butler writes:

> The notion of Force thus distinguishes the inner and outer 'moments' of thought inasmuch as Force is a constant movement between an inner reality and a determinate manifestation; in effect, Force is the compulsion that a nascent reality exhibits to find a determinate manifestation for itself—Hegel's reformulation of Spinoza's *conatus*. Force characterizes relations in the physical world as well as within consciousness itself, and thus becomes the ontological basis of consciousness' bond with the sensuous and perceptual world that it initially encountered as ontologically disparate from itself.[35]

Butler's reading of Force illuminates two of the main threads that I wish to follow. The first is to think about Force as a form of drive towards life, here characterized by Butler as Spinoza's drive (compulsion) towards self-preservation. Although I will not be pursuing the Spinozistic elements of Butler's claim, in Chapter Two I turn to the introduction of Life in the "Self-Consciousness" chapter of the *Phenomenology* and in Chapter Three to a consideration of Eros, of the life drive (as unifying Force; as drive to self-preservation/equilibrium), as discussed by André Green, in order to elaborate on this interpretation of Force. Secondly, there is great resonance in Butler's use of the term *bond* and my formulations of Force as a binding material. Again, these links will come to fruition in the following chapters. What is key to keep in mind is the link between Force and the "ontological basis" of consciousness' relationship with the external world. With the activity of Force, not only does consciousness now know of the difference between its internal and external realities, but it also must now live with, be with, this new set of relations as part of its own becoming. Hegel's ontology, then, is an ontology of "relation."

It is also this very work of the play of Forces which helps to give the inner world its substance, its meaning. Before moving into the concept of the inner world as we can abstractly conceptualise it, let me briefly recap how it has been illustrated and alluded to in my discussion thus far and elaborate on those moments of contact. This will then allow me to re-enter the text, moving in the slightly circuitous, non-linear manner required and weave into my understanding of Force the notion of the inner world.

So far I have noted that not only is Force "the middle term which unites the two extremes, the Understanding and the inner world" but also that it is through Force as "a vanishing" that the inner world can be viewed (*PS*, 86). This is not Force as a vanishing moment but is Force as vanishing itself. What we saw this vanishing accomplish was the disappearance of the world of appearance only to show us the inner world. Yet this inner world has as its "filling" this very world that has just vanished. Thus, as we are beginning to understand, this vanishing is not a true disappearance, an unrecoverable loss, but is simply an intrinsic stage in the process of discovery of the inner world.

We have also seen that the realm in which self-consciousness takes its first breath, where being "posits itself as an inner being containing different moments, but for which equally these moments are immediately not different," the realm in which this being exists *as* self-consciousness, is the realm of the inner world. We saw the "curtain of appearance" pulled back and saw the inner world and this inner being come into contact, thus indicating, and in a manner that is hard to pin down, that the "inner being" and the "inner world" were two separate entities (*PS*, 103). Reiterated in the same concluding passage is the fact that in order for there to be something behind the curtain, in order that there is something in this inner world, we must not only take responsibility and pull back the curtain, but we must also be responsible for that which lies behind it, for we are responsible for the filling of this inner world. With what, we must consider, are we filling it? As we can recall, "appearance" is certainly one of the fillings of the inner world, but what is this inner world when appearance vanishes, as it does to reveal this inner world itself?

It is in working through this notion of "filling" that we can continue to elaborate upon our understanding of Hegel's relationship with language in this section. We will re-encounter, most predominately, my own discussion of Explanation and of the gap between language and meaning with which Hegel struggles. But before doing so, it will be profitable to examine the moment where Hegel refers to the inner world as a "complete void." It is here that one begins to see a prefiguring of a model of the unconscious.[36] Pushing our conceptual speculations even further, we can see this inner world as a generative space out of which meaning is created or where meaning lies, after we have filled it with our external experience, waiting for articulation. In Chapters Three and Four I will be exploring in more depth the links between the inner and external worlds in the psychoanalytic realm and how the "articulation" of this link creates a new shape of knowing.

It is central to an understanding of the inner world that we are again reliant upon the movement of Force both to gain access to this inner world and for the constitution of the inner itself. We must look again at Force in its capacity as mediator, and as a binding agent. As noted previously, it is Force that is the middle term uniting the Understanding and the inner world. Hegel pushes us further and supplies us with another conception of Force when he states that the "developed being of Force" is "called appearance" and, furthermore, that this appearance is a "totality," is a "universal," and is what "constitutes the inner [of Things], the play of Forces as a reflection of the inner into itself" (*PS*, 87). So, as previously noted in my discussion of vanishing, here we have appearance offered to us as one of the fillings of the inner world. We also re-encounter here the idea of reflection, to which I have already referred briefly. As we can recall, when discussing the idea of "universal medium" and specifically our (as Hegel's "we") role as this universal medium, we saw that "we regard the characteristic of being a universal medium as *our* reflection" and in so doing we are the "truth of the Thing, its being a One" (*PS*, 72). We can now take this idea of reflection further when we see that the inner world, which has been filled with "appearance," reflects itself to itself and that this, in a sense, defines the play of Forces. Here the notion of the play of Forces as an agent of reflection is reinforced, and we recognise that we can only know Force in its appearance.

What is critical to my study, however, is not necessarily the knowledge that appearance can now be thought of as a constituent substance of sorts but the relationship between consciousness and what it now sees as "True": this inner world. As before, we can bear witness to the not-yet agonizing but quite obvious split between what consciousness is at this given stage and what it knows of itself when Hegel writes:

> This inner is, therefore, for consciousness an extreme over against it; but it is for consciousness the True, since in the inner, as the in-itself, it possesses at the same time the certainty of itself, or the moment of its being-for-self. But it is not yet conscious of this ground or basis, for the *being-for-self* which the inner was supposed to possess in its own self would be nothing else but the negative movement. (*PS*, 87)

Prior to this point, what was True for consciousness was the Thing as it was perceived. Now we see that it is the Thing(s), or rather the appearance of the Thing, that constitutes the inner world; this inner world is what is True for consciousness. We mark the move that consciousness is making in its understanding of its own reality, of its own supposed truth, of its attempts to locate itself as a ground or basis from which it relates to the world. It is only through the play of Forces that these leaps are enacted. Without Force as the agent of negation here, as the mediator of this "negative movement," consciousness would remain forever on the surface. Force, and its ability to effect such change as it does, gives life to consciousness, gives it an ability to ascertain the truth both of itself and of its inner relation to the Thing, the other, the outside world. Hegel writes of the inner world:

> In it, the Things of perception are expressly present for consciousness as they are in themselves, viz. as moments which immediately and without rest or stay turn into their opposite, the One immediately into the universal, the essential immediately into the unessential and vice versa. This play of Forces is consequently the developed negative; but its truth is the positive, viz. the *universal*, the object that, *in itself*, possesses being. (*PS*, 87)

There are two main points that are important to take from this. The first pertains to my forthcoming discussion of the episode of "The Unhappy Consciousness" and the notion of the shift between the Essential and the Unessential. As I will show, self-consciousness experiences a painful struggle for stability, recognition, and a much sought after reconciliation of its essential and unessential nature. Hegel's examples above, used to illustrate of the power of the play of Forces to convert Things into their opposite, were not, in any way, arbitrarily chosen; Hegel is not a thinker of the arbitrary. He is laying the ground for how we, his philosophical partners, should be threading the use of Force through the *Phenomenology* and the power that Force has in relation to the fundamental concepts of his system. Furthermore, he is preparing us for an understanding of the fundamental shift in and struggle for identity consciousness undergoes as the unhappy consciousness.

Secondly, it is key to understanding the concept of the negative, and how it is used in the *Phenomenology*, to mark that the play of Forces is consequently the "developed negative." The action of Force—the double nature of its being Force itself and Force driven back into itself, its activity as simultaneously that which is solicited and the solicitor and equally that which expresses and that which represses—is the very action of the negative, perhaps of negation itself. This is a topic to which I will return in Chapter Three.

In my discussion of vanishing, I noted before being fully equipped to delve into the concept of the inner world, we had to discover that one of the facets of vanishing was that entire worlds vanished; in the prior example, we discussed the "vanishing *present* world." We noted that when the present world vanished, a "supersensible world," the "true" world, opened up. This was also noted as the "permanent beyond," and the "first, and therefore imperfect, appearance of Reason" was introduced (*PS*, 87–88). This is all essential to understanding what Hegel means when he then posits, "The inner world is, for consciousness, still a *pure beyond*, because consciousness does not yet find itself in it. It is *empty*, for it is merely the nothingness of appearance, and positively the *simple* or *unitary* universal" (*PS*, 88). Again, we have the split inherent in consciousness at this stage, between what consciousness is and what it knows. Consciousness has recognised this inner world but does not yet realise that it is part of this inner world or rather that this inner world is part of it. Consciousness needs to recognise this world as its own, must take responsibility for it, in order that it not remain empty, in order to bring it back from this "beyond." The act of vanishing causes these splits to occur because it does away with the illusion of unity and reveals that which appearance is and that which lies behind, or rather beyond, appearance itself.

Hegel is not satisfied with leaving the inner world as an unknowable beyond but realises that it will take a new and deeper kind of work to reach it. He states:

> Certainly, we have no knowledge of this inner world as it is here in its immediacy; but not because Reason is too short-sighted or is limited, or however else one likes to call it—on this point, we know nothing as yet because we have not yet gone deep enough—but because of the simple nature of the matter in hand, that is to say, because in the *void* nothing is known, or, expressed from the other side, just because this inner world is determined as the *beyond* of consciousness. (*PS*, 88)

Although Reason has just taken its first, imperfect, jagged breath, Hegel is already in pursuit of the preservation of its integrity. The nature of the inner world, its void-ness, does not, at this stage, fall within the bounds of Reason's fledgling authority, but through no fault of Reason. It is its very nature as a void, albeit in a rather more complicated manner as we will soon see, that allows the inner world to exist. The question can be posed, however, as to whether this inner world could ever truly be known in its "immediacy" or whether the immediate of the inner world is that which escapes knowledge. We are clearly moving beyond the realms of perception and sense-certainty when we ask this question, and that is precisely the point. Rather than having the immediacy of this inner world as the object of knowledge for consciousness, it is the Explanation, or the expression of the inner world, that becomes that which can be known or can be put into language; the notion of immediacy is shifting. We would have again to take seriously into consideration the idea that we have begun to formulate regarding Hegel's relationship to language and proceed with the possibility that there will always be a gap between language and meaning, that something, some essence, will always remain "beyond." We begin to see the expression of the "immediate" as necessarily being mediated by language. When talking about knowing the immediacy of experience outside the realm of perception and sense-certainty, we must see language as the mediator. This is one reason why there will always be a gap: because there must always be a mediator present in order to bring the inner world into the realm of the outer world. We cannot remain in the world of sense-certainty or perception alone and must move into the realm of understanding via the action of Force. Thus the relationship we inevitably have with language is complicated. Is this inner world and its immediacy, then, a home, even if temporary, of this essence? Let me push this idea even further.

In an incredibly rich moment, Hegel attempts to formulate the nature of this void:

> Or, in order that there may yet be something in the void—which, though it first came about as devoid of *objective* Things must, however, as *empty in itself,* be taken as also void of all spiritual relationships and distinctions of consciousness qua consciousness—in order, then, that in this *complete void,* which is even called the *holy of holies,* there may yet be something, we must fill it up with reveries, *appearances,* produced by consciousness itself. It would have to be content with being treated so badly for it would not deserve anything better, since even reveries are better than its own emptiness. (*PS*, 88–89)

What is striking here is that what Hegel asks for instead of a space devoted to direct communion with God is a "holy of holies" "void of all spiritual relationships." It seems that in order that the void truly function as such, it must not have pre-existing notions of a relationship with the world on any other level than its own. Furthermore, Hegel states that it is void of all distinctions of consciousness, and we can find here a resonance with the notion that within the movement of Force itself all differences, all distinctions of consciousness, are done away with. There is a strange urgency to not let the void remain an empty space and a simultaneous admission that there is some sort of judgement being made regarding the potential worth of this inner world. The idea that it would not "deserve anything better" is slightly puzzling. In order, though, for it to be filled, it must first be a void, a space stripped of all distinctions. It is the movement of Forces that allows for this void to exist, but it is also the play of Forces that will ultimately provide it with the substances that fill it. It is the production of appearances and reveries by consciousness itself that fills this void and this inner world "comes into being" through the mediation of the world of appearances (*PS*, 89).

What is not clear at this point is what happens when the movement shifts the other way; that is, when the inner world expresses itself, when it comes into contact with language. It is helpful here to attempt to make a link between the topic of language and the inner world and our discussions both of expression and repression, and with my discussion of Explanation. I noted previously that through the process of Explanation the flux, the to-ing and fro-ing that existed outside the inner world was able to penetrate into the inner world, into this "supersensible beyond." For consciousness, this was a move from the "inner being" as object into the Understanding. Much as we began to understand expression as a form of penetration and repression as a form of condensation, we can look at this filling of the inner world, of this holy of holies, as a form of repression of appearance, of the condensation of the outer in the realm of the inner. Thus, it follows that the expression of the inner world would be the reverse of this process. If we, through a philosophical sleight of hand, inverted the process, then it follows that Explanation could affect the change of the contents of the inner world, driving them back out to penetrate the outer world. This brings another level of Understanding to the becoming of consciousness, and it is only possible, clearly, when self-consciousness has entered the picture.

We must take into consideration the distinction between the notions of "inner being" and "inner world." As we have witnessed, in the final barrage of vanishing acts that concludes the "Force and the Understanding" section, the "curtain [of appearance] hanging before the inner world is therefore drawn away and we have the inner being [the I] gazing into the inner world" (*PS*, 103). Here, in the vanishing of the distinction between the inner being and its inner world, is born self-consciousness. Therefore, once self-consciousness arises, the distinctions between the "I," this inner being, and its inner world do not carry the weight that by necessity they had to carry in the realms of sense-certainty and perception. The distinctions do not disappear but are simply vanished in order that self-consciousness can exist. As readers, we must, as with all the others, carry these distinctions with us and allow them to subsist but not interpenetrate.

CONCLUSION

A close reading of the "Force and the Understanding" portion of the *Phenomenology* allowed me to build a conceptual foundation for understanding how consciousness is bound and thus relates not only to itself, to its own process, but also to the external world. In his discussion of Force, Hegel is supplying us with a way of conceiving of processes that take place in the becoming of consciousness but that must, by necessity, exist outside of, free from, thought itself. It is a tricky proposition, this attempt to think a process of movement, of Force, that must be thought of yet understood outside of thought itself. In so doing, we will gain a better understanding of the movement of consciousness and of the dialectic itself. I have begun to tease out of these early sections of the *Phenomenology* the conflicts that Hegel himself saw inherent in language. Language cannot be relied upon as the only means through which subjects communicate, and so I am looking at Force as a model for that which exists outside of language but operates to bind, to connect, consciousness to itself and to the external world. The notion of vanishing has in many ways been my primary guide throughout this chapter, and I have formulated the sites of vanishing as moments of transition and transformation. These moments allow for the dynamic movement of consciousness to realise new shapes of knowing and being. The manner in which I can translate these sites of vanishing into the psychoanalytic context will become more apparent in Chapters Three and Four.

I have also located the points of contact with the concept of Explanation as it pertains to our psychoanalytic investigations and as will be relevant to "The Unhappy Consciousness" episode. Through Explanation, through what can be seen as the verbalization of consciousness' inner self to itself, there is a breakthrough in the realm of the Understanding that gives life to self-consciousness. I will explore the paradigmatic situation of the theoretical analytic episode, where two consciousnesses interact, forming an intersubjective, dialectical pair, where there is an inevitable interaction between Forces, an analytic play of Forces, one of which is soliciting a potential "explanation" from the other. The articulation of the contents of the inner world is attempted. In the case of psychoanalysis, the aim is unearthing the unconscious, and in Hegel the inner world as the "beyond" of consciousness is pursued. This, I will argue, entails the turning of self into an object of sorts (the third) via explanation, through language, so that a return to the self can be made by a reincorporation of the object. This necessarily involves a process of reflection and recognition in language, a closing of the gap between the self and its created object. The unhappy consciousness will soon represent for us a subject who, in its painful splitting of self from both its own self and from the external world, and by turning itself into an object, creates a reflective gap that it then uses to further its knowledge of itself. By reflective gap I mean a space of transition and transformation that consciousness experiences, or rather finds itself in, as a consequence of its alienation, and through which, once it emerges, consciousness finds itself as a new shape.[37] When I turn to the work of Christopher Bollas in Chapter Four, I will explore the concept of analytic genera (Bollas's version of the third) as an "object" created out of the play of Forces that takes place in the analytic setting and that is fashioned out of both the exchange of unconscious material and the language of the analytic dialectic. I will also touch upon how these transformational/transitional spaces are figured in psychoanalytic theory.

Before turning in the second half of my investigation to the psychoanalytic notions of negation, the binding process, and the notion of the third, let me in my next chapter move the play of Forces out of what has been, for the most part, a model of intrapsychic functioning. This is a move into the realm of intersubjectivity, a reading of the movement of self-consciousness in the *Phenomenology* as a play of Forces and the activity of Force as a model for the concepts of recognition and desire. I begin to ask, what is it that is created out of this play of Forces? What is it that subsists, that survives, this play, and what is its use and activity in the process of becoming? As we move toward "cognition of *what consciousness knows in knowing itself*," consciousness, in its form of self-consciousness, will come to know the "truth" of its previous shapes of knowing, and is that much more prepared for that which lies ahead (*PS*, 103).

2 Hegel's Re-Running of the Play of Forces as a Way of Understanding Intersubjectivity and Its Discontents

In this movement we see repeated the process which presented itself as the play of Forces, but repeated now in consciousness. (*PS*, 112)

INTRODUCTION

From my reading of "Force and the Understanding" I have constructed a framework out of a handful of key concepts. These are vanishing (*Verschwinden*), gazing (*Schauen*), solicitation (*Sollizitieren*), preservation (*Aufbewahren*), explanation (*Erklären*), expression (*Aussprechen* or *Äußerung*), and suppression/repression (*Unterdrückung/ Zurückhalten*). My previous interrogation of these terms enables me to now enter the realm of self-consciousness, where a model of intersubjectivity is presented.[1] The binding nature I am attributing to Force as a universal medium and the play of Forces (*das Spiel der Kräfte*) finds practical application and illustration in the relationship between subjects. This is represented by the figures of the lord and bondsman, the stoic, the sceptic, the unhappy consciousness, and ultimately in the third consciousness introduced by Hegel to rescue the unhappy consciousness from itself.

The aim of this chapter is to understand the entire movement of the play of Forces as it is translated into the interaction between consciousnesses. To do so, I cannot simply examine the manifestation of Force in the isolated and overly well-trodden ground of the "Lordship and Bondage" section that is, as Paul Ricoeur says, "an unjustified example if taken in isolation from the total movement."[2] The birth of the unhappy consciousness must be traced from the preceding moments of self-consciousness to see how this movement works. In so doing, the famous "life-and-death struggle" has to be rethought in order to incorporate the idea that, along with a drive towards death that can be read in the *Phenomenology*, there is equally a drive towards life. This can be found shot straight through the movement of consciousness, which begins to take shape in the form of "Life as a process" that arises with the birth of self-consciousness.

What I am also setting forth here is a philosophical method for reading the concept of the third or thirdness in psychoanalytic theory that I will address in the second half of this book. The concept of vanishing lays the groundwork for the designation of this third as a vanishing mediator enacting, in the intersubjective realm, the work of the vanishing that has been occurring throughout the preceding chapters of the *Phenomenology*.[3] Although it is not the only role that I will assign to the concept of the vanishing mediator, this will lead me to a formulation of the analyst figure as a vanishing mediator. In "The Unhappy Consciousness" episode, I will read the third (*das Dritte*), the counsellor, as this vanishing mediator, thus positing the presence of a proto-analyst figure in the *Phenomenology*. However, the concept of the vanishing mediator could potentially designate various elements of the intersubjective encounter, the unique instance of which is illustrated in the analytic setting. Therefore, I argue that the vanishing mediator can also be discussed in the language of the third that I take out of André Green's and through Christopher Bollas's work. This shifting and malleable nature of the term *the third* indicates the complexities and the difficulties of attempting to think through the question of intersubjectivity. By reading Hegel and psychoanalytic material together, I aim to illuminate potential methods for navigating our way around this territory. With all of this in mind, let us turn to the work at hand.

THE FORCE OF SELF-CONSCIOUSNESS OR THE BINDING OF DESIRE

Recall that Judith Butler highlighted the lack of attention paid to the transition from the freedom of the "Lordship and Bondage" episode to the self-enslavement of the unhappy consciousness. I have argued that what Butler does not recognise is that Hegel negotiates the escape by consciousness from this state of self-enslavement via the introduction of the third, what I am designating as a form of the vanishing mediator. With this in mind, a re-interrogation of these episodes, and the transition between them, is important, in order to see how Hegel's subjects are bound to one another and further to show how consciousness is bound to its own process and to the external world. Alongside the notion of self-enslavement that Butler highlighted, what warrants attention is how in the movement of becoming *pre*-desire, two consciousnesses might be bound by the interaction of their play of Forces. This is a movement that is prefigured by the notion of solicitation in Force, before the moment of recognition arising from the play of Forces occurs, and serves to further bind the duelling consciousnesses. It is here that two consciousnesses begin the process of binding, initiated by their play of Forces. In other words, the link between Force and the way in which consciousnesses are bound by the universal medium that *is* Force needs to be examined.

In the light of this, we can better understand how the process of recognition itself can be seen as an integral facet of the concept of the play of Forces and that it is, in some sense, a manifestation of this play. This is an elaboration on my assertion in the last chapter that Hegel was using Force and its activity as a model for this recognition. Recognition, and the acknowledgement that arises therein, is the "appearance" of Force in the intersubjective realm. Henry Sussman writes,

> [The episodes of self-consciousness] comprise particularly striking instances of one of the most vibrant forms of the Hegelian coordination: translation. Translation, for Hegel, is a substitution of terms that takes place in conjunction with a structural continuity. 'Lordship and Bondage' and the 'Unhappy Consciousness' *translate* the dynamics of the physical world into intersubjective relations and the history initiated by them while sustaining the operations that define the text's possibility.[4]

As I have discussed, Force can only be known in its appearance and is solicited only by another Force, and, as we know, self-consciousness can only be recognised by another self-consciousness. Hegel's understanding of this link culminates in his resolution of the predicament of the self-enslavement of the subject that finds itself as the unhappy consciousness.

In Chapter Three I will elaborate upon the links between the concept of negation as found in Freudian theory (via a Hegelian lens offered by Hyppolite) and my discussion of Force and the unhappy consciousness. In addition to the act of negation, of self-splitting, that gives motion to the process of consciousness, there is always a lack in consciousness that it desires to fill, catching itself in a perpetual state of "not yet," of aiming for that "something beyond itself." This notion of the beyond has its roots in the "Force and the Understanding," and I will expand in this chapter on the notion of the seeking by consciousness for this "beyond" that has always already vanished. Therefore, I will begin to conceptualise the unhappy consciousness as the manifestation of the potential breakdown in an internal play of Forces that, in turn, necessitates the play of another consciousness, the third consciousness, in order to resume its play. I will simultaneously draw out the implications for a reading of the unhappy consciousness as the epitome of the split, suffering, lacking consciousness.

This is a formulation that I have already tracked in my consideration of Force. Hyppolite writes: "Just as the forces discovered by understanding, which appeared to be alien to each other, proved to be a unique force divided within itself—each force being itself and its other—so the duality of living self-consciousness becomes the splitting and reproduction of self-consciousness within itself."[5] This replication of the work of Force in living self-consciousness constitutes the movement of the entire dialectic, the heart of which Hyppolite sees as lying in the unhappy consciousness. Exploring the notions of Force and of splitting, both as generative and binding processes, and focussing on "The Unhappy Consciousness" episode itself will allow a reading of the *Phenomenology* that lets it open up beyond the readings which focus on the end of history and help to splinter notions of absolute totality. Instead, I am opening the text to readings such as I perform in Chapters Three and Four, where the dynamic notions of movement and process can be explored.

To further ground us in the reading of "The Unhappy Consciousness" from which I take my lead, I turn to Jean Wahl. The generative quality that the splitting of the self holds, the primary negation, works in conjunction with the nature of motion in the self's process of becoming. Wahl's concept of unhappy consciousness as "motor" is therefore of particular importance. Wahl asserts, "What Hegel dealt with in the *Phenomenology* were not philosophies but ways of living; or rather, the two were not separated."[6] This is the basis for a reading of the *Phenomenology* that permits the theoretical moves I will make. I will be focussing on the experience of suffering of the unhappy consciousness as one of the generative forces behind the *process* of becoming that is traced through the *Phenomenology*.

According to Bruce Baugh, Wahl read this moment as a way into Hegel that aided in understanding the concepts of the essence of human nature, of consciousness, that lay embedded in the *Phenomenology*. Wahl, therefore, did not rely solely on the framework of historical or political determinations of self-consciousness and its moments. In *Le Malheur* Wahl states, "The beginning of philosophy, as of religion, is less wonder than non-satisfaction and the divided consciousness [*la conscience déchirée*]." Elaborating on this, Baugh writes, "Before being a method, the dialectic is the experience of a divided consciousness striving for unity."[7] In other words, what Hegel is setting forth is a way of understanding how our consciousness functions using a method based on this functioning; experience comes before method. Wahl further asserts that our activity, when we reach the stage of the unhappy consciousness, is taken up with,

> watching the perpetual passage of one idea into another; since the opposites are not held together in spirit, we watch a play of forces in the spiritual domain analogous to the play of forces in the material world (and to what will be, much later, a play of hypocrisy in the domain of morality). Every time that consciousness believes that it has achieved rest and rolled its stone up to the summit of unity, it is rolled back again towards division and the abyss.[8]

Here we can use Wahl to further bolster our interpretation of this moment as the re-running of the play of Forces. Additionally, Wahl's Sisyphean analogy, taken seriously and to its limit, would do away with the "end of history" claims and would rather designate the work and movement of consciousness as infinite, interminable. In other words, if the unhappy consciousness is the central figure of consciousness, and its action is as Wahl describes it, then consciousness will always have within it this sense of unrest and incompletion. I am arguing in this chapter that this sense of unrest can be generative, yet that the danger lies in this moment of consciousness becoming isolated and separated out from its relation to the movement of which it is part.

Wahl performs his reading of Hegel on two levels, thus historically introducing a way of understanding Hegel's work at a level of existential analysis. The first is a straightforward reading of the episode that locates the unhappy consciousness in the context of religion. This is the level at which most conventional interpretations of the *Phenomenology*, before and since Wahl, stop, and certainly this is faithful to one element of the text.[9] However, to remain at such a level of analysis is to not unpack the rich paradigmatic potential of envisioning all consciousness as always containing within it the potential for extreme alienation and agony as one of its moments. It can be argued that Hegel intended for it to be read on both of these levels. Wahl seems to have taken this approach and thus treated the religious context as an illustration of Hegel's more essential point regarding consciousness.[10] Barry Cooper remarks,

> The religious and the philosophical were, according to Wahl's Hegel, aspects of the same incomplete historical self-consciousness. Only 'philosophy,' or more precisely, 'science,' could unite the two. It is for this reason, according to Wahl, that Hegel undertook the study of the unhappy consciousness. Wahl's argument is straightforward: only when consciousness has descended to the absolute depths of separation could it recover its own unity.[11]

The level I choose to read the text is at that of the philosophical (secular), exploring what the descent to the "absolute depths" looks like. Since I am looking at the *Phenomenology* as philosophies intertwined with "ways of living," I interpret Wahl's "spiritual" domain within my understanding of consciousness in the intersubjective realm. Such an interpretation of terms is not necessarily that straightforward but is done so that there is no confusion between the spiritual and its religious implications and an understanding of the subject and Spirit. Hyppolite also discusses Hegel's use of the implicit examples of Judaism and Christianity to illustrate unhappy consciousness. However, he reads these as historical *examples* only and chooses to interpret this moment in much the same manner as Wahl: "What Hegel really wants to describe is the education of self-consciousness, the elaboration of subjectivity, which leads back to the consciousness of being."[12] This is precisely the manner in which I will be reading "The Unhappy Consciousness" episode and the episodes leading up to it, leaving aside the historical context of Stoicism and the Scepticism and the historical and religious contexts of the unhappy consciousness.[13] It is to an understanding of the generative and binding nature of Force, of the play of Forces, that I now turn, as I move through the episodes that lead up to the introduction of the unhappy consciousness.

With the shift into "Self-Consciousness," we are entering a realm of a rather more violent set of relations. My focus, however, is not on the reading of physical violence inherent in the "life-and-death struggle" of the master/slave dialectic. This is the site where most readings place the emphasis on bodies and power relations, thus neglecting the remaining movements of self-consciousness. Instead, I am looking at a sort of psychic violence that consciousness, as a burgeoning self-consciousness, both puts itself through and experiences as it (its inner world) begins to relate to the (external) world *as* this self-consciousness. As noted in my discussion of the "Force and the Understanding" chapter, the key to this shift to the internal division that comes about as a result of the play of Forces, and the unrest engendered, can be located in the introduction of desire (*Begierde*). I have suggested that the notion of solicitation, as an activity of Force, could be viewed as a model for desire. This is important to recall since it reminds us that in the movement of Force there exists, built into its very essential nature, the seeking of that which is other than itself but which, ultimately, turns out only to be Force itself. We will find this also occurring with the concept of desire proper. At this stage we can locate the introduction of desire as a product of another series of vanishings.

The crucial shift that has occurred in the move into self-consciousness is from consciousness knowing itself in relation to an "other," to a realm in which this other has vanished, at least momentarily. This is, for Hegel, a "new shape of knowing." Here I flag an anticipation of my argument regarding the third that is produced in the psychoanalytic setting. My elaboration upon the "shapes of knowing" will take place most significantly in Chapter Four. There I will argue that what is created in the interaction between the analyst and the analysand, through their communications, both unconscious and in/through language, is the analytic third. This third survives the analytic encounter, preserving its moments and altering ways in which the two subjects involved think and know. For now, we can understand that "if we consider this new shape of knowing, the knowing of itself, in relation to that which preceded, viz. the knowing of an other, then we see that though this other has indeed vanished, its moments have at the same time no less been preserved, and the loss consists in this, that here they are present as they are in themselves" (*PS*, 104–05). It is not, then, that the other, in its entirety/wholeness, itself has been preserved within self-consciousness, but its *moments* have, and it is thus not "other" to consciousness but is part of consciousness itself.

This notion of preservation within the self-consciousness is akin to Force *preserving* within it all of the moments of difference. What self-consciousness holds, then, are these moments that remain from its interaction with the other; they are the products of this previous form of knowing. It might be said that the other simply *is* these moments, and thus, the other is preserved within the self even though it has vanished. Hegel continues:

> The [mere] *being* of what is merely 'meant,' the *singleness* and the *universality* opposed to it of perception, as also the *empty inner being* of

> the Understanding, these are no longer essences, but are moments of self-consciousness, i.e. abstractions or distinctions which at the same time have no reality *for* consciousness itself, and are purely vanishing essences. (*PS*, 105)

As we shift into the realm of self-consciousness, Hegel is preparing us for the intersubjective battle to come. Because it has vanished for self-consciousness, Hegel has made vanish for us the world of abstraction and distinction and has designated these as "vanishing essences." In so doing, however, these abstractions and distinctions are preserved within our movement of reading as they are in the new movement of self-consciousness. Self-consciousness now not only holds within itself the other/otherness (the sensuous world) as a "distinct moment" but also holds the notion of the "unity of itself with this difference" (*PS*, 105). Above all, it has within it the new knowledge (the new shape of knowing) that it was precisely its movement that caused this other to vanish and that it is within the properties of this vanishing that the other never fully disappears but remains as a trace, a subsistence.

It is self-consciousness' holding of these two moments within itself, via the movement of vanishing, which introduces the concept of desire.[14] It is also here that the seed has been sown for the subsequent pain of its being *as* a double object which takes place when the unhappy consciousness attempts to reconcile just how the containment of these two moments within itself must inevitably manifest. The notion of unity "must become essential to self-consciousness, i.e. self-consciousness is *Desire* in general" (*PS*, 105). Thus we can see desire as the desire of self-consciousness for the unification of self, much like we saw the notion of the *solicitation* of Force by Force as the "desire" of Force for the unification of its two moments (of Force proper and Force driven back into itself). It is at this point that Hegel introduces the concept of Life through which we can trace another level of understanding that consciousness gains about itself. If we find desire as, in Butler's words, the subject's "movement towards the world, consumption and externalization, appropriation and dispersal," then we are about to find in the Life of the subject "the constant consolidation and dissolution of itself."[15] What we are to find in the concept of Life is another way in which to articulate how the subject binds (consolidates) and unbinds (dissolves) itself and an emphasis on the importance of constant becoming.

THE CONCEPT OF LIFE

I will spend a brief time here gesturing towards an understanding of the concept of Life. My discussion will by no means be complete but will allow the move into the psychoanalytic theory of Eros as a binding force in Chapter Three, thus reinforcing my discussion of binding in Hegel. Although desire has its roots in the desire of self-consciousness for its own unity, to illustrate how desire functions in an intersubjective realm Hegel posits that just as self-consciousness is the reflection out of the being of the world and is a return from otherness, the object has a moment of reflection into itself and "has become Life." Thus "the object of immediate desire is a *living thing*" (*PS*, 106). Songsuk Susan Hahn writes,

> But if life in its human form is something essentially linked to desire and self-consciousness, as it is in the dialectic that unfolds in the self-consciousness chapter of Hegel's *Phenomenology*, then, like self-consciousness, becoming a living subject is something that must be achieved. That's why Hegel thinks it's not an empty tautology to refer to the achievement of 'Life as a *living* thing.'[16]

We will soon come to see how Hegel describes the emergence of "Life as a living thing" (*Leben als Lebendiges*). What Hahn articulates is that for Hegel one can be alive, but to be truly *living* is to constantly *become*. The significance of the concept of Life is that we can see in the *Phenomenology* an inevitable drive towards life, a form of Eros. We can see this existing alongside the heaviness of death, despair, and negation that is traditionally focussed upon in readings of it.[17] Robert Williams traces the concept back as a category to Hegel's earliest writing. In language similar to the language he uses to discuss Force, Hegel, as translated by Williams, writes, "Life cannot be considered as union alone, or as relation alone, but must be regarded as including opposition as well [. . .]. Life is the union [*Verbindung*] of union and non-union."[18] Here in Hegel I find the language for the positing of Life, of Eros, in his work that can be read as a unifying/binding force to be found at play simultaneously with the drive towards death, or unbinding (non-union).

Herbert Marcuse offers a remarkable reading of the introduction of Life in the *Phenomenology* and argues that it is the original foundation of Hegelian ontology. He also tracks the concept from the *Early Theological Writings* through the *Phenomenology*. What Marcuse finds, writes Seyla Benhabib, is, "Life is that form of being that can only sustain itself by initiating difference, by externalizing itself, and by reabsorbing such difference and externality once more into its unity. *Activity* is thus central to the mode of being of Life, and it is on account of such activity that Life always unfolds in a 'world.'"[19] This is the distinction between being alive and actually living. It is through action, through active becoming, that one is truly living. This active becoming involves an awareness and acceptance of the notion of process and of one's responsibility for this life. There is resonance to be found here with the description of the activity of Force, although I am by no means attempting to equate the categories of Force and Life by linking them together. Instead, I am suggesting that by introducing both categories as categories of relation in the early stages of the *Phenomenology*, Hegel is setting forth the manner in which we are to consider the *activity* of the subject as a living thing that is responsible for its own becoming but not entirely capable of becoming on its own.

Along the lines of Hyppolite's thinking, Marcuse, although heavily invested in the "historicity" of consciousness, does not see that the primary focus of the *Phenomenology* as tracing a particular history as such. Rather, he regards it as a treatise on Being and the way in which history replicates the activity of Being.[20] He therefore places a great importance on the introduction of "Life as a process" (*Leben als Prozeß*):

> The development of this process is governed by the question of *Being* (*die Frage nach dem Sein*), and in the final analysis, by the question of the most *authentic* form of beings. The *Phenomenology of Spirit* by no means concerns, therefore, sociological laws, historical processes, or the like. The temporality of this process, the 'moments' of the movement of Life must not be interpreted as if they were actual historical periods. Rather, historical periods correspond to moments of the *Being* of historical Life (with what justification cannot be discussed here). When the history of Life as self-consciousness is analyzed into its different moments, then it will be seen that this is a history which is repeated by every existing, living being, which has already always occurred, and which is sustained in the unity and integrity of every life context. (*HO*, 248–49)

Marcuse sees the entire *Phenomenology*, all of the categories, all of the moments, as an unfolding of Life as a process towards its "fulfilment as 'Spirit.'" He further claims that the "we-like process of life" and the "movement of life and thus the being of life" was Hegel's greatest discovery in relation to historical processes (*HO*, 248). Although I am not discussing the nature of historical processes as such, what is compelling about Marcuse's reading is the emphasis on the notion of a collective or shared existence, of the "we" embedded into and essential to the movement of every living being. My aim is to see the movement of the self through the lens of the binding process, which is the creation of a "we," and thus come to recognise the importance of the category of Life for Hegel's thinking.

Marcuse's reading offers a rich and stimulating way into Hegel's text, and while I will not be able to do justice to his entire treatment of the concept, let me just touch upon two more key points he articulates. First, if we recall from the last chapter that "simple infinity" was for Hegel the "simple essence of Life," and that further found in the *Jena System* was the idea that Force was the "cause of infinity," with Marcuse's help here there is a strong link to be made between Force and the concept of Life. Marcuse writes of "simple infinity" that it "refers to those characteristics of the motility of Life as a unifying unity, already familiar to us from the Jena System and referred to there as 'relation-to-self.' This motility is called 'infinite' for it never runs merely along or afoul but is sustained and carried by the *unity* of the living"

(*HO*, 230). Marcuse, in his discussion of Hegel's notion of Being, states that it can be conceived of as *energia* in the Aristotelian sense and that Force is a category of Being. He further argues that in order for Being to be actual, it must "absorb into its own very existence the essential relationality within which it already exists" (*HO*, 92). Although Marcuse does not draw the concept of Force into this passage regarding infinity and Life, if one takes Life as a unifying property in which the infinite finds itself sustained, then claims about Force as a unifying property (and the cause of infinity) are bolstered. Furthermore Force, as a category of Being, has an ontological basis that can be seen as part of the self-movement of Spirit.

For my purposes, the second significant point that I will draw from Marcuse is that Life, for Hegel, is the "ontological condition and the presupposition of cognitive activity" and of the unity of "I and the animated world" (*HO*, 161). This shift to an emphasis on Life is important in order to illuminate the ontological possibilities, which are often overlooked in Hegel, specifically those of Force in my investigation. Marcuse writes:

> The unity of I and the world, or the prior bonding between the subject who cognizes and beings, does not merely result from knowledge; nor is it grounded in the accidental constitution of human knowledge and experience. This is rather an ontological relation, one that holds among beings themselves, one that is true of the 'thing-in-itself' (*Ding an Sich*). This bond precedes all knowledge and in fact makes factual knowledge possible. (*HO*, 161–62)

What I have tracked in my consideration of Force thus far is the burgeoning realisation that the subject is gaining from this bond between itself and the world. Ultimately, what Marcuse so nicely illuminates is that not only can we read the concept of Life as an ontological concept in the *Phenomenology* but also that it is "a form of knowledge." It is "through the act of knowing, through the knowledge of itself and of its 'world'" that Life becomes the unifying principle between "I and the world" (*HO*, 305). Each shape of consciousness, each new shape of knowing, is equally a shape of Life. When I come to discuss more fully the shapes of consciousness in Chapter Four, the importance of this formulation will become more apparent. Additionally, intrinsic to the concept of Life, as Marcuse reads it, is the very "internal process of movement" (*HO*, 309). For my purposes there are two things to add regarding the concept of Life as a process of movement that is essential to the process of becoming of consciousness. Both will help develop our understanding of "Life as a process" and the importance of Spirit's emergence as it is grounded in the activity of Life. Moreover, both points concern the generative collapse of difference. The first is a reintroduction of the concept of flux.

As we can recall from the discussion of Force, consciousness entered a state of "absolute flux" when, in an act of vanishing of "separate, mutually contrasted Forces," consciousness collapsed itself into one Force. Here Force, in an act of generative negation, momentarily moved from its capacity as a differentiated, stable medium into a *movement* wherein difference was simply universal difference, and which generated the "law of force." Here, in self-consciousness, once the object has become Life, *essence* is introduced as having the status of "infinity as the *supersession* of all distinctions, the pure movement of axial rotation" (*PS*, 106). "*Independence*" is posited as that "in which the differences of the movement are resolved," and we are brought into the notion of "universal flux" (*allgemeinen Flüssigkeit*). In the universal flux, as opposed to the "absolute flux" (*absolute Wechselnde*) of Force, the differences *do not* collapse in and of themselves but subsist and are potentially superseded by becoming part of a "pure movement" (*PS*, 106).[21] Being no longer means simply abstract being; pure essentiality no longer means abstract universality. Being "is precisely that simple fluid substance of pure movement within itself." Furthermore, as concerns difference, it too becomes intrinsically a part of the movement of being, the process of becoming. Hegel writes: "The difference, however, *qua* difference, of these members with respect to one another consists in general in no other *determinateness* than that of the moments of infinity or of the pure movement itself" (*PS*, 107).

The concept of Life, much like the concept of Force, is supplying us with a way of discussing the manner in which self and other relate and, indeed, how the existence of the self is undeniably bound up in the other. Hans-Georg Gadamer writes, "Life is the identity of identity and difference. Everything alive is bound to its 'other,' the world around it, in the constant exchange of assimilation and secretion."[22] We could view in Gadamer's biological language of assimilation and secretion forms of binding and unbinding respectively and note that we, as living things, are thus bound to the other by this "constant" process of Life as a series of these bindings/unbindings. This formulation will become more important as we proceed, especially for the various ways in which I conceive of the binding process through psychoanalytic theory.

The second point of importance, especially in view consciousness as a process of becoming and in view of the notion of Force as a universal medium, is that Hegel posits Life not only as a substance that subsists in a "fluid medium," as part of this "pure movement," but also as a *process*:

> Life in the universal fluid medium, a *passive* separating-out of the shapes becomes, just by so doing, a movement of those shapes or becomes Life as a *process*. The simple universal fluid medium is the *in-itself*, and the difference of the shapes is the *other*. But this fluid medium itself becomes the *other* through this difference; for now it is *for the difference* which exists in and for itself, and consequently is the ceaseless movement by which this passive medium is consumed: Life as a *living thing*. (*PS*, 107)

These two concepts of "pure movement" and "Life as a process" will then help us to understand the next key moment in self-consciousness, that of the "articulation" of the individual shape which has as its *essence* universal Life. Individuality is born of the introduction of the other into this simple substance, of the division that this other causes to this "differenceless fluid medium" (*PS*, 108). For Hyppolite, this means that "life is the medium in which self-consciousness experiences and seeks itself."[23] Life is this splitting of itself into individual shapes and the collapse of the very differences it has created. This recalls the nature of Force as the universal medium that collapses the differences yet in its expression creates the split, establishing the multiplicity of difference once again.

There are two moments, however, that are essential to the concept of "Life as a process" and that will recall the discussion of Force. The first is the moment of the "subsistence of the independent shapes," an effectual "suppression" of diremption, and the second is the moment of the exposure of existence, which is no "enduring" existence, to the "infinity of difference" (*PS*, 107). In the suppression of the splitting into difference, the individual shapes are able to subsist, much as we saw difference subsist within Force, where they were held in perfect tension, without "interpenetrating." Here again we can understand suppression as a generative act or at the very least a sustaining power. In the suppression of the self-splitting, the existent shape is able to assert its being-for-itself and is able to "preserve" itself by separating itself from and by the "consuming" of universal substance, the essence. Consequently, the "supersession of individual existence is equally the production of it" (*PS*, 108). As we saw with Force, because of the moment of suppression, what we are faced with is "supersession" as a generative force. The subsistence of these shapes is the creation of individuality.

In light of this, we might wish to consider Hegel's formulation of the "articulation" (*Gliederung*) of the shapes into individual form along the same lines as we considered the notion of expression in the Force section (*PS*, 108). Force itself is constituted by a series of expressions and repressions, Force itself and Force driven back into itself. Much in the same manner, if we are to simplify Hegel's formulation, there are two moments of Life that gives it its movement: the moment that is the "articulation" of itself and the moment which is simultaneously a "splitting up of what is articulated into form or a dissolution of it." We cannot, nor should we, Hegel warns, take either of these moments as ever existing without the other. For, he states, "Life consists rather in being the self-developing whole which dissolves its development and in this movement simply preserves itself" (*PS*, 108). Again, note the generative quality of dissolution evident in the preservation of self through an element of negation. Life consists of a perpetual series of sublations/supersessions (*Aufhebung*), and, as Charles Taylor writes, "Life only exists in an articulation (*Gliederung*) into existing individual forms (*bestehende Gestalten*). They seem to be independent, and yet they only exist in the process of life itself."[24] So, too, we found that Force existed in its appearance, in its expression.

By no means do I wish to argue, nor would Hegel, that Force itself can be articulated into different, permanent shapes. It is the very nature of Force that, while it might "belong" in some senses to the Understanding, it must exist outside of thought, outside of any formulation of object or subject. Force exists as Force. Even if we locate it as a binding, universal medium, it must remain outside of spatial and temporal designation in order that it exists *as* this medium, as this binding force. This is not to say, however, that Force cannot be found to exist *within* shapes. It might be argued that the articulation of Force is in the "play," in the interaction between Forces, thus between subject and object, or subject and subject. As Butler notes: "Moreover, it is not that articulation offers forth a 'content' which is then reflected upon by a consciousness doggedly watching from an ontological elsewhere, but consciousness reveals itself as *an articulated phenomenon*, that which only becomes itself *as* articulation."[25] Consciousness, then, in its process of becoming, in its many plays of Force, is thus involved in a process of articulation of self *as* this process. As I move out of my direct discussion of the concept of Life, I maintain the idea that Life, as a living thing, is a form of knowing and is above all a process.

DESIRE AND THE BIRTH OF SPIRIT

Let us return to the connection being drawn between solicitation and desire in order to flesh it out. Although Hegel has declared that, "self-consciousness is Desire in general," it would be a mistake to take this as the full formulation of desire (*PS*, 105). We must understand the *essence* of desire as "something other than self-consciousness" (*PS*, 109), as existing *outside* of self-consciousness, in the object, the other itself, in the finitude of its content. Self-consciousness only gains its truth, its self-certainty, by "superseding" and ultimately destroying this other, this object, which has presented itself "to self-consciousness as an independent life." Therefore it is simultaneously this object, this other, that conditions the entire process (*PS*, 109). It calls forth, solicits, self-consciousness and in its destruction by self-consciousness the other grants self-consciousness the self-certainty it needs.

We witnessed with Force that what appeared to be other to it and solicited it both into its expression and to drive back into itself was Force itself. Force is that which solicits and that which is solicited. Force exists in and for Force. We are given the well-known formulation, "*Self-consciousness achieves its satisfaction only in another self-consciousness*" and that the "satisfaction of Desire is, it is true, the reflection of self-consciousness into itself, or the certainty that has become truth" and still further that "a self-consciousness exists *for a self-consciousness*" (*PS*, 110). We begin to better understand the formulations of self-consciousness as manifesting the model of the play of Forces. Even if the essence of desire exists in something outside of self-consciousness, even if self-consciousness is solicited by this outside object to ultimately destroy it, it is all in the service of ascertaining certainty of self. It confirms Life, "which is the object of Desire" (*PS*, 110), in confirming unity between the self and the object. As Butler writes, "For Hegel, desire is a negating activity that both distinguishes and binds consciousness and its world."[26] It is this bind that is the appearance of the Force that is desire. In Chapter Three I will pursue in more detail what this seemingly paradoxical formulation of binding as a negating might look like in psychoanalytic theory and see how we can use that theory to better understand the concept in Hegel. At the root of both activities is the potential for binding and negating to give rise to shapes of thought and knowledge in the subject.

Crucially, out of this process of Desiring, the notion of *Spirit* is born:

> The 'I' which is the object of its Notion is in fact not 'object'; the object of Desire however, is only independent, for it is the universal indestructible substance, the fluid self-identical essence. A self-consciousness, in being an object, is just as much 'I' as 'object.' With this, we already have before us the Notion of *Spirit*. (*PS*, 110)

What the "I" desires, in desiring the object, in allowing this object as the essence of desire to solicit it, is as much this essence as it is itself. Furthermore, we must note the formulation of the "'I' that is 'We' and 'We' that is 'I'," the opposition of independent self-consciousnesses, is ontologically constitutive of the "I" (*PS*, 110). Here is the heart of intersubjectivity in the *Phenomenology*. My aim is not to make a simple equation of Force and self-consciousness and solicitation and desire but to show how the play of Forces is that which is the model for the labour of the Desiring subject.

The work of desire as it is transformed in the intersubjective play of Forces then takes the model of Force a step further. My reading that the move from the abstract world of Force to the intersubjective world that stages, in consciousness, the play of Forces is a logical one and will allow for another understanding of recognition which finds support in Sussman's:

> The pure relativity and functional nature of the counterforces is an effect of the physical and mechanical metaphor of force. Yet it is only a brief step from this reciprocal mechanics to the operating principle of Hegelian intersubjectivity. Purely functional vectors may disappear into each other, but this self-consuming physics lays the groundwork for the recognition of self in an other, and the complementary identification of the other through the self. This scenario of recognition not only will condition all subsequent Hegelian interactions but will reverberate well beyond Hegel.[27]

As discussed in the Introduction, I am, however, reading Force as part of Hegel's metaphysical thinking about the world and for the way in which he used it as a model for consciousness. It is in this manner that I turn to the intersubjective world of the *Phenomenology*. It is these reverberations that I will then continue to trace, but more to the point, it is the root in

Force of these reverberations that will be a guide. I am looking here for a theoretical framework for considering how a consciousness is bound to itself and to the external world. Further, how might two consciousnesses be bound together, and what might the process of this binding look like? With this approach in mind, I will look at three aspects of this section. First, my aim is to understand how Hegel formulates the struggle between the lord and the bondsman as a play of Forces in light of the previous investigation into the nature of Force. Alongside this line of inquiry, I will show how and where the concept of vanishing is used here and how it is essential to this play. Finally, I will interrogate the activity of the bondsman where in the "fashioning of the thing" (*PS*, 118) he turns his own negativity, his being-for-self, into an object. I will be using this "fashioning" of the object out of the self as one of the key elements for a discussion of the fashioning of the third in Chapters Three and Four.

LORDSHIP AND BONDAGE: THE INTERSUBJECTIVE PLAY OF FORCES OR THE BINDING TO THE OTHER

I begin, then, with the introduction of the "process of Recognition" (*die Bewegung des Anerkennens*). This process of self-consciousness being acknowledged by another self-consciousness has the structure of Force: "Its moments, then, must on the one hand be held strictly apart, and on the other hand must be in this differentiation at the same time also be taken and known as not distinct, or in their opposite significance" (*PS*, 111). This is the process that we saw in Force, where the moments must not only subsist in the universal medium that is Force and thus create the movement but also must not interpenetrate and thus remain distinct. What we understood as a movement of Force and then understood as the movement of a single self-consciousness, we now see as the "double significance" of recognition in that what is action for one will be the action of the other. We have entered a "mirror phase" of sorts in Hegel's *Phenomenology*, where "each sees the *other* do the same as it does; each does itself what it demands of the other, and therefore also does what it does only in so far as the other does the same. Action by one side only would be useless because what is to happen can only be brought about by both" (*PS*, 112).[28] This mirroring is the action of Force recognising its other as itself, as Force, in the movement of its solicitation. As we have seen, Force can only come about if called forth by another Force. Much in the same manner self-consciousness only exists "in being acknowledged." As seen in the epigraph to this chapter, Hegel brings us here: "In this movement we see repeated the process which presented itself as the play of Forces, but repeated now in consciousness" (*PS*, 112). Of key importance, then, is the formulation that Hegel proceeds to give of the other as the "middle term," the mediator, that which *binds* the self to its own process and to itself. Each is for the other this middle term. This middle term is that which "mediates itself with itself and unites with itself" (*PS*, 112). This movement, this process of mutual recognition, is the root of the binding process.

Here, in the process of recognising, we see the process of the play of Forces. The middle term, the medium, is split up into extremes where one is recognised and the other is recognising. Likewise, we had Force as a medium split into the extremes of Force expressed and Force repressed, or Force that was solicited and Force that was the solicitor. In a sense, each consciousness is its own Force and within this Force is a distinct set of the play of Forces. Through the process of recognition, these Forces come into play. We might wonder how this play shifts when the desire for the death of the other becomes necessary for self-consciousness. We must recall that this desire for death only came about because of the introduction of desire proper. Butler writes, "If there is a *telos* to the movement of desire, an end and motivating force, it can be understood only as death."[29] The implications of this for a reading of the Freudian death drive and the articulation of Hegelian Force will be drawn out in Chapter Four. Equally, however, the drive towards life as Eros suggested above should be kept in mind. It is in this manner that Merleau-Ponty discusses recognition: "I discover myself in the other, just as I discover consciousness of life in consciousness of death, because I am from the start this mixture of life and death, solitude and communication, which is heading towards its resolution."[30] For now, we can posit that this seeking of the death of the other and thus the staking of the life of the self lies at the root of how the self-consciousnesses are bound to one another.

It is in a consideration of this "life-and-death struggle" in which the two self-conscious individuals are engaged that we can see the work of the vanishing as it is manifested in the "Lordship and Bondage" episode. Each self-consciousness seeks, *for itself*, truth through this struggle. Further,

> It is only through staking one's life that freedom is won; only thus is it proved that for self-consciousness, its essential being is not [just] being, not the *immediate* form in which it appears, not its submergence in the expanse of life, but rather that there is nothing present in it which could not be regarded as a vanishing moment, that is only pure *being-for-self*. (*PS*, 114)

Unpacking this formulation, we can see that all moments in self-consciousness can be seen as vanishing moments. All vanishing moments are moments that leave behind the trace of "pure being-for-self." In staking its life, self-consciousness finds that it is not simply appearance, nor is it simply just part of the fluid movement that is life. Although its activity is a submission to, or "submergence" in, the process of Life, we must keep in mind that it is not a powerless acquiescence. To be truly living, consciousness must actively choose this submergence and in so doing recognise its vulnerability to losing this life. Self-consciousness knows, however, that in winning its freedom, its process of becoming is a series of vanishing moments, that its essential truth is "pure being-for-self." Its independence is dependent upon acknowledging the vanishing potential of the moments of its being. Yet this "essential being is present to it in the form of an 'other,'" and so it must also regard this "otherness as a pure being-for-self or as an absolute negation" (*PS*, 114). Therefore, its independence is bound to the other.

What we witness in the next, and last, sight of vanishing that occurs in the "Lordship and Bondage" episode is the vanishing of extremes and a collapse into unity. This is the form of vanishing most familiar to us from the investigation of Force. In the "life-and-death struggle," those that "survive"

> put an end to their consciousness in its alien setting of natural existence, that is to say, they put an end to themselves, and are done away with as *extremes* wanting to be *for themselves,* or to have an existence of their own. But with this there vanishes from their interplay the essential moment of splitting into extremes with opposite characteristics; and the middle term collapses into a lifeless unity which is split into lifeless, merely immediate, unopposed extremes; and the two do not reciprocally give and receive one another back from each other consciously, but leave each other free only indifferently, like things. (*PS*, 114)

This collapse into "lifeless unity," this vanishing of the moment of splitting into the extremes of difference, is an essential moment that leaves the battling self-consciousnesses deactivated, existing only as inanimate objects to one another. This abstract negation does not come from the activity of the play of Forces as such but through this vanishing of the splitting into extremes. In the pause of the resulting inertia, self-consciousness comes to learn that it needs life in the form of and thus given to it by another self-consciousness. The moment of the splitting, of difference, is therefore recognised as entirely essential to its existence. This key vanishing and the knowledge gained are fundamental to the movement of the *Phenomenology*. This is not only for the knowledge gained by self-consciousness but also for the fact that it is out of this vanishing that Hegel introduces the lord and the bondsman, the independent consciousness and dependent consciousness (or so it seems at first), respectively. Here we find, as we did with key moments of vanishing in "Force and the Understanding," that with an essential vanishing arises a new moment of understanding, the birth of a new shape of consciousness.

Because I am exploring the notion of binding and what it means for two consciousnesses to be bound to one another, it is important to focus on the idea that the lord is bound to itself and to the world by a process of mediation through another consciousness, the bondsman, who is, in turn, "bound up with an existence that is independent, or thinghood in general" (*PS*, 115). The true "mediator" in this relationship is this being (this thing), by which the bondsman is chained to the lord and that the lord uses to mediate his existence in the world. The bondsman, however, creates the thing, and thus we have the well-known formulation that the essential nature of the lord is exactly the reverse of what it wishes to be. For in its work, the bondsman is free, and in its dependency upon the work of the bondsman the lord is *not* truly free. We can see this in the statement, "So too servitude in its consummation will really turn into the opposite of what it immediately is; as a consciousness forced back into itself, it will withdraw into itself and be transformed into a truly independent consciousness" (*PS*, 117). Here we can see the concept of Force at work if we recall that Force is itself comprised of two moments, that of the *expression* of Force and Force *proper*.

Force proper, as we have seen, is the moment into which the independent matters have disappeared, or "Force which has been driven back into itself from its expression." The expression of Force is that moment that holds the "dispersal of independent 'matters'" (*PS*, 81). Through its work, the bondsman creates its own expression, its own independent matter (the thing) and the object of independence. It is only through being driven into itself that this transformation can occur. Thus, we see Force, the play of these Forces, as the binding, universal medium. On top of this, we now have the existence of the product of this work, the "object" as binding. We must, however, be slightly cautious about designating the object as the *only* thing that binds. It should be, rather, designated as the manifestation, as the appearance, of the bind, thus the *appearance* of the play of Forces, or of the particular Force of the bondsman. Butler offers a compelling formulation of the relationship between the bondsman and the object in terms of vanishing:

> Hence, if the object defines him, reflects back what he is, is the signatory text by which he acquires a sense of who he is, and if those objects are relentlessly sacrificed, then he is a relentlessly self-sacrificing being. He can recognize his own signature only as what is constantly being erased, as a persistent site of vanishing [. . .] His signature is an act of self-erasure: he reads that the signature is his, that his own existence appears to be irreducibly his own, that what is irreducibly his own is his own vanishing, and that this vanishing is effected by another—that is, that this is a socially compelled form of self-erasure.[31]

Ultimately, what we must continuously acknowledge is that Force is only *visible* in its appearance, only known when solicited by another Force. Thus, the object of the bondsman is the manifestation of his solicitation by the lord and by their play. The seeming independence of the object, then, has its origin in the entirely dependent relationship with the lord and, if we agree with Butler, as I believe we should, the truth of the bondsman is his vanishing. Our understanding of vanishing thus far would then lead us to say that this vanishing is never a true disappearance but a transformation, a marking of the existence of another moment; in this case, the truth of the vanishing of the bondsman is the marker that the lord (Butler's "socially compelling" force) exists.

Without attempting to delve any further into the relationship between the lord and the bondsman, one last moment must be considered so that a theoretical move into the psychoanalytic realm has further basis. This moment is the creation of the being-for-self of the bondsman in the form of an object. When I turn to psychoanalytic theory to examine what the third is, what it is that is created out of the intersubjective, analytic setting, I will investigate the creation of an object of sorts, a co-creation between analyst and analysand, and offer an illustration of what this object as bind might look like in psychoanalytic theory. That being said, I will certainly not be making an equation between the lord and bondsman and the analyst and analysand. One significant difference is that in Hegel the creation of this object for the bondsman would not occur without the "negative significance of fear." Fear is, in some senses, the motivating factor, the generative motor behind the existence of the bondsman's object. Furthermore, "in fashioning the thing, the bondsman's own negativity, his being-for-self, becomes an object for him only through his setting at nought the existing *shape* confronting him" (*PS*, 118). The bondsman can only "articulate" or express its own being-for-self as an object by using the fear constructively. Firstly, however, he must make the confronting, external object (the life in the form of the master) a "nothingness." In turning his internal being-for-self into an object, the bondsman is articulating its existence. This articulation is simultaneously a refashioning of the bind of servitude and a binding of the self with its own truth.

What can be extrapolated from this element of fear in Hegel is the notion of affective binding that will be explored in Chapter Three. Hegel writes: "Without the formative activity, fear remains inward and mute, and consciousness does not become explicitly *for itself*. If consciousness fashions the thing without that initial and absolute fear, it is only an empty self-centred attitude" (*PS*, 119). What can be traced, in a move into the unhappy consciousness, is what occurs when this work of transformation of self, the process of becoming, stops occurring, when the consciousness finds itself at a critical, painful, and potentially damaging moment of stasis. Without articulation, when fear (or anxiety or another affective state) remains "mute" and there is no attempt to use it constructively, consciousness does not realise the potential fullness of being-for-self. Again, we can mark what could be read as Hegel's investment in "articulation," whether on a physical or a potentially linguistic level.

With that said, I move into "Freedom of Self-Consciousness" and into the realms of "Stoicism, Scepticism and the Unhappy Consciousness." Again, much as my examination of the "Lordship and Bondage" episode concentrated on those elements of Force and the notion of the play of Forces that can be found therein, a swift move through the episodes of Stoicism and Scepticism will concentrate primarily on the element of vanishing and on the shifts in the play of Force. In the realm of the sceptic, an unparalleled flurry of vanishing activity occurs, leading us into the unhappy consciousness.

STOICISM AND SCEPTICISM: TESTING THE LIMITS OF FORCE AND THE PROCESS OF UNBINDING

I am beginning to track the process of unbinding, both of the self from itself and from the external world, which begins with the stoic and culminates in the frenzied liberation of the sceptic. In the next chapter I will compare this unbinding with the same process articulated in psychoanalytic theory by André Green. In Stoicism we have entered the realm of freedom and of thought and are in the "presence of consciousness in a new shape" (*PS*, 120). This is a shape of consciousness in which the object presents itself in *Notions* and not in what Hegel terms "picture-thoughts." This is a clear shift into a new kind of representation of the self to the self, a new kind of language of consciousness. Self-consciousness holds the other within itself but this time not as an image, not just as part of the appearance of the world, but in the form of *thought*. The freedom it finds is a freedom that is the result of pure unity of self with self: "In thinking, I am *free*, because I am not in an *other*, but remain simply and solely in communion with myself, and the object, which is for me the *essential* being, is in undivided unity my being-for-myself; and my activity in conceptual thinking is a movement within myself" (*PS*, 120). Here the work, the activity, is internal, intrapsychic. It is not the creation of an object, for the object is already unified with the being-for-self, but it is an internal movement of thinking.

But this selfsame consciousness that is Stoicism also has the movement that "repels itself from itself" and thus becomes aware of itself as a second moment, "as the element of *being-in-itself*" (*PS*, 121). It is not yet aware, however, that this second moment is also an intrinsic part of its own process of being. This simultaneous attraction and repulsion of self that is illustrated by the stoic can be understood here in the light of attraction as drawn from the discussion of Force. We are experiencing another translation of the properties of Force. Here in Stoicism the attraction of self to itself is this communion with self. Both the movement of attraction and repulsion in the activity of Force and the movement of the same in Stoicism produce moments of difference. From Force we see that "it is the *selfsame* which repels itself from itself, and therefore what is repelled is essentially self-attractive for it is the *same*; the difference created, since it is no difference therefore cancels itself again" (*PS*, 96). The activity of attraction and repulsion here in self-consciousness produces the awareness in consciousness of "the element of *being-in-itself*" but in this case within the universal. This manifests the freedom of self-consciousness of the stoic. The difference created here is also no difference but is a manifestation of itself using the new tool of "thought." As Hegel writes: "What alone has importance is the difference posited by *thought,* or the difference which from the very first is not distinct from myself" (*PS*, 121). Through its reality as freedom, this new form of consciousness has released itself from bondage and has entered into the universality of thought and an undivided unity of being-for-self that contains otherness within it *as* thought.

Yet this freedom is not yet true freedom but is only the "Notion of Freedom" (*PS*, 122). In order to have the "realization" of that Notion, we must make the transition into Scepticism and into the "actual experience of what the freedom of thought is." This is another shift out of the abstract and into the concrete, the actual. Concrete thinking destroys the being of the world, as "manifold determinateness," and the negativity of free self-consciousness turns into the understanding of itself as "a real negativity" (*PS*, 123). When I turn to a close reading of the psychoanalytic concept of negation in Chapter Three, I will begin to draw links with the Hegelian concepts of negativity/ negation and the process of thought as such. What is remarkable about this section on the figure of the sceptic is that Hegel employs the concept of vanishing ten times in an incredibly short space of time. If, as I have argued, each site of vanishing brings about a new moment of and shift in understanding (however slight it might be given the particular circumstances of the particular vanishing) for consciousness, then we can locate in Scepticism an environment of heightened, nearly frenzied activity and transformation. The result of this is the creation of the polarity that will cause the agonizing split of the unhappy consciousness. Remember the roots of this polarity from the movement of Force, subsequently replicated in the movement of desire and soon to be found in the self-splitting of the unhappy consciousness. An examination of these moments of vanishing will locate for us the pathway of the confusion, contradiction, and unrest that leads us to the unhappy consciousness.

In the first instance, we find that consciousness, in the new form of Scepticism, because it is *thinking*, is in itself infinite and sees independent things and their differences as only "vanishing magnitudes" (*PS*, 123). In his discussion of the "mathematics of the infinite" in the *Science of Logic*, Hegel describes vanishing magnitudes as "magnitudes which are no longer any particular quantum and yet are not yet nothing but are still a *determinateness* relatively to an other" (*SL*, 254). Far from wishing to confuse this present consideration with the "mathematics of the infinite," I wish only to elucidate what the nature of this particular instance of vanishing might be. Let us take the idea that these vanishing magnitudes do not become *nothing*, do not disappear, but are still in a bond of sorts with an other, with self-consciousness. Again, we find here the familiar vanishing of differences in their abstraction but not a vanishing of the relationship between these differences and the infinitude of thought. In this same passage of the *Logic*, Hegel goes on to discuss the relationship of the space of the intermediate state *between* being and nothing and the mis-designation of this as a "state." Recall here the way in which we understood the state of "in-between" with the assistance of Stephen Houlgate's thoughts on vanishing, being, and nothing discussed in the last chapter. What is important for my purposes in this chapter is not the entire scope of that discussion but that a step is taken towards understanding Hegel's relationship between the "infinite" and vanishing. This is an understanding that it is not the state or the designation of the space between being and nothing that is the truth but that "the vanishing or equally the becoming is alone their *truth*" (*SL*, 254).

At this stage in the *Phenomenology*, as a result of the introduction of vanishing magnitudes, what was before the abstraction of differences now becomes "the *entirety* of the differences, and the whole of differentiated being becomes a difference of self-consciousness" (*PS*, 123). It is possible to conceive of the vanishing magnitudes as markers of a sort, points of location for the shift in consciousness. Our sites of vanishing exist as (potentially) invisible but somehow traceable indicators of the sites of transformation. It is to this notion of between-ness, of the between, that is the space of transformation and transition that I will return to again when I delve further into the notion of the third and the analytic third in Chapters Three and Four. Speculatively speaking, I will explore the idea that if there is an object that is created between subjects, composed of their intersubjective relating, and if this object is incorporated into one of the subjects, then it has vanished from the space between and has become part of the subject. This creation, what can be seen as the third, is the marker of intersubjectivity at work in the analytic setting.

The striking element of the next set of vanishings is that self-consciousness, as Scepticism, is entirely aware of its agency in the situation, of its knowledge that it has the power to make things vanish. Recall the idea of agency as it pertained to the vanishings that occurred in the "Sense-Certainty" chapter. I discussed that the "I," in its relationship to the "Now," the "Here" and the "This," has the ability to actively cause these "truths" to vanish (by turning around) or prevent them from vanishing (by holding fast to its senses). With the narrative of the sceptic, Hegel seems to build upon this notion of agency and marks this fundamental shift in the dialectic of consciousness in the intersubjective realm:

> Dialectic as a negative movement, just as it immediately *is*, at first appears to consciousness as something which has it at its mercy, and which does not have its source in consciousness itself. As Scepticism, on the other hand, it is a moment of self-consciousness, to which it does not *happen* that its truth and reality vanish without its knowing how, but which in the certainty of its freedom, *makes* this 'other' which claims to be real, vanish. What Scepticism causes to vanish is not only objective reality as such, but its own relationship to it, in which the 'other' is held to be objective and is established as such. (*PS*, 124)

Particularly jarring is the fact that Scepticism not only vanishes objective reality but also its *relationship* to it. It is, in a sense, severing its bind with the object and the reality in which it is found, thus generating, by this severe negation, its own freedom, its truth. There is clearly a distinction in Hegel's system between negation and vanishing. I am not equating them here but simply suggesting that the two might have similar qualities that have not yet been considered.

Regardless, Scepticism is a consciousness that is fully aware of the power of its actions, that it is the cause of these vanishings. However, it is not yet aware of the consequences. Hegel continues:

> What vanishes is the determinate element, or the moment of difference, which, whatever its mode of being and whatever its source, sets itself up as something fixed and immutable. It contains no permanent element, and must vanish before thought, because the 'different' is just this, not to be in possession of itself, but to have its essential being only in an other. (*PS*, 124)

In the vanishing of the moment of difference, the moment that gives structure by its very nature as that which is fixed and unchangeable, the sceptical self-consciousness has now led itself again into the "flux" wherein it alone is responsible for the *preservation* and constitution of itself. In the moment of difference, its being was preserved only by being in an other. In a sense, Scepticism is a Force playing on its own. Here, consciousness is the "*absolute dialectical unrest*" (*PS*, 124). Hegel in another generously simple move tells us that Scepticism exhibits the dialectical movement "which Sense-certainty, Perception, and the Understanding each is" (*PS*, 123). We as readers are offered some sense of grounding so that we do not find ourselves in the flux alongside the consciousness that we are observing.

With full knowledge, consciousness has just destroyed for itself a sense of grounding in its activity *as* this unrest. It is now a "confused medley" of "sensuous and intellectual representations" and suffers from the "dizziness of a perpetually self-engendered disorder" which it itself "maintains and creates" (*PS*, 125). It takes itself to be simultaneously a contingent, animal life and holds the power of converting itself into universality. It is consciousness testing the power of its own Force.

> This consciousness is therefore the unconscious, thoughtless rambling which passes back and forth from the one extreme of self-identical self-consciousness to the other extreme of the contingent consciousness that is both bewildered and bewildering. It does not itself bring these two thoughts of itself together. (*PS*, 125)

The pain of the sceptic is engendered by the knowledge that it has inflicted this state upon itself, in the heady aftermath of the battle to attain the very freedom that now torments it. Shklar writes that the escape from Scepticism into the unhappy consciousness is "not a logical necessity, but an emotional one. The psychic tension of Scepticism is overwhelming and the distracted ego chooses some avenue of escape. It yearns for some point of spiritual peace far from the world of doubt."[32] As we move towards the unhappy consciousness, it is to the realm of *unconscious* thought that the sceptic seeks to escape. It is as though there is a necessary retreat to a "thoughtless" space in search of a sort of safety from the potential pain of recognizing and living, with this absolute freedom as the only reality. A distinction must be made between the notion of the unconscious as a property of the inner world, the void, the abyss to which both Hegel himself and Wahl's reading of Hegel refers, and unconscious ramblings, which seem to have a linguistic and not spatial relationship to self-consciousness. This is the thoughtless rambling of a consciousness that has broken itself down, seemingly both mentally and linguistically.

There are three remaining instances of vanishing that occur in the "Scepticism" episode and we see, in the second instance, consciousness declaring itself to *be* the vanishing which it effects. The link here to the relationship between language and meaning warrants attention. The first two sites of vanishing occur because Scepticism "lets the unessential content in its thinking vanish; but just in doing so it is the consciousness of something unessential. It pronounces an absolute vanishing, but the pronouncement *is*, and this consciousness is the vanishing that is pronounced" (*PS*, 125). Here we have the sceptic consciousness allowing the unessential to vanish, thus making itself consciousness *of* this unessential. Swiftly following this comes a "pronouncement" of vanishing, but because the vanishing is given form, given shape, because it is articulated, consciousness then *is* this pronouncement. Consciousness is the form that it gives itself, but paradoxically, this "form" is a vanishing, an invisible designation.

As we began to see in "Sense-certainty," however, the problematic relationship between language and meaning, the location of the gap that inevitably lies *between* the two, is one that Hegel traces throughout. Here, the consciousness that has pronounced itself to be this vanishing does not escape. In fact, it even creates this difficulty. "Its deeds and its words always belie one another and equally it has itself the doubly contradictory consciousness of unchangeableness and sameness, of utter contingency and non-identity with itself" (*PS*, 125). It affirms the nullity of that which it is (seeing, hearing) and that by which it lives (ethical principles), thus causing a gap between itself and its own meaning, a gap between the world and the meaning of the world. The contradictory nature of consciousness and how it articulates this contradiction at this stage Hegel likens to the action of self-willed children who "buy for themselves the pleasure" of purposefully contradicting one another (*PS*, 126). This type of "pleasure" gained could be grouped with the feeling of "self-satisfaction" gained by consciousness in the process of explanation as we saw in "Force and the Understanding." Both are feelings of purely selfish satisfaction that are gained by linguistic means exercised by consciousness at each different stage. Again, we can here see the pleasure gained by a Force in testing the limits of its power. This testing is a simultaneous gaining of moments of self-consciousness.

The very last act of vanishing that takes place in Scepticism is one that leads us into the unhappy consciousness. Although consciousness in Scepticism truly experiences this internal contradiction, it is essential for a "*new form* of consciousness" to come forth in order for the process of becoming to continue. Thus Hegel utilizes another vanishing, leading us to another stage of understanding. Here, "Scepticism's lack of thought about itself must vanish, because it is in fact *one* consciousness which contains within itself these two modes" (*PS*, 126). There is no longer the option of retreat into the safety of "lack of thought," for this safety has vanished. Consciousness must now acknowledge the fact that it is one consciousness that simultaneously contains a duality. With this knowledge self-consciousness becomes the unhappy consciousness, "the consciousness of self as a dual-natured, merely contradictory being" (*PS*, 126). Ultimately, the recognition and resolution of the knowledge is at stake.

This shift into the discussion of a dual-natured being is also the shift from the divisions that came about due to the play of Forces in the intersubjective realm, the realm of the lord and the bondsman, to the intrapsychic realm of a single, individual consciousness. All that we have learned up until this point we are now to apply to an understanding of the internal struggle of consciousness with its own self. As we saw that the movement into the "Lordship and Bondage" episode was the process of the play of Forces repeated in consciousness, so now we see a similar mode of repetition in action. What Hegel advances here, in light of my investigation, is not simply an elaboration of the pattern of repetition, although I will trace the aspects most pertinent to the present discussion, but a warning, a paradigm for what a consciousness would look like if its movement stopped, if its Force was somehow not able to manifest itself. Here we find a case study of sorts that illustrates what occurs when the play of Forces becomes too internalised, and we are able to examine the dangerous implications of such a shift. An understanding of the potentiality and importance of this stage in the development of consciousness is key for the reasons that were touched upon earlier. A turn now to "The Unhappy Consciousness" episode will enable a further understanding of the key concepts that have been pursued throughout the discussion thus far.

THE UNHAPPY CONSCIOUSNESS: THE INTERNALISED PLAY OF FORCE, THE INTRODUCTION OF THE VANISHING MEDIATOR AND THE PROCESS OF REBINDING

To begin with, recall that at the end of the "Force and the Understanding" section we were left with the inner being, the "I," *gazing* into the inner world, attempting to see what it was that lay behind the curtain of appearances. Here, with the birth of the unhappy consciousness, Hegel writes that this unhappy consciousness "itself *is* the gazing of one self-consciousness into another, and itself *is* both, and the unity of both is also its essential nature. But it is not as yet explicitly aware that this is its essential nature, or that it is the unity of both" (*PS*, 126). What is important about the gazing

(*Schauen)* at this juncture is that, instead of the "I" gazing into an inner world, following the vanishing of "appearance" as mediator, we have a self-consciousness gazing into another self-consciousness, both of which are part of the same unity. This is the world of "Force and the Understanding" mirrored in the intersubjective realm and the intersubjective realm shifted into the *intra*subjective realm. Although a small point, it is significant that this is a gazing *into* and not *at*. This is not simply the cool observation of "at" but is an intensely involved introspection.

There are very few other times in the *Phenomenology* when Hegel employs the action of gazing. To my knowledge, we encounter moments of gazing on only three more occasions. The first is found in the Preface, and the remaining two are found in the "Culture" section of the "Spirit" chapter. These latter two instances, in a similar manner to those I am presently discussing, involve a turn inward. The second example, found in "Absolute Freedom and Terror" is also a looking *into* and is furthermore recognition by the self of itself as "doubled." It is of the most interest to us as it mirrors the gazing of the unhappy consciousness but with the important distinction that it has full knowledge of itself as this doubled being and a "certainty" in this knowledge. In contrast, the fundamental point about the unhappy consciousness is that it is not aware of its essential nature and is certain of nothing. Consciousness, at the stage at which it finds itself at this point in the "Culture" section, is "pure insight, is not a single self which could be confronted by the object as equally having a self of its own, but is pure Notion, the gazing of the self into the self, the absolute seeing of *itself* doubled; the certainty of itself is the universal Subject, and its conscious Notion is the essence of all actuality" (*PS*, 356). Without taking attention away from the interrogation of the unhappy consciousness for long, I pause for two more remarks. The first is that what we find here is the absolutely fundamental role that this gazing plays in the progression of consciousness. The long, hard look that the self has into itself *is* pure Notion, and this pure Notion is the *essence* of all actuality. Secondly, out of this moment of Absolute Freedom and all that the movement that created it entails is born the new shape of Spirit that is the *moral* Spirit.

So the act of gazing has taken us from the "I" looking into the inner world, to self-consciousness gazing into another self-consciousness, to the self, gazing into the self, with full recognition of what it sees. This is precisely the kind of gazing that Hegel asks of philosophy. He writes in the Preface of the progression of ways of knowing as a series of attempts to redirect the gaze of those pursuing truths—that is, the "gaze" of science and philosophy up to that point. There was the turn from a "preoccupation with the sensuous, ordinary, private affairs" to "gaze at the stars" and a shift when then the "eye of Spirit had to be forcibly turned and held fast to the things of this world," to empirical science (*PS*, 5). However, Hegel sees that the Spirit is impoverished by the misdirection of its gaze, and we can read his *Phenomenology* as an attempt to train the "eye of Spirit" to gaze again and anew into the ways of knowing itself. This process intrinsically involves the moments of not knowing, of agonizing splits and of the longing for the beyond that is always just out of reach. Without these moments, we can argue, there would be no progression, no transformation, and no cause for change. I return to the unhappy consciousness as the epitome of such a moment and thus as the paradigmatic "motor of the dialectic."

As I have shown so far, a summary of the narrative of the consciousness enables us to extract rich conceptual material that can be taken into the psychoanalytic realm. In this section on the unhappy consciousness, then, my aims are as follows. Firstly, I will give an overview of the relationship between consciousness and the "simple Unchangeable" with which it comes into contact in this episode. Then I will mine it in particular for the occasions of vanishing and the notion of the beyond that have been shadowing this discussion and with them the concept of lack. The desire to fill this lack lies behind this "motor of the dialectic." In so understanding this notion of lack that consciousness feels, prompting it in its seemingly perpetual search for a "beyond" that is always already out of reach, we will be better able to see how the play of Forces is enacted within it and to what unhappy consciousness is bound or from what it unbinds itself. This will bring us to the heart of the importance of "The Unhappy Consciousness" episode and to the notion of thirdness and the introduction of the third consciousness.

The birth of the unhappy consciousness is, in many ways, the manifestation, the actualisation, of the potential for the pain that the play of Forces holds intrinsically within it. It is a product of the movements of the stoic and the sceptic that have come before. It is the culmination of the fear and the terror of the "life-and-death struggle" and the frenzy of its preceding stages. It is, in some senses, the affective response of consciousness articulated and made apparent since we have now turned to the idea of the activity of consciousness as it occurs in one individual rather than between two. Here we encounter consciousness that is experiencing a crisis of existence. Daniel Berthold-Bond writes of the state of the unhappy consciousness,

> Hegel's commitment to an account of human existence as subject to 'infinite pain' is what motivates him to see the state of despair, or the 'unhappy consciousness,' as the central shape of consciousness in its quest for unity, and we might say that madness is the most extreme gesture open to consciousness when it is unable to resolve this despair.[33]

I will not necessarily be focusing on the idea of madness itself in any great detail at this stage but will need to examine the idea of what it is that is left "open to consciousness" when the progressive movement of its becoming ceases. The stoic and the sceptic can also be considered as individuals, in that their respective activities are that of a stage of "consciousness forced back into itself" and the preliminary explorations of what could be considered the internalised, individual play of Force. However, it is the unhappy consciousness that illustrates the full extent of what this internal play might look like. The stoic and the sceptic are, in relation to the fuller exploration in unhappy consciousness, simply the illustrations of a singular Force exploring the notion of Freedom and independence but not fully realising what truth of either is. When we come to the unhappy consciousness, we are now tracking the quest for unity in a consciousness that does not know that its object is its own self, is itself the "individuality of consciousness" (*PS*, 131). Let me quickly sketch the root of the problem for the unhappy consciousness so that I might draw out the implications for my current investigation.

At the base of the struggle of the unhappy consciousness is the relationship of consciousness with the Unchangeable (*das Unwandelbar*), the essential being (*das Wesen*). In opposition to the Unchangeable is found to be the Changeable (*das Wandelbare*), the unessential being (*das Unwesenliche*). These two positions are, according to the unhappy consciousness, "alien to one another"; it identifies itself with the changeable but finds itself to be the unessential being and "sets about freeing itself from the unessential, i.e. from itself" (*PS*, 127). Unlike the sceptic that set about freeing itself, with a miscalculated coldness, from itself and from the world in which it existed, the attitude of the unhappy consciousness is not one of indifference. If anything, it could be accused of feeling too intensely its own existence. It holds both the Unchangeable and the Changeable to be entirely essential to its being but does not yet understand how to reconcile the opposition, both sides of which are part of its self. This very opposition, this "contradictory movement" allows for no rest and only "produces itself afresh as an opposite." Thus is engendered the pain of the unhappy consciousness, involved as it is in the "struggle against an enemy, to vanquish whom is really to suffer defeat" (*PS*, 127). This internalisation of the enemy, where the enemy is, unbeknownst to it, itself, not only brings the play of Forces that is the battle between lord and bondsman into the individual consciousness, but it also illustrates the nature of the interdependence of each side.

What the unhappy consciousness is bound to at this stage is the *feeling* of its own meaninglessness. Hegel writes: "Consciousness of life, of its existence and activity, is only an agonizing over this existence and activity, for therein it is conscious that its essence is only its opposite, is conscious only of its own nothingness" (*PS*, 127). What it is also bound to, then, is a different sort of flux, a movement wherein it becomes aware that it must bring itself out of its nothingness to the side of the Unchangeable only to realise that although its individuality emerges out of this essential, it can never *be* the Unchangeable. It experiences momentary joy when it finds itself with the Unchangeable that is in its "form of individuality like itself." However, this joy is fleeting and is simply a moment in the "*experience* through which the divided self consciousness passes in its wretchedness" (*PS*, 128). The essence of its activity is the *desire* for its own self as this essential being. What it finds is that what it seeks, the essential, the other in an individual form, will necessarily always be out of its reach. Ultimately, the lack it feels, the *desire* to fill this lack in its consummation with the essential, is its activity. This leads us to the notion of the "beyond" and to the main activity of vanishing as we find it in the "The Unhappy Consciousness" episode.

The first instance in which we encounter the activity of vanishing in this section occurs in fact with the introduction of the "moment of the beyond" (*das Moment des Jenseits*). Consciousness wishes to be unified with the Unchangeable in its definite form. Hegel introduces the notion of hope (*Hoffnung*) in a way that we can read it as another sort of catalyst, another kind of "motor" to the dialectic (*PS*, 129). The existence of hope is, in some senses, the signpost that true unity has not yet been reached. Hegel posits that the hope of becoming one with the Unchangeable must always remain hope, "for between the hope and its fulfilment there stands precisely the absolute contingency or inflexible indifference which lies in the very assumption of a definite form, which was the ground of hope" (*PS*, 129). The "moment of the beyond," although it has been brought closer to consciousness, still remains an "opaque sensuous *unit*" and, furthermore, is an "*immediately present unit.*" As such, "in the world of time it has vanished," and "in space it had a remote existence and remains utterly remote" (*PS*, 129). Thus, consciousness has no temporal relationship to this beyond because in the world of time it does not exist as such. The world of time, of course, does not vanish for consciousness, but this remarkable instance of the vanishing of the beyond as an actuality in the world of time necessarily marks a moment of understanding for consciousness as to the temporal and spatial parameters of its relationship with this beyond.

Just as "hope" must remain unfulfilled, the beyond must necessarily always remain just out of reach. The unhappy consciousness is the "unity of pure thinking and individuality" and as such has advanced beyond the "abstract thinking" of the stoic and the "unsettled thinking" of the sceptic. It has also advanced beyond these two stages in terms of what could be considered its affective, emotional state. It is the "pure inner feeling" of consciousness that in its full manifestation keeps the unhappy consciousness from knowing that it is the unity that it already is and from knowing that its "object" is its own self. We are faced with "the pure heart which *feels* itself, but itself as agonizingly self-divided, the movement of an infinite yearning which is certain that its essence is such a pure heart." This essence is, however, simultaneously the "unattainable *beyond,* which, in being laid hold of, flees, or rather has already flown" (*PS*, 131). This feeling is a retreat of sorts into the inner self, the "abyss" as noted by Wahl. Instead of laying hold of the Unchangeable, consciousness has really only laid hold of itself, of the unessential.

We are now prepared to encounter one of the richest and most despairing moments in the movement of consciousness and are confronted with illuminating implications for our consideration of vanishing:

> Where that 'other' is sought, it cannot be found, for it is supposed to be just a *beyond,* something that can *not* be found. When sought as

> a particular individual, it is not a *universal* individuality in the form of thought, not a *Notion,* but an individual in the form of an object, or an *actual* individual; an object of immediate sense-certainty, and for that very reason only something that has already vanished. Consciousness, therefore, can only find as a present reality the *grave* of its life [. . .] But having learned from experience that *the grave* of its *actual* unchangeable being has *no actuality,* that the *vanished individuality,* because it has vanished, is not the true individuality, consciousness will abandon its quest for the unchangeable individuality as an *actual* existence, or will stop trying to hold on to what has vanished. Only then is it capable of finding individuality in its genuine or universal form. (*PS*, 131–32)

It is necessary that the other remains a "beyond" so that consciousness can be driven by this lack, by the process of *desiring* that which is always already out of its reach. The existence of individuality depends both on the vanishing of that which is not true individuality and on the letting go of that which has vanished. The purpose of the vanishing at this point is to bring to consciousness the knowledge of itself *as* an individual. Consciousness, in a way that we have not truly witnessed prior to this point, is aware that not only is the activity of vanishing essential to its being but also that it must relinquish the notion that it can "possess" the other, this "individual in the form of an object" in order for it to find its individuality. This other, however, must somehow subsist as a trace in the process of becoming. These sites of vanishing are the indelible marks within consciousness.

With this knowledge of itself as an individual, in having let go of what has vanished, the "feeling heart" of consciousness has returned to itself. It has passed through the moments of agony, and in realising that the presence of the "grave of its life" is not its true self, it has come to a point where it has "felt the object of its pure feeling and this object is itself" (*PS*, 132). What remains for the unhappy consciousness, then, is to realise that the confirmation of its inner certainty that is its current state comes in not just *finding* itself *desiring* and *working* but in knowing that its activity is its own confirmation and is the certainty that it seeks. Yet its inner life remains incomplete self-certainty. Consciousness still remains divided within itself, and in itself the divisions subsist. On one side, it "stands actively present" while simultaneously "confronting it is a passive actuality." Here we have consciousness as Force acting only on itself:

> The [passive] extreme of actuality is set aside by the active extreme; but the actuality, on its side, can only be set aside because its own unchangeable essence sets it aside, repels itself from itself, and hands over what is repelled to the active extreme. The active force appears as the *power* in which actuality is dissolved; for this very reason, however, the consciousness to

which the *intrinsic* or essential Being is an 'other,' regards this power which it displays in its activity to be the beyond of itself. (*PS*, 133–34)

So here, the "active force" is taken one step further and made a power and is, more importantly, designated as a "beyond." We see the mechanisms of Force at play here in the action of repelling illuminated in the discussion of attraction and repulsion above. Instead of the idea of attraction, however, we seem to have that of the "active extreme," but in the notions of "activity" and "passivity," we seem to have the play of the expression of Force and Force driven back into itself. The fundamental point to be taken is that with the knowledge that the "active force" of consciousness now gives itself by regarding this very power the "beyond" of itself, it has just taken away from itself its own force. Here we have seen how the generative activity of the play of Forces has broken down in the unhappy consciousness, which can be seen, as Donald Philip Verene notes, as "evidence of the breakdown of the self's certainty of itself."[34] We have moved from the assurance of the stoic and the sceptic to the uncertainty of the unhappy consciousness.

Because my interest here is not in the nature of the Unchangeable as such but is more in the mechanisms at play, I will move swiftly over the following moments that lead to the introduction of the third consciousness, the mediator, the external force called in to save the movement of consciousness from utter collapse. The renouncing by consciousness of the power of itself into a "beyond" coincides with the renouncing and surrendering by the Unchangeable of its embodied form. Consciousness here still refuses to acknowledge its independence, and thus Hegel designates this a moment of "reciprocal self-surrender" (*PS*, 134). The activity of consciousness as a desiring, working, and enjoying being becomes one of destruction as consciousness takes itself again as a nothingness and sets about reducing all particularities to nothingness. The relationship with the internalised enemy is reinvigorated, and we must echo Berthold-Bond and ask, what is left to consciousness now? The unhappy consciousness must to return to itself, to escape itself as "a personality confined to its own self and its own petty actions, a personality brooding over itself, as wretched as it is impoverished" (*PS*, 136). This is a twofold process of the introduction of the "third consciousness" and the turning of self-consciousness by itself into a Thing (*einem Dinge*). It is not that the unhappy consciousness is unaware that it needs a way out of its pain. As Simon Jarvis writes:

> It is usually remembered that unhappy consciousness is restless self-consciousness. But what is as often forgotten is that what powers this restlessness is precisely the attempt of self-consciousness to fix itself, to become a real actuality amongst other real actualities. It is vain to tell unhappy consciousness to pull itself together since it is just by trying to pull *itself* together that it falls apart.[35]

It is simply that the unhappy consciousness cannot "pull *itself* together" without assistance and therefore requires the introduction of "the Third."

In considering the activity of the unhappy consciousness, we have seen the play of Forces manifest themselves within an individual and have witnessed the danger of what occurs when the play of Forces ceases. The unhappy consciousness has internalised the enemy and has broken itself down by placing its own Force, its own power, as a "beyond." Because it has relinquished its force and is "confined to its own self," the mechanism of the play of Forces needs the activation of another being, another self-consciousness. The presence of this other being will *unbind* the unhappy consciousness from these solipsistic, particular confines, from itself, in order to *rebind* it simultaneously to the universal once again, thus reactivating the movement that is its becoming. The unhappy consciousness is already in an unbound state. It is unbound from the external world and is bound only to itself. What we find here is a sort of *doubly* unbound state that the counsellor is called into fix. It must unbind the unhappy consciousness from itself (from its unbound state) and rebind it to the external world. This is necessary because, as Peter Dews writes, "the longing of the Unhappy Consciousness of religion for an unattainable beyond [. . .] can only be definitively overcome when self-consciousness abandons its insistence upon its own absolute autonomy, and accepts its belonging to and dependence upon the human community which constitutes its substance."[36] As I will elaborate on more fully in the next two chapters, this means that true freedom, especially from the confines of despair, comes only from being bound to others and in acknowledging and accepting these binds.

Thus, Hegel introduces the force of the "mediator" into the economy of forces. This third term, this mediator (*dieser Vermittler*), has the ability to bring into relation the two extremes of the Unchangeable and the unessential consciousness and thus has the potential to bring unity to the unhappy consciousness. This mediator is explicitly a "conscious being" to whom, because it has next to nothing left to relinquish, the unhappy consciousness hands over its own will and "freedom of decision and herewith the responsibility for its own action" (*PS*, 136). In order to fully surrender to this mediator, the unhappy consciousness also "casts upon" the mediator the "*actuality* it received in work and enjoyment," thus denying itself any *feeling* it may have had left to it. As such, it is now bound, through this act of surrender, to this mediator, and is now completely deprived of "consciousness of inner and outer freedom, of the actuality in which consciousness exists *for itself*" (*PS*, 137). It has become fully *unbound* from its own existence as consciousness.

The unhappy consciousness is a new bondsman of sorts. "It has the certainty of having truly divested itself of its '*I*,' and of having turned its immediate self-consciousness into a *Thing*, into an *objective* existence" (*PS*, 137). In the discussion of the relationship between the lord and bondsman, I noted that the bondsman was motivated by fear to "fashion" its own into an object. By thus confronting the lord as a nothingness, the bondsman attained freedom and truth in binding its own self to the object of its creation. In much the same way, the unhappy consciousness recognises the necessity to refashion its own self-bind through the turning of itself into an "objective existence." This is one of the only options "left open" to it and is the initial stage of the way out of the binds of despair. Walter Davis, in his work *Inwardness and Existence*, illuminates this point:

> Unhappy consciousness desperately seeks some way to objectify itself; only by so doing can it preserve the power it senses beneath its discord, arrest its self-diffusion, and posit an image in which it might eventually remake and know itself. Objectification is a necessary release from inner pain; it prevents a suicidal enclosure of unhappy consciousness in its own inwardness. Unable to master itself, subject can still develop its possibilities by externalising them.[37]

Thus we see this objectification as the first gesture towards the reclamation of the "I." Only in renouncing this "I," only in going to the "absolute depths of separation," in unbinding itself, will consciousness be able to find its unity again. In the turning of immediate self-consciousness into a thing, we also encounter the notion that with this act of self-renunciation "therein does *deception* vanish." The deception that vanishes is the life of consciousness as beholden to a "gift from above," a deception that results in a disclaiming of the power (force) of its own existence while still holding itself to be its own particular existence (*PS*, 137). In the vanishing of this deception and the turning of itself into an object, it has entered a state of rawness and vulnerability. In this raw state of self-sacrifice, it has delegated all power of understanding and action to this mediator. In exchange, however, it has obtained momentary relief from its misery.

Hegel does not wish this action of self-renunciation to be seen as a purely negative act. He states that it is at the same time generative, because, in the handing over of the will of the self to an other, to this mediator, the will itself becomes "other" to consciousness and thus becomes actual. But it is "not through the Unhappy Consciousness itself, but through a Third, the mediator as counsellor" (*den Vermittler, als Rat wird*) that this change comes about, that the self begins to become actual, to truly live again (*PS*, 138). It is here that we have now the true activity of what Walter Davis calls "the priests, the first mental health professionals."[38]

In this book, I am performing a secular reading and therefore am moving away from the designation of "the priests." I am, instead, positing the birth of our vanishing mediator, a figure that might be seen as the prototype of an analyst figure. The will becomes universal and essential will, but consciousness *still* does not take itself to be this essential will. It is the mediator that knows of the certainty of this bind, that consciousness is both objectivity and being-for-self and as such is bound both to itself (inner world) and to the universal (outer world). Along with the power of understanding, the mediator also has the power of "expression" of this certainty that the unhappy consciousness does not yet know. As Hegel writes, "*For itself,* action and its own actual doing remain pitiable, its enjoyment remains pain, and the overcoming of these in a positive sense remains a *beyond*" (*PS*, 138). This sense of the "beyond" serves a similar function to the other notions of beyond that we have encountered with the notion of hope and with the other that consciousness sought. It is this sense that the satisfaction of this lack, here the positive sense that consciousness seeks, always already eludes consciousness and spurs the dialectic ever onward. Here, consciousness is moved to escape the pain of its existence.

Yet, the mediator has saved the unhappy consciousness from itself and rescued the play of Forces from the internal collapse that threatened to become a permanent state. The idea of Reason has been born *in* and *for* consciousness and with it the certainty that "in its particular individuality, it has being absolutely *in itself,* or is all reality" (*PS*, 138). Recall Frederic Jameson's definition of the vanishing mediator. He writes that it is "in the strictest sense of the word a catalytic agent that permits an exchange of energies between two otherwise mutually exclusive terms" and that it "serves in its turn as a kind of overall bracket or framework within which change takes place and which can be dismantled and removed when its usefulness is over."[39] As we shift out of the realm of "Self-consciousness" and into "Reason," where consciousness has returned to itself because it has grasped the thought "that the *single* individual consciousness is *in itself* Absolute Essence," we have again what could be conceived of as the "exchange of energies" (in Jameson's terms) between the two terms that the unhappy consciousness had thought were mutually exclusive (*PS*, 139). Due to the work of the vanishing mediator, our proto-analyst, this exchange of energies, this play of Forces, can begin again. Furthermore, as we slip into the realm of Reason, this mediator silently vanishes and Self-Consciousness finds itself *as* Reason and "its hitherto negative relation to otherness turns round into a positive relation" (*PS*, 139). Consciousness is once again bound to itself in its new state and to unity with the universal.

CONCLUSION

With this groundwork in place, we are prepared to move into the psychoanalytic realm. Of primary importance is the understanding of the intersubjective play of Forces that led to the unhappy consciousness wherein we witnessed the intrinsic danger of the breakdown in this play. This led to a consideration of the fundamentals behind the moments of binding that we witnessed throughout the "Self-Consciousness" chapter and for which we were prepared given our work with the concept of Force. These culminated with the birth of the third, of the vanishing mediator. The first binding witnessed was of the self to the self with the birth of Self-consciousness. The second occurred in the recognition of the "object" of the other, which in its nature as a "life-and-death struggle" is simultaneously a binding and an unbinding. The third moment in the process is the rebinding. This is where the work of the vanishing mediator first makes its appearance. Because the unhappy consciousness is unable to enact rebinding on its own, it requires help from the third consciousness to find its unity again. Through the mechanisms of alienation, and the subsequent loss of self that can be seen as a true unbinding from both itself and the world, consciousness can generate for itself a reflective gap, the discussion of which was begun in the last chapter. It is in this gap, in the alienation from itself, that self-consciousness gains a new level of understanding, a more advanced way of knowing its own self and process. When it has emerged, with the help of the Third consciousness, from this transitional state in which transformation occurs, it is once again an active, thinking, feeling consciousness. With this framework in place, I will now explore how the Hegelian economy of relation, that of which the play of Forces is part, can be read alongside similar concepts in psychoanalysis. In so doing I will illustrate what an exploration of the psychoanalytic concept of binding does to an understanding of Hegel. I will further consider the notion of the third as it can be formulated in psychoanalytic theory. Moreover, as I have been gesturing towards thus far, I will find, alongside formulations of the analyst as the third, the various ways in which the term of the third can be used to designate that which is created in the analytic setting.

3 Negation, Binding, and Thirdness
The André Green– Hegel Couple

> It has been maintained that Hegel's work marked the end of the era of philosophy. It seems to me, however, that something is continuing which started with Hegel: the idea of consciousness as a process which is self-revelatory through its discourse, the path from latency to actuality [. . .]. For it is indeed with Hegel that alterity inhabited consciousness, not as the result of an exteriority which, coming from the outside, leaves its imprint on the subject, but as a different development of the figures of consciousness which henceforth see their unity constantly challenged by its own discursiveness. (*WN*, 41)

INTRODUCTION

I am using the work of André Green as the first of my two psychoanalytic "case studies" to examine three primary theoretical concepts. The first is the idea of the negative and of negation. It is with the concept of the negative that the only explicit parallel is drawn by Green between Hegel's philosophical thought and Freud's psychoanalytic thought. This will be my point of departure from which to pursue the next two concepts of binding, and the third, and the form of thirdness that Green elaborates on, in varying degrees, in nearly all of his work.

The Hegelian framework I have constructed out of the notions of Force, vanishing, and, further, the speculative figure of the vanishing mediator will allow me to move in and out of the two fields. In this chapter I will further develop the links between the work of the negative, of negation, and the ties it has with the work of vanishing to see how they both are moments of transformation. I made, however, a distinction between negation and vanishing in that I argued that the notion of "abstract negation" was born out of moments of vanishing, and thus I was careful not to equate the two. Rather, my suggestion was that these two moments could be found to function in strikingly similar ways within Hegel's system and that the potential correlation deserved a more detailed examination. Furthermore, I suggested in the previous chapters that the action of Force could be seen as not only a model for recognition and desire but also as a model of the very action of the negative, or of negation. Along these lines I noted that the play of Forces could also be understood as the "developed negative." Finally, I began to make associations between modes of negation, self-splitting (especially in my discussion of the unhappy consciousness), and Force as generative and binding processes. In particular, I located the link between Hegel's discussion of Life and negation, wherein Life consists of a series of sublations (*Aufheben*), and also explored the correspondence of these terms to the notion of Force. In the initial stages of the present discussion of negation, it is the properties of *Aufhebung* and both Freud's and Hegel's use of the term that is the clearest point of departure for a comparison. Ultimately in this chapter, I am exploring both the origin of "thought as such" and of judgement and will be using the figure of the unhappy consciousness to illuminate these theoretical formulations in order to build my model of the role of the third.

The "Hyppolite-Lacan couple," the "exchange between the philosopher who was an authority on Hegelian studies and the psychoanalyst who was cultivating an affinity with philosophy," is Green's point of departure for his thinking on the concept of the negative, as it will be mine (*WN*, 1). Although Green does take Hyppolite and Lacan's exchange as his catalyst, he does not discuss Hyppolite's (Hegel-infused) reading of Freud's *Verneinung* ('Negation') in any detail; I will do so here. In addition, because my book is not centred specifically on the concept of the negative but rather on how the negative can be seen in light of Force, especially as Hegel's formulation of the negative as the "energy of thought," this chapter will by no means be an exhaustive discussion of the topic in isolation (*PS*, 19).[1]

At the heart of my argument is the claim that intrapsychic life and subsequently, intersubjective life, in both the *Phenomenology* and psychoanalytic theory, is a movement that relies in great part on the processes of binding. My aim here is to build a model of intersubjectivity with a strong concentration upon the concept of binding as it is found in psychoanalytic theory that takes into account the entire process (binding, unbinding, rebinding) and not simply the first moment of recognition and struggle with the other that is illustrated by the master/slave paradigm. In Chapter Four I will more fully flesh out the notions of intersubjectivity that are formulated in this chapter. Therefore, the majority of the time spent here will be in the intrapsychic realm and in locating the point at which a shift can be made into a consideration of the interpsychic/intersubjective sphere. This will be a process that can be observed as "functioning in the field of language" as well as along more economically centred lines.

As I note when I come to discuss the notion of binding, seen through the work of Green, Freud's concept of energy is reinvested with an importance and validity that most post-Freudian psychoanalytic theory seems to avoid. Green, in his work *The Chains of Eros*, in a chapter titled "Towards a Metabiology," points to Freud's early attempts to root his psychoanalysis in the language and structure of biology. For Green, the importance of Freud's metabiological origins should not be so easily cast aside, for they are the foundation upon which Freud builds his entire system. Furthermore, he argues, these roots help us to problematize and understand both the "limits of the analysable" and the "limits of the psyche" and the underlying textures of psychical activity. Under the heading of "metabiology," Green places the subheadings of Force, Binding and Unbinding, the Work of the Negative, and Energy (as well as three categories that are of slightly less interest to us: quantity [although this is related to Energy], "the loss of bipolar flexibility," and "the problematisation of categorisation and its distinctions"). Of Freud's relation to the category of Force, he writes that the psyche is a process of movement of forces and that this is not simply the model for an individual psyche but for the development of culture. Importantly, this process holds the potential for collapse, for the breakdown of Force's generative capability:

> If it must be recalled that Freud always insisted on describing the foundations of the psyche as 'psychical forces,' it nonetheless remains that this starting-point is also characterised by its potential transformations, which extend to the most advanced cultural sublimations, and for which Freud always refused to envisage a separate or distinct origin. It is as if the dynamic quality—the main property or force, the conductor of psychical energy—could on occasions become jammed, fixed into positions that hold back the psyche's capacity for movement, remaining caught up in a repetition compulsion that blocks the possibilities of development.[2]

I am concerned with the role that Force plays as a model for the foundations of consciousness, with the transitions of and transformations within the process, and with how such a model of consciousness might play itself out in the intersubjective and thus more social realm. Significantly, as explored through the figure of the unhappy consciousness, I am most interested in those moments when the capacity for movement is "jammed."

In addition, while recognising that he was amongst the very first to bring Hegel and psychoanalysis together, Green believes that Lacan tied his subject too "narrowly to language" and that there is something more elusive and powerful in the psychic life of the subject that exists outside of its relationship to linguistic structures. As noted in Chapter One, Hegel believed that language needed to be helped along and that it could not ever truly convey the essence of things. I clearly recognise the importance of language for Hegel and for the development of the subject with and through language but wish to see what else is at play alongside it. Green acknowledges, however, that Lacan uses in his system the "fundamental theoretical fact of psychoanalysis which Freud calls *binding* (when he talks of energy) [. . .] whilst seeking to give it a conceptual base." Although he grants that Lacan's "procedure appears perfectly correct," Green sees that "it is faulty insofar as Lacan seems obliged to lean on the structure of language to make his theoretical system work."[3] My interest here lies neither in agreeing with Green in his repudiation of Lacan, nor in tracing the intellectual arguments behind such repudiation. My work with Green simply allows me to perform the reading of Hegel that is the endeavour of my book.[4] I will turn to Lacan in order to help frame my discussion of the links I am tracing between Hegel and psychoanalytic theory, for his work, as mentioned above, lies very much at the origins of these connections. Following Green's theory, then, there are multiple levels of bindings that occur, of which linguistic binds will be included. I will not, however, necessarily be looking at these linguistic binds from a purely Lacanian angle.

My final aim in this chapter is an examination of concepts of thirdness and the third alternatively referred to as the analytic third. For Green, "the whole of psychic structure is based on thirdness."[5] However, there are two main models of the third that appear in psychoanalytic theory and then several variations on these primary models that will be touched upon in Chapter Four. On a basic level, the first is the Lacanian model that is manifested most prominently in the "Law of the Father" and whose emphasis is on the linguistic sphere, in the realm of the symbolic. The second is that of Green, Thomas Ogden, and others of the intersubjective school such as Jessica Benjamin who locate the origins of thirdness in the mother/infant relationship and in a space prior to the child's participation in language. I will touch briefly on the Lacanian interpretation in Chapter Four, but my interest in this chapter lies in the speculative model that I can draw out of the Green/Ogden version. However, I will be approaching it not from the angle of infantile development but from an elaboration of that blueprint.

IMPLICIT VERSUS EXPLICIT CONNECTIONS: GREEN'S HEGEL-FREUD COUPLE

Green's work on the concept of the negative marks him as a practising psychoanalyst who incorporates Hegelian philosophy into his own theory and writing. Investigating the mechanisms and structures of the negative, what Green terms "the work of the negative," as it is found in psychoanalysis and then reading this structure through and alongside Hegel will prove to be essential grounding for my subsequent exploration of the concepts of binding and thirdness. The tripartite process of binding, unbinding, and rebinding has its origins in the process of the drives, which, in turn, can be seen at play in the work of the negative. Furthermore, it is the way in which Green *frames* his discussion of a comparison between Hegel and psychoanalysis that gives my own argument a structural foundation.

On one level, Green states that any comparative study of Hegel and Freud would have to make the distinction between direct and indirect connections in their thought. Lacan's use and interpretation of Hegel in his own writing, to which Green is, in part, indebted, is based more on what is implicit in the connections than what is explicit, "i.e., on the intuition that the psychoanalytic process might be resonant with Hegel's thought" (*WN*, 3).That is to say, Freud famously did not read Hegel, and thus we are not misguidedly to go looking in the reading of Freud for direct reference to Hegel as his predecessor. On another level, Green wishes to read both Hegel and Freud in this comparison within the "context of a history of ideas which itself owes something to the Hegelian concept of the development and creation of theoretical systems" (*WN*, 4). He acknowledges that psychoanalytic thinking has since put distance between itself and the Hegelian ideas that influenced Lacan. In many ways, this return to the root of the negative as it is found in Hegel serves to enforce Green's claim that "something is continuing which started with Hegel: the idea of consciousness as a process which is self-revelatory through its discourse, the path from latency to actuality." This basic positioning of Hegel as a thinker of "process" is, of course, not unique to Green, but his connection between the idea of process in philosophy and process in psychoanalysis makes his work extremely well-suited for my purposes.[6]

My concern is the way in which Green conceives of the negative with the help of Hegel. Green writes:

> We shall see how the work of the negative seeks accomplishment by expressing itself in different ways depending on the circumstances: as a passage, a procession, a figure, a moment of transformation, the significance and extent of which will only become clear retrospectively, a moment in the process or, conversely, as obstruction, rigidity, blockage, the illusion of stopping the process as if trying ahead of time to appropriate an end which is beyond the object's reach. Henceforth, the entire activity of analysis aims to restore freedom of movement to the structure of the psyche leaving the analysand responsible for his decisions. (*WN*, 11)

Links can begin to be drawn between Green's thinking here and the discussions in Chapter Two regarding the transitions and the moments of transformations that occur between the stages of self-consciousness and also regarding the potential for the dangers to consciousness when the play of Forces is internalised, as epitomised in the figure of the unhappy consciousness. My introduction of the vanishing mediator (the "counsellor") in many ways casts this figure as the agent of movement, a motor for re-instigating the freedom of movement for a psyche experiencing the agony of a split self whose process of becoming has ceased moving. I am now in a better position to address the question of the potential *necessity* for these moments of stasis in the process of becoming. In other words, I can ask, If it is not a permanent state, is this alienation, despair, self-estrangement essential to the relationship between the self and the world, internal consciousness and external existence? Following Wahl, we have situated the figure of the unhappy consciousness as the "motor of the dialectic" and argued that all consciousness is unhappy consciousness. The question, then, is not about the necessity of such a moment, of such a figure of consciousness, as this necessity is already established with the introduction of the idea of reflective gaps and the need for the state of alienation as providing the catalyst for transformation. The question now revolves around the need to move out of such a stage, about the necessity for the third, for the vanishing mediator. In this chapter I will argue that the unhappy consciousness is a necessary *moment* in the process of consciousness but should not, and cannot, remain a permanent state.

In the *Phenomenology*, although it initially shifts into the shape of Reason as a result of the intervention of the Third, the unhappy consciousness will return in various forms (most significantly as a precursor to the "beautiful soul") and remains the model for the suffering, split consciousness. In my discussion of Force I argued that the lack that Hegel sees at the heart of any attempt at self-sufficiency makes an external Force a necessary agent in resituating the play of Forces within the context of the outer world. It is not, therefore, simply that the vanishing mediator saves consciousness from itself but that the introduction of the unhappy consciousness is a way of rescuing consciousness from the unbound state of the sceptic (although it, too, is in a state of extreme unboundedness). I will examine the work of the negative as a moment of transformation and as an integral part of a binding process that will then serve to expand a way of thinking about how it is that consciousness is bound to itself and its own processes of knowing and understanding its existence.

For Green, Hegel's importance to psychoanalysis is in the way he "lays down the premises on which knowledge is based." In essence, according to Green, the usefulness of any comparison between Hegel and psychoanalysis would lie in mutual appreciation of each methodology, since he believes that Hegel and Freud are moving towards their goals in opposite directions: Hegel forward towards Absolute Knowledge, and Freud backwards to the "basic elements out of which the psyche is constructed." He acknowledges, however, that "Hegel returns to the most obscure and modest forms of consciousness," and thus Green offers a way of reading Hegel that allows for him to break out of the role traditionally assigned to him (*WN*, 29, 32). Like Jon Mills, Green also sees the shadow of an unconscious in Hegel.[7] His is not a detailed exposition of Hegel's philosophy but relies more upon the notion of movement and the application of this movement to the processes of consciousness. Green sees in the very antithesis, in the very gap between consciousness and self-consciousness, the "conceptual position of the unconscious." It is, most fundamentally, in the "movement which attempts to unite them—because it is difficult to imagine a consciousness which is not self-consciousness—that we encounter the shadow of an unconscious." He therefore asks for a conceptualisation of an "unconscious-consciousness" which would not be "an inferior form of consciousness, but a state of consciousness which would not involve referring either to a self (ego) or to a reflexivity and yet would be a form of investment" (*WN*, 31). Hyppolite had already prefigured this formulation:

> A radical unconsciousness of self might be called a *function of unconsciousness of consciousness* [. . .]. We have perhaps here a key to the problem of the unconscious; it is not a thing behind a thing, but fundamentally a certain spirit of consciousness, a certain inevitable way for natural consciousness to be itself. Hence, we might speak of a certain ontological unconsciousness of consciousness.[8]

Hyppolite links this form of consciousness, this unconscious-consciousness, to the element of the process of knowing that is recognition. I will discuss recognition and the implications for this formulation in the section on binding.

Thus far, there is little to dispute with Green's thinking. Where he begins to construct an artificial distinction between Hegel and Freud is in his failure to realise the full potential of reading a notion of the intrapsychic into Hegel that he attributes only to Freud. Green does not stray far from the standard reading of Hegel's concept of desire, where desire is desire of the Other and where in Hegel's system this formulation brings with it the idea of struggle and conflict. Nor does he stray far from the reading that what in Hegel is the master and slave in opposition (thus demarcating the boundaries of the intersubjective territory), in Freud is the conflict that "takes place intrapsychically between the demands of the drive and the ego organisation, before acquiring an intersubjective form which results in the formation of the super-ego" (*WN*, 33). Recalling my discussion of the play of Forces that is the "Lordship and Bondage" episode, note that it is possible to read this episode with both intrapsychic and intersubjective models in mind. Moreover, in the interrogation of the transitions between the lord and bondsman and the subsequent three stages of "Self-Consciousness," it can be seen that Hegel does, in the manner in which I am reading him, move very much intrapsychically. As I move further into the psychoanalytic realm, I continue to resist the artificial distinctions that formulations like Green's above make between the two systems of thought and instead let the two systems play off one another.

It is the very notion of intersubjectivity that allows me to make a transition into my discussion of the negative. Green gives full credit to Hegel's notions of alterity and wishes only to emphasise that it is the moments of conflict, of the "clashes" between the self and the Other (an alterity by which we are "doubly inhabited" both within ourselves and "with respect to what is not me") that give rise to the negative. As Green writes, "It is the relationship between these two polarities, intrapsychic and intersubjective, which constitutes the essence of the work of the negative" (*WN*, 43–44). It is here that I locate myself alongside Green, at the crossroads of the two poles, at the intersection of philosophy and psychoanalysis, in order to examine the generative elements behind the movement of becoming, the process of consciousness, and to investigate what occurs when this movement ceases, if only temporarily. Following the lead of Paul Ricoeur, I wish "to show in each discipline of thought, considered in and for itself, the presence of its other."[9]

What I have, then, is the idea that in returning to Hegel's philosophy in order to re-examine psychoanalytic theory, we "turn, rather, towards the evolutionary movement or to the perspectives of reversal which are an essential feature of this movement, to the relation between the products of historicity and the historical subject, and examine the formative stages of the hierarchy of meaning" (*WN*, 4). It is the work of the negative that is responsible for this reversal of perspective, and for Green it works to show the movement of the figure of consciousness as it coincides with its essence and that this figure is marked temporally and with its own progress, the marks of which are made evident by the movement itself. Songsuk Susan Hahn posits that Hegel argues for what could also be termed a reversal of perspective:

> It is crucial for Hegel that as a result of this dialectical movement we get a 'reversal of consciousness itself' (PS §87). We get a new kind of knowledge and a new 'object' to which that knowledge corresponds and a new set of standards for evaluating them (PS §85, §86). The new standard for evaluating knowledge claims involves the 'nothingness' of the original object of the previous form of consciousness.[10]

This reading of what the "reversal" gives us coincides with the "shapes of knowing" that I discussed in the first portion of this book and that I will approach again in Chapter Four. What the negative expresses, Green says, is "the reversal of the perspective that essence is immutable and invariable" (*WN*, 36). Essence is, instead, movement and change.

LOCATING THE ORIGINS OF THOUGHT AND JUDGEMENT: A READING OF 'NEGATION' THROUGH THE LENS OF FORCE

Hyppolite, in his address on Freud's 'Negation' (*Verneinung*) to Lacan's seminar, performs the task of elucidating what he sees as the "prodigious philosophical importance" of Freud's rather short but incredibly dense text.[11] He was invited by Lacan to do so because Lacan saw that Freud's paper "concerns nothing less than the entire theory, if not of knowledge, at least of judgment."[12] In his introduction to Hyppolite's presentation, Lacan acknowledges that a (Hegelian) philosopher, especially one "practised in the analysis of language," is most suited to take on the task of unpacking Freud's text and expresses an esteem for Hyppolite that he rarely seems to offer to the rest of his seminar attendees. The importance of the Hyppolite-Lacan couple will, for my purposes, be heavily weighed on the side of Hyppolite. What Lacan did with his reading of 'Negation' was not as rich and wonderfully

Hegelian as Hyppolite's, and so my aim is really to re-centre the reading of the concept of negation away from its "symbolic" importance, even though this was an important element of Hyppolite's reading, and to look instead at how it actually functions on a structural basis. In working through his main points, I find embedded rather important links to my analysis of Force.

To begin with, the basis for Freud's formulation of negation lies in the linguistic expression of that which is repressed, where one presents "one's mode of being in the mode of not being it." This is the famous Freudian formulation whereby when the patient says, "It is not about my mother," the analyst has no doubt that of course it is. What interests me here is not necessarily whether we agree with Freud's view of repression or not but rather the mechanisms of how negation functions and how repression, as found under the heading "the work of the negative," might be seen through the lens of Hegelian negation, to operate in more affirmative, generative ways.

This mode of locating *being* through *non-being*, says Hyppolite, is where Freud, in order to "engage with the function of negation" uses the word *Aufhebung*. We are already aware of the crucial role this word plays in Hegel's system, this word which Hyppolite himself cannot "but feel at home with," and its power to "deny, to suppress, and to conserve, and fundamentally to raise up."[13] The Hegel that the audience of the seminar would be familiar with would have been a Kojève-saturated Hegel and what would have been (and still is) refreshing about Hyppolite is his liberation of and expansion upon Hegel's philosophy from the confines of the master/slave dialectic.[14]

Freud states that negation "is already a lifting [*Aufhebung*] of the repression, though not, of course, an acceptance of what is repressed."[15] What is ultimately at stake here, according to Hyppolite, is that even when the repressed is no longer repressed due to the *Aufhebung* (via, on one level, the work of the interaction between the analyst and the analysand), it does not mean that the *content* has been accepted. Freud further states: "With the help of the symbol of negation, thinking frees itself from the restrictions of repression and enriches itself with the material that is indispensable for its proper functioning."[16] Here Hyppolite locates the process that separates the "intellectual function" from the "affective process" and notes that in this process, "what is born here is thought as such; but not before the content has been affected by a negation."[17] Through my reading of Hegel's unhappy consciousness, it is possible to see this stage of self-consciousness, which lies on the cusp of Reason, as not holding the "freedom of thought" and as not yet enriched with what Hegel sees as the proper material for its functioning. This helps to further an understanding of what it means for the movement of consciousness to cease functioning properly. The unhappy consciousness is consumed by its affective experience and is an improperly functioning intellect or, rather, an intellect that has ceased, momentarily, to become.

A critical passage from the preface to the *Phenomenology* will give us another angle on this movement: "But that an accident as such, detached from what circumscribes it, what is bound and is actual only in its context with others, should attain an existence of its own and a separate freedom—this is the tremendous power of the negative; it is the energy (*Energie*) of thought, of the pure 'I'" (*PS*, 19). Here, too, the negative is that which lies behind the freedom of thought. As we know, according to Hegel, once an idea is broken up into its elements, into moments, we have arrived at thought. It is then Understanding that has the power to dissolve (again) these thoughts, which in themselves are "familiar, fixed, and inert determinations" further into their own self-movement (*PS*, 18). The work of the negative is essential in order to attain this freedom for thought so that Understanding can properly function. As we will also recall, it is Force that belongs to the Understanding. Can further links be formulated here between the idea of Force as holding properties of negation and Hyppolite's reading of Freud in that both notions seem to serve towards the idea of "freedom" of thought? Moreover, it would seem from Hegel's formulation that the negative has the power to unbind, to detach the "I," consciousness (eventually self-consciousness), from the context defining its existence and allow it a separate existence as an autonomous "I." The act of negation is a return to a state prior to the binding of the self to its objects and to the external world of contingency. However fleeting the freedom afforded by negation may be, we must recognise these moments as flights of transition; these are the moments that, as I have traced in the first two chapters, the activity of vanishing affords. These are the gaps on which the entire movement of consciousness depends. Without the space created in the movement of negation, there would be no state of transformation, no moment in which a retrospective understanding of the preceding shapes of consciousness could be gained.

We can see that it is the work of Force, in conjunction with the work of the negative, which saves consciousness from slipping irretrievably into these gaps by binding it to its own movement. Negation is the "energy" that is behind the movement of the "I." One might question the notion that the "I" could in any way be "pure" and untouched by its connection to the external world but only if we refuse to constantly acknowledge the fundamental importance and strength of Hegel's conviction that consciousness is a *process* and that within the process there will be *moments* where consciousness is unbound before the transition into a new, bound moment (of understanding). Accordingly, free thought is this pure "I." If I were to make one final speculative turn with this rather remarkable passage, then it would be to reflect upon Hegel's use of the notion of "energy" to describe the function of the negative. Here we can begin to follow connections between the notion of Force and the dynamic, generative movement of consciousness and the notion that Hegel is asserting that there is something at work *in* this movement, there is something that is giving life to thought. This energy, for Hegel, is the work of the negative.

Julia Kristeva argues that in the *Phenomenology of Spirit*, negativity "appears most material and independent—closest to what we have called a semiotic *chora* (energy discharges and their functioning) [. . .] when it appears as Force [*Kraft*]" (*RPL*, 114). Two points here are crucial for my argument. The first is that Kristeva sees Force as the material expression of negativity, and the second is that, therefore, Force can be thought of in terms of energy. She goes on to posit, as I have, that Force constitutes "freedom from thought" and further that it "acts in a space that is *other* which (Hegelian) speculation, unable to situate it within a concrete signifying practice—in the materiality of the signifying process—ends up superseding not only under the unity of the Understanding, but also under that of reason" (*RPL*, 114). Accordingly, Kristeva argues, what happens to Force in so doing is that the "subsisting essence" of Force is recognised, but the supersession of it "represses its material negativity, free energy" (*RPL*, 114). While I agree with the idea that Hegel's own system in some senses shifts focus from an energetic notion of Force, I do not think that it is a complete and static repression. By this I mean that in its repression, Force does not cease in its work. It is still there implicitly, in every moment of recognition that occurs and in every stage of Spirit's movement, which, as John Burbidge articulated, *is* a play of Forces. Once we enter the realm of Reason, it is simply that the designation of the play of Forces is understood to be at work rather than explicitly referenced. Importantly, Kristeva concludes that the "negativity that was sketched out albeit already repressed in Hegel" was buried by Hegel's phenomenological and logical philosophical descendants (Husserl and Frege) and that what "made its materialist overturning possible, in our view, was the key notion of drives in Freudian theory" (*RPL*, 116).

I can align this thread of argument with my own in order to reinforce my claim that what is already at work in Hegel's theory of Force, a kind of economic system running through the *Phenomenology*, can be illuminated by a consideration of theory of drives as found in psychoanalytic theory. I am certainly not going to argue for a comparison of Freud's notion of "energy" and Hegel's notion of Force that aims to *equate* them but rather one that sees them as maintaining a structural and metaphorical isomorphism with one another. They are the building blocks of the respective systems of consciousness that are only too easily dismissed or overlooked, perhaps because they are considered too metaphysical, too speculative.

There are two types of negativity that need to be considered and with this distinction, Hyppolite begins to elucidate the philosophical potentials implicit in Freud's paper, to point to the "mythical" structures behind the psychoanalytic. He uses the example of Hegel's master/slave episode to show how "genuine negativity" is different from an "ideal negation." At this stage in the development of self-consciousness, he says, a shift occurs in that "genuine negativity" is substituted by the "destructive appetite which takes hold of desire," thus modifying Hegel's movement from a "psychological manner" to that of a "mythical" manner, creating the possibility of the "ideal negation" in which, in the struggle to the death between the master and the slave, there is "no one left to remark the victory of the defeat of the one or the other." In other words, this negation is "ideal" and is able to remain so simply because it is "mythical" and therefore does not truly take place on a physical level but on a psychic level.[18] Rather, it exists in order to show the full potential of negation itself. It is in this "mythical" manner that Hyppolite believes Freud offers to us a striking, asymmetrical formulation of the drives.

Freud, according to Hyppolite, at once gives us the idea of the unifying, affirmative drive of love and additionally the "genesis" of the destructive drive, "of that negation whose true function is that of giving rise to intelligence and the very starting point of thought."[19] We thus have in both systems the action of negation as giving rise to thought. This is the structural level on which a comparison must be based. As I have already noted, the acceptance of the negation in the psychoanalytic process, and the designation of the origins of thought there, does not necessarily lift the repression. In further staking his Hegelian investment in Freud's text, Hyppolite writes: "I conclude from this that one must do what Freud didn't do: call what happens here by a philosophical term—the negation of the negation. Literally, what appears here is intellectual affirmation, which is only intellectual, in so far as it is negation of the negation." He then asks: "What does that imply? Behind affirmation [*Bejahung*] what is there? *Vereinigung*, which is Eros."[20] Judith Butler notes that Hyppolite grasps an ultimate confirmation of dialectical logic at play in the psychoanalytic context. The double negation that takes place in transference is the unity that only comes about due to the work of the negative. Crucially, Butler defines *Vereinigung* as "binding," a considered choice of translation that Hyppolite does not explicitly make but one that I follow Butler in making.[21] In positioning Eros, the life drive, as a binding activity, I am in a better position to understand what its relationship to the destructive drive as a form of unbinding will soon look like in Green's reading of Freud. However, there is a bit more work to do with the negative before I reach that point.

For Freud, to affirm or to negate the content of thought is an act of intellectual judgement. With this act of judgement comes the primal set of responses of "introjection" and "ejection," where the "pleasure-ego" wishes to introject (take into itself) everything that is good and eject (to keep out, expel) everything that is "alien" or "bad." So here, too, comes the distinction of the internal and the external. There is an instinct here for preservation of wholeness, of unity (internal) and the destruction of that which is alien, other (external). Judging, then, is the intellectual act that decides upon what stays out and what comes in. "Judging is a continuation, along lines of expediency, of the original process by which the ego took things into itself or expelled them from itself, according to the pleasure principle."[22] Recall that in the *Phenomenology* it is in the movement of Force and the work of the Understanding that consciousness begins to make clear the distinctions between the internal and the external world and to understand its agency and the part it plays in this creation.

As it moves out of Sense-Certainty and Perception, and into the realm of the Understanding, consciousness begins to explore the relationship between "appearance" and that which constructs the inner world. The generative movement of Force, both as a universal medium or a binding substance, and a preserving matter, allows consciousness to hold within itself this outside world and to create the distinctions between the inner and outer worlds. It is, simultaneously, the play of Forces that allows the "inner being" (the "I") to "gaze" into the inner world. The work that remains, for the *Phenomenology*, for consciousness, is the exposition of "what consciousness knows in knowing itself" (*PS*, 103). In knowing itself, consciousness learns to take the other into itself and to eject this other from its internal world in order to keep the distinction between the two within the realm of its understanding. For consciousness, it is a process of defining itself by that which it is not. This can be seen as akin to negation or the presentation of "one's mode of being in the mode of not being it."

It is by the means of negation that this act of judgement finds meaning. At the tail end of his paper, Freud writes, "Affirmation—as a substitute for uniting—belongs to Eros; negation—the successor to expulsion—belongs to the instinct of destruction."[23] I want to hold onto here this last idea of the destructive drive as giving birth to the very genesis of thought and see what might be made of it in terms of the activity of vanishing. The correlation of vanishing with negation carries us towards the idea that both mechanisms allow for new moments of understanding, of thought, to be born in the transformation (through destruction and incorporation) of previously held truths and/or moments. As I have noted, these moments create the space into which consciousness slips in its new shape, without which consciousness could not grow.

I cannot help but recall that, famously, for Hegel, the life of Spirit is "not the life that shrinks from death and keeps itself untouched by devastation but rather the life that endures it and maintains itself in it [. . .] Spirit is this power only by looking the negative in the face, and tarrying with it. This tarrying with the negative is the magical power that converts it into being" (*PS*, 19).[24] Behind, or rather inextricably bound to life, for Hegel, is this destructive drive, this bond with death, this drive to dismemberment. Hyppolite must have recognised this, even if he did not explicitly make this link when presenting his paper. There is something startlingly akin to the treatment of the negative and the process of consciousness as it is found in Hegel and to the destructive drive later formulated by Freud, which Hyppolite begins to touch upon. For Hyppolite, it is Eros that lies behind affirmation. As I argued in Chapter Two, this drive towards life through the double negation, this Eros as a binding force, exists in the *Phenomenology* and is simultaneously at work with the "drive towards death" that is the "tarrying with the negative." While Daniel Berthold-Bond also sees a clear anticipation of Freud's primitive death instinct in Hegel's "destructive character of nostalgic desire" and, furthermore, in "the element of desire which seeks the destruction of the other," he simultaneously emphasises that we "cannot lose sight of the fact that Hegel himself almost always emphasizes the positive, evolutionary character of desire." He sees in Hegel that the acts of "destruction and death [are] always a prelude to the reincarnation of life" and pulls from Hegel's *Philosophy of History* the notion that "life proceeds from death." Berthold-Bond sees Hegel emphasising the "power of the life instinct to emerge from death" and sees desire as a "vicious cycle of yearning, a movement outwards, a cathexis (binding) of an other so as to satisfy its need for content, and yet, in the confrontation with alienation, an anxious attempt to retreat to itself so as to protect itself from the pain of self-opposition." Here we see the activity of attraction and repulsion at play, a binding as well as an unbinding in the form of retreat. Neither Butler nor Berthold-Bond, however, elaborates on the concept of binding in the manner in which I do.[25]

I thus return to Hyppolite's assertion that one of the significant features of Freud's text is the split between the affective and the intellectual. We see here his further assessment:

> The process which leads to that point, which has been translated by *rejet* [rejection], without Freud having used the term *Verwerfung*, is still yet more forcefully accented, since he uses *Ausstossung*, which means expulsion. Here, then, in some ways one finds <the formal couple> of two primary forces: the force of attraction [*Einbeziehung*] and the force of repulsion, both, it appears, under the domination of the pleasure principle, which in this text cannot but strike one.[26]

There are two points to make here. Firstly, this passage should recall for us that one of the properties of Hegel's notion of Force was its movement of attraction and repulsion. I argued that this activity is wonderfully illustrated in consciousness with the appearance of Stoicism, where the stoic was by turns attracted and repulsed by its own self. I further argued that this movement was the internalised movement of Force and that it was the stage in the process of binding in which consciousness unbound itself from the other but was not yet entirely unbound from its relationship with the external world. In this particular play of Forces, we saw that "what is not selfsame is self-attractive" and saw the advent of a law in which "like becomes unlike and unlike becomes like." This movement is "absolute transition and pure change," where the "*selfsame* which repels itself from itself, and therefore what is repelled is essentially self-attractive, for it is the *same*" (*PS*, 96). It is crucial here to think about this movement as "absolute transition" in light of my discussion of negation as the genesis of thought. Through these moments of transition, in the attracting and then repelling movement of consciousness, thought as such is born.

Secondly, we see here the first of Hyppolite's striking assertions of "the tendency to destruction with the pleasure principle." Lacan (and his editor, Jacques-Alain Miller) took great pains to indicate the originality of Hyppolite's thought.[27] Hyppolite's second comment on this connection is even more explicit and follows on the heels of his discussion of unification and destruction and their links to affirmation and negation. He states:

> In fact this explains how there can be a pleasure in negation, a negativism which results straightforwardly from the suppression of the libidinal components; that is to say what has disappeared in this pleasure in negating (disappeared = repressed) are the libidinal components. As a consequence, does the instinct of destruction also depend upon <the> pleasure <principle>? I think this is very important, crucial for technique.[28]

In his notes, Lacan states that Hyppolite's location of the instinct of destruction being bound to the pleasure principle was "all the more important given that I had not as yet produced these theses that I was to develop in the following year in my commentary on 'Beyond the Pleasure Principle,' on the death instinct, which is simultaneously both so elusive and so present in this text."[29] It is difficult not to propose that Hyppolite got to his formulations first because he was so closely reading Freud from his Hegelian perspective, suggesting that Hyppolite was aware that there was embedded in Hegel work on the intertwined nature of the life and death drives.[30] In locating this pleasure in negation, Hyppolite finds a way to read into Freud a *use* for the repressed. The repressed therefore can be seen to possess dynamic qualities of generative force.

> From then on, what does this asymmetry between affirmation and negation (*négation*) signify? It signifies that all of the repressed can once again be taken up and used again in a sort of suspension and that, in some way, instead of being under the domination of the instincts of attraction and repulsion, a margin of thought can be generated, an appearance of being in the form of non-being, which is generated with negation—that is to say, when the symbol of negation is linked up with the concrete attitude of negation.[31]

The idea of a "sort of suspension" can recall those "matters" in Hegel's concept of Force that subsisted, "mutually interpenetrating" without coming into contact. They, too, were "used" to generate movement; they *were* the movement of Force. The margins of thought arise in these suspended states, emerging out of the gaps created by the movement of negation.

Kristeva offers a way of combining thinking about the activities of attraction and repulsion as I am reading them in the concept of Force, in light of a discussion of "rejection." It should be noted, however, that Kristeva's discussion of attraction and repulsion (and Hegel's response to Kant's analytics of force) is grounded in Hegel's *Science of Logic* and not the *Phenomenology*. This strikes me as slightly odd considering her treatment of Force later in her book that I will soon touch upon. She sees in her reading of Freud's 'Negation' that the notion of "rejection" is equivalent to expulsion but that Freud himself "says nothing about rejection." She states, "Although it is destructive—a 'death drive'—rejection is the very mechanism of reactivation, tension, life; aiming toward the equalization of tension, toward a state of inertia and death, it *perpetuates* tension and life" (*RPL*, 150). This reading of rejection can recall my discussion in Chapter Two of the maintenance of "tension" via the movement of Force. I argued that matters subsist in this movement and that it was the activities of attraction and repulsion of Force that allowed them to do so. "In Hegel," Kristeva writes, "the term *Repulsion* designates a movement within negativity that comes close to what we have called *rejection* yet does not coincide with it" (*RPL*, 157–58). I am attempting to draw these designations just a bit closer.

One of the incontrovertible differences, of course, when considering the language of psychoanalysis in a Hegelian context lies in the idea of instincts. What Hyppolite terms the instincts of attraction and repulsion exist in Hegel's "inner world" but are certainly not considered as instincts. The difference in translation between *Trieb* as drive and as instinct as it is given in the *Standard Edition* should, however, be noted. It seems clear that Kristeva uses the translation of drive, which as many have argued, was Freud's intention. Kristeva argues that it is the matter of drives that delineates the difference between Hegel and Freud and that for Freud what "activates expulsion is 'another scene' based on the drives" (*RPL*, 158). She will link the activities of rejection and binding "only to the extent that it is the *precondition* of the binding that takes place on another scene" (*RPL*, 147). I am, however, attempting to find this other "scene" in Hegel as well.

In the next portion of this chapter the connection between the destructive and affirmative drives, between Eros and the death drive, will be key for an understanding of how the structure of binding and unbinding works and how this can illuminate a discussion of binding in the *Phenomenology*. Binding for Freud, according to Green, is "synonymous with mitigation" and unbinding "always appears in terms of an increase in destructiveness" (*CE*, 54). By mitigation, we can understand that binding is at work to maintain stability, to reduce the pain and potential severity of trauma, to negotiate the effects of the external world, in essence to reduce the presence of "unpleasure" in the psychic apparatus. Is there something of "mitigation" in the act of mediation? Is Hegel's dependency on mediated Being recognition of the boundedness of existence? In an elaboration of an understanding of figure of the unhappy consciousness, one can see that this state of being bound is by no means one-dimensional and a move can be made ever closer to the conclusion that for Hegel the paradox is that the boundedness of existence is essential to freedom.

There is one last point to make before moving to a summary of Green's writing on the "work of the negative." For Hyppolite, the fundamental importance of Freud's paper is that it marks "a genesis of everything which occurs on the level of the primal, and in consequence the origin of judgement and of thought itself (in the form of thought as such, since thought is already there before, in the primal, but it does not figure as thought there)—grasped by means of negation."[32] The act of negation for Freud finds its symbol in the articulation of that which is repressed, in the language of the "no." Psychoanalytically speaking, negation in many senses brings to the surface points of origin that then allow for the birth of thought. It is a generative act. A return to other aspects of Hyppolite's Hegelian reading can restore this notion of the generative act of negation, so that it is not simply seen as a linguistic act that resides in the symbolic realm.

This is certainly not to say that the two readings are entirely incompatible and that Lacan's reading sees something that isn't there. Clearly this is not the case; both Hyppolite and Lacan unmistakably locate the symbolic function of the negative. It is to suggest that moving the emphasis back to what is happening on a structural level in Freud's paper illuminates a remarkable argument about the origins of subjectivity and invigorates my reading of Hegel's concept of negation. Jacqueline Rose highlights the appropriation by Lacan of this aspect of Hyppolite's reading. She draws out the implications for the "symbol-making capacity" in a manner that perfectly illustrates how the paradoxically generative nature of negation exists for Lacan, but in the realm of speech. Rose writes:

> Negation, for Lacan, is death in the structure, or what he also calls the 'real,' which, for symbolization to be possible, has to subsist outside its domain. Negation shows the subject, and its world, arising in an act of demolition. For the subject to enter into the possibilities of language and judgement, something has to be discarded, something has to fall away. For Lacan, therefore, negativity resides on the edge of speech.[33]

It is this notion of the subject "arising in an act of demolition" that has been my main interest. The most important piece of Lacan's response to Hyppolite's commentary, however, allows for a Hegelian link that Hyppolite did not articulate so succinctly. Lacan contributes, "In other words, the relation to the other, in so far as the primitive desire of the subject strives to manifest itself in it, always contains in itself this fundamental, original element of negation, which here takes the form of inversion."[34] Again, we are left with the notion of the primacy of negation, not only for the formation of consciousness and the drives but also in its being drawn out into the relation to the other. All of this will serve profitable when I return to my discussion of intersubjectivity in the *Phenomenology*.

GREEN AND THE WORK OF THE NEGATIVE

For Green, consciousness is a process that reveals itself to itself as it progresses. The movement is that of uncovering (often retroactively) that which has been present all along.[35] In this light, negation is the activity behind the moments of revelation. Green writes:

> With Hegel, to the extent that the phenomenology of consciousness distinguishes the figures which represent the different stages of a journey, each of them implies the negation of the stage preceding it, even if it cannot be apprehended as negation and results in creation. In the same way, one should realise that what comes at the end of the process is already present from the outset in an invisible or unconscious form. This state can therefore be qualified as negative (the absolute exists 'in a negative form' = a shadow in the common phenomenal consciousness). (*WN*, 39)

How far can we go along with Green's assessment that the absolute exists, even from the very first moments of sense-certainty in Hegel's consciousness? For Hegel, the journey of consciousness to self-consciousness and through the subsequent stages as illustrated in the *Phenomenology* can be seen as a process of consciousness not only revealing itself to itself and to the observing consciousness. It can also be seen as the path of consciousness learning how to reflect on these moments of revelation. In each moment of vanishing, as I argued in the first two chapters, there comes a new moment of understanding, wherein a new moment of consciousness is born. Here, too, a link can be found between negation and vanishing as acts of "creation," even if they "cannot be apprehended" as such. We only know of their act of creation retrospectively, once we already possess the knowledge they have given us. However, we might question whether the time of retrospection acts simultaneously with the immediate experience of consciousness. Is the space created for reflection or rather the act of creating this space, created concurrently with the act of reflection itself? Each new stage of consciousness, and each new moment along the movement, acts as the mark, the trace of the negation.

Therefore, even before we have the affirmation of the Hegelian "negation of negation," we have the positivity of "creation" that comes from one act of negation. I can agree wholeheartedly with Green when he states that, for Hegel, "negativity is the stage necessary for the emergence of consciousness, of the process and of the relations by which it is woven into the positivity of its connections" (*WN*, 39). As Kristeva reminds us, however, we must be careful in our formulations and acknowledge the difference between "negation" and "negativity" as they come out of Hegel. Negativity as Green has it here can be read alongside the concept as Kristeva sees it, as "both the cause and the organizing principle of the *process* ." It is the "mediation" that "reformulates the static *terms* of pure abstraction as a process, dissolving and binding them within a mobile law." Negativity, according to Kristeva, "underlies" both negation and the "negation of negation" (*RPL*, 109). It is key to keep in mind this distinction and designation of negativity as both a stage and as an "organizing principle" of the process.

Thus far there is no dispute about the necessity of the work of the negative for the activity of consciousness both in Hegel (where its role is indispensable) and in Freud. Green asks for a reading of three aspects of the negative. The first is to be found in language, and it is here that Green locates the philosophical derivatives of the concept, starting with Hegel. Given our exploration of the concept through Hyppolite's commentary, it can be argued that Green is stopping short when he proceeds to base the distinction between the philosophical and the psychoanalytic approach in an assertion that the negative for Hegel is located very much in the movement of consciousness, and for Freud it is traced back to "a subsumable un-conscious" (*WN*, 40). The connections go much deeper than Green allows here. The second aspect Green locates as "negation in the psyche," and the third he locates as "negation in thought" (*WN*, 25). As I have noted, the importance of the function of the negative is that it is an act of creation in both systems, that from it, thought, as such, is born. Thus, my line of thinking has derived predominantly from this last element of Green's approach.

For Freud and for psychoanalytic thinkers like Green, the idea of movement comes in the form of drives. The idea that there is a notion of Forces moving in the action of negation, those of attraction and repulsion, seems to be the very suggestion that Hyppolite was making in his commentary. The manifestation of this movement is found in the distinction between the internal and the external, between the introjection and the expulsion. Green states that for Freud, "The movement of the drives relates both to what is necessary for my continued existence and to my relation with my counterpart who, even before becoming an object of desire, was essential for my survival" (*WN*, 46).The drives, then, are intrinsic to the subject/object relationship even before the object is the object of desire. Here we find resonance with Hegel's notion of Force, as it is in operation before desire is introduced into self-consciousness. Our existence, our very survival, is dependent upon the energy (the work of the negative) that is the motor of consciousness and its relations.

As I have argued, Hegel's model for recognition is Force. Much like Force can only be attracted by another Force, self-consciousness can only be truly recognised by another self-consciousness. Drive and Force, then, are both movements that exist and are used as models for subsequent states of consciousness in both Freud and Hegel, preceding the introduction of desire proper. In *Less than Nothing*, Žižek asks, 'Can Hegel think the drive?' and argues, "Hegel comes close to the Freudian drive in his elaboration of the notion of Force."[36] In the subsequent reading of the concept of Force that he performs, Žižek then asks: "Does this being 'driven back into itself' of the Force already point towards the Freudo-Lacanian drive? Is the drive a Force in its being-driven-back-into-itself? Does the rhythm of Force point towards the repetitive movement of the drive?" My own reading of this section, which took place in Chapter Two, suggests such a reading, as well as a prefiguration of the workings of desire.

What we cannot overlook, however, is that there is a fundamental *lack* out of which consciousness is orientating itself and a "beyond" towards which it is reaching. It is the work of the negative that aims to first capture and then destroy this beyond. Because the beyond can never be reached, the work of the negative has no end and the beyond is never truly destroyed. Žižek offers a further way of framing and nuancing the discussion, not around the work of the negative per se but around the correlation between Freudian drive and Hegelian Force. He characterizes the drive by arguing that it is neither Power nor Force but is "Force thwarted in its goal, finding its aim in repeating the very failure to reach its goal. [. . .] It is not driven back to itself through overcoming or annihilating its expressions, but through *not being able to do so.*"[37]

This, ultimately, is Green's main point about the negative. Whatever form it might take in psychoanalysis, and in *The Work of the Negative* he outlines the ways in which it can be seen to work in "negative Narcissism, borderline cases, hallucinatory activity, and sublimation," it is always operating within the framework of this lack and desire for that which cannot be attained. To this extent, Green is perhaps betraying his adherence to certain fundamentals of Lacanian thought. Psychoanalytic theory, according to Green, has been linked to the negative "from the outset" (*WN*, 56). So, too, has the speculative philosophy at play in Hegel's *Phenomenology*. It is, however, the "negation of negation" that is the generative power of the dialectic. Thus, I believe that criticism launched at Hegel as a thinker of the negative that does not then allow him the affirmation of creation is founded on a somewhat forced misconception.

As witnessed through Hyppolite's reading of Freud's 'Negation,' the activity of negation gives rise to the theory of the drives of both Life (Eros) and death (destructive) and as Green writes, "We must bear in mind Freud's idea that the major mechanisms which he described as being characteristic of the life and death drives are binding and unbinding" (*WN*, 85). For my purposes in this chapter, I had to make my way carefully, but certainly not exhaustively, through the concept of negation so that I could come closer to an understanding of its relationship with this formulation. In so doing, I have built the necessary framework for an interrogation of the activity of binding. It is this move that I will make through the work of Green and his work on the binding, unbinding, and rebinding processes. He is heavily invested in the "metabiology" of Freud's work because it allows for a more heavily philosophical angle to be brought back into a reading of Freud.

INTRAPSYCHIC BINDING AND UNBINDING

> We thus arrive at a theory which is less concerned with describing singular entities than with attempting to reinsert these unities within a dynamic spectrum or within a range of states which are in a permanent state of potential transformation (*KI*, 122).

Green locates the origin of the tripartite process of binding in the process of the drives. In examining this origin, I will be better able to situate it alongside my claim that the process of the drives can be found in the work of the negative. I will also pursue the notion of "origin" of thought and of judgement in psychoanalytic theory by tracking how it is first located in the economic and dynamic framework of Freud's 'Project for Scientific Psychology' (1895). I designated the work of the negative for Hegel as giving rise to the birthplace of thought or at least acting as the "energy" behind the emergence of thought as such. For Green, the notion of binding belongs to the "relations between Eros and the destructive drives" (*CE*, 54). We have already seen that following Freud, Green sees binding as a form of mitigation, and we have found with the negative that it is, on one level, an act of creation illustrating the potentially generative nature of destruction. In the movement of attraction and repulsion, in the strenuous work of externalisation and internalisation, we found a remarkable manifestation of the drives. With all of this in place, we will now find in the activity of binding another, inextricably related, process of generativity and its links with the destructive drives.

One of the difficulties in writing about the process of binding (including the stages of unbinding and rebinding) is that, much like Force, we can only see the effects of the process of binding, which on a basic level *are* the binding itself (its appearance). Therefore, we can describe the *mechanisms* of the activity of binding and in so doing incorporate other theoretical frameworks in order to illustrate its manifestation. Although Green does not devote any single work to the discussion of binding, it is an integral concept in his own psychoanalytic theory, which is based on his return to and reworking of Freud's ideas.

Freud's 'Project for Scientific Psychology' and 'Beyond the Pleasure Principle': The Origin and Later Articulation of the Binding Process

Green predominantly locates the origins of the concept of binding in 'Beyond the Pleasure Principle,' where we also find a lucid articulation of the relationship between the drive towards death and the life drive, or Eros, and the notion of binding upon which Green is building his own theory. He spends less time, however, locating the origins of the concept in the 'Project.' As is well-known, Freud himself cast aside the 'Project' in an unfinished state and never formally returned to it. The aim, then, is not to turn to the 'Project' for a finished theoretical framework, for it is widely acknowledged that this text is but a "torso"[38] and not a fully fleshed out body of thought. For my purpose I argue that a return to the 'Project' not only gives us an anchor for understanding the model for the "economy" of psychical phenomena and the introduction of binding as an integral part of this economy as Freud first saw it but also supplies an essential link to my discussion of negation.[39] The second aim is the location of the origin of "judgement" (and, in particular, of the movement of attraction and repulsion and the internal/external split that can be found here) as well as the "process of thought." I will find an illuminating link to my reading, via

Hyppolite, of Freud's 'Negation.' A third point of focus is what I see as a form of the process of recognition (via a "fellow human being") that gives rise to true "cognition" and that bears a striking structural resemblance to the Hegelian form of recognition.

The 'Project' is indisputably a difficult text to read, with its combination of neurological/biological, theoretical, and early psychoanalytical language. It is more difficult still to summarise. It is necessary, however, to designate it as a foundational text for this economic line of thinking and to take from it a handful of key ideas. Richard Wollheim offers a succinct reading of Freud's 'Project.' While many discard the 'Project' as a strange, highly flawed, and dated fragment of Freud's thought, Wollheim, although not alone in his reading, considers it for its theoretical importance. Teresa Brennan also offers an elegant and lucid discussion of the 'Project' along energetic and economic lines, as does Peter Dews who comments upon Freud's lifelong commitment to "energetic and causal modes of explanation." Dews further points to the inability of Freud's practice to ever "approximate the epistemological ideal" aimed for when he used natural science as a prototype for knowledge.[40] It is following thinkers such as these that this thesis reads the 'Project' for its energetic and economic elements, without attempting to follow each twist and turn of the rather dense scientific formulations to a logical end and without duplicating the invaluable and detailed summary that Wollheim gives in *Freud*. While Wollheim argues for an economic reading of the 'Project,' he also wishes to give a place for a "dynamic" reading which expands beyond a concentration on the "part of the theory which concerns the discharge of energy or the eruption of it from the system" to an examination that also "concerns shifts or transfers of energy within the system." As I have noted, Paul Ricoeur likewise reads the 'Project' for its theoretical formulations of the economic/energy discourse that Freud traces throughout his writings. I will be using both of these complementary methods of reading as my starting point and am especially interested in pursuing notions of "shifts" and "transfers" of energy and force as suggested by Wollheim.[41]

'Project for a Scientific Psychology'

To begin, what we are given in the 'Project' is, on one level, an energy discourse. It is an economic model for how, through the movement of energy, both created and stored, the "psychic apparatus" (including the "ego" and "consciousness") negotiates and processes its relationship to the external world and with the internal reactions based on experience.[42] At stake is the facilitation of pleasure and the avoidance and/or mitigation of unpleasure, both sensations belonging to consciousness, so that the psychical apparatus will find itself in a state, or as close to this state as possible, of equilibrium. Thus we find in the 'Project' the seeds for what will later become the "pleasure principle." Furthermore, this negotiation of stimulus from the external world has as one of its main purposes the testing of reality and the avoidance of the tendency towards hallucinatory wish-fulfilment.

In this discourse, Freud attempts to work out the mechanisms of the psychic apparatus based on the movement of neurones (permeable/ϕ, impermeable/Ψ, and perceptual/ω) and of the distinction between activity and rest "subject to the general laws of motion."[43] It is in terms of ("energy" or) "*Q*" ("quantity" or "of the order of magnitude in the external world") and "*Qη*" ("quantity of the intercellular order of magnitude") that Freud negotiates the movement of the apparatus. The apparatus moves towards a reduction of tension, a discharge, of the energy that comes from both internal and external stimuli. Integral to this movement is the process of the investment of this energy, the process (or activity) translated by Strachey as *cathexis*. The cathexis, this investment, or what Wollheim refers to as the "filling" of energy and Ricoeur has as the "placement and displacement of energy," is the activity that is the agent of the binding process.[44] The processes of the apparatus, in fact the construction of the apparatus, and the process of thought, are facilitated by a series of these bindings. The ideal state would be, for Freud, a state of constancy or, in other words, of movement of the system towards equilibrium and ultimately wholeness.

With this rather basic framework in place, let me tease out of the text itself the theoretical threads I wish to follow. First, I will sketch the origins of judgement in the 'Project' as it relates to my previous discussion. I noted that judgement, as found in the 'Negation' paper, was the intellectual act that decided on what stays out and what comes in.[45] We can examine what the origins of this might look like in terms of an economic (energetic) model:

> Thus judging, which is later a means for the *cognition* of an object that may possibly be of practical importance, is originally an associative process between cathexes coming from outside and arising from one's own body—an *identification of information or cathexes from φ and from within*.[46]

The first level of judgement, then, is a process that has to negotiate the "energy" that arises outside of the body alongside that which is generated on the inside. This seems to involve, on one hand, distinguishing between the two worlds (of the external and the internal) and, on the other, processing the information. For Freud, this is the model for what will later be "cognition." When recalling the process of consciousness in the "Force and the Understanding" chapter in the *Phenomenology* at this point, there is an initial link that can be made between the texts. After consciousness has gone through the stages of Sense-certainty and Perception, it has reached a point in its development where it must begin to understand the relationship between its external experience and its internal world. Force, as we saw, was brought in to broker the negotiations, to act as both mediator and binding agent. Consciousness must now understand both the objects external to it and what effect those objects have on its internal life and must judge if, in fact, its internal life has anything to do with the creation of those external objects. With the introduction of this new stage of the "intellectual process," consciousness becomes aware of its split nature and has the burgeoning knowledge that this split means there is always something *beyond* which is required for its existence and to which its existence is thus bound.

Freud's first use of the term *bind* follows very shortly after this description of judging and after he introduces the "process of thought." In the 'Project' we first see that "activity of thought" arises from the disjunction between a wishful (hallucinatory) state of memory and the perceptual reality that presents itself to an inhibited ego.[47] The aim of the thought process is therefore to "bring about a state of identity," and it is here that we see its role in the testing of reality. Freud writes: "If after the conclusion of the act of thought the indication of reality reaches the perception, then a *judgement of reality, belief*, has been achieved and the aim of the whole activity attained."[48] The process of thought is brought about by "side-cathexes from the ego." These "side-cathexes," this additional movement of energy, "*binds* a quota of the $Q\eta$ flowing through the neurone."[49]

Now, it is not essential for my purposes to follow the intricacies of this technical argument. What is important to note is that the process of thought, mechanically speaking, is made possible by a series of binds upon excitations coming both from within and from outside. Freud's interest in the methodology of "reality testing" is, in some senses, what lies at the heart of the 'Project.' Recall the concluding images from the Force and the Understanding chapter. In the pulling back of the "curtain," consciousness is testing the limits of appearance, of that which it has perceived, and finds that anything that it knows at this stage in its existence, that it has retained, it has put there itself. Could this be examined in the language of consciousness testing its own reality? There is something akin, I would suggest, in the first stages of judgement in Freud's system and in Hegel's description of Force as it is brought in to negotiate the split between the internal and the external worlds of appearance. Isn't this, too, what consciousness was doing in Sense-certainty and Perception? What we observed was consciousness testing the "Thises" and the "Heres" by altering its physical position and causing the world to vanish; this is a version of reality testing. Indeed, what the activity of vanishing proved to attain for consciousness was a trace of what reality was for it. The moments of new forms of knowing were the marks of this experience.[50] The Introduction to the *Phenomenology* helps bolster any claims to a method of "reality testing" behind Hegel's enterprise. A prime example:

> Since consciousness thus finds that its knowledge does not correspond to its object, the object itself does not stand the test; in other words, the criterion for testing is altered when that for which it was to have been

> the criterion failed to pass the test; and the testing is not only a testing of what we know, but also a testing of the criterion of what knowing is. (*PS*, 54–55)

What Hegel takes issue with in the "Sense-Certainty" and "Perception" chapters is the way in which reality, or rather the knowing of reality, has been tested incorrectly, and he wishes to introduce the right and true way of going about it. However, it is not my aim to follow the compelling process of "reality testing" beyond these initial gestures towards a comparison, so I must leave our remarks on the topic at this cursory stage so that I can move to the second, and perhaps most significant, illustration of binding that Freud supplies. He writes:

> We arrive at the hypothesis of what is, as it were, a *bound state* in the neurone, *which, though there is a high cathexis, permits only a small current* [. . .]. Now the ego itself is a mass like this of neurones which hold fast to their cathexis—are, that is, in a bound state; and this, surely, can only happen as a result of the effect they have on one another. [. . .] We may perhaps suppose that as a result of this binding precisely the external Q remains free to flow while the cathexis of attention is bound [. . .]. *This bound state, which combines high cathexis with small current, would thus characterize processes of thought mechanically.*[51]

Although he has already introduced the concept of binding, what Freud encapsulates is the process of binding as it pertains to thought and the explanation of what the "bound state" is. The first striking feature of these formulations is that Freud posits that the ego, which he introduced earlier in the paper, is itself a highly bound state, a complex in which there is an amount of external energy left to freely flow and in which the internal energy, that of attention, is bound and thus fixed and holds fast to this binding process. Furthermore, this state of being bound, he says, explains the mechanisms of thought. This can recall Hegel's notion that thought is fixed until broken up into its separate elements, and we can see that in some senses it is a highly charged mass, a product of the process of binding. Freud acknowledges his anxiety about these speculations actually being "mechanically tenable."[52] However, Freud will take the notion of binding and its agency a step further and assert that it is through "repeated binding" on the part of the ego that unpleasure (affective, in the realm of memory) can be mitigated or counterbalanced.[53] As we will shortly see when we turn to 'Beyond the Pleasure Principle,' this model of binding, and of repeated binding, will remain an integral part of the economic system that Freud sets forth.

Related to this idea of the "bound state" is the introduction of the psychical primary and secondary processes. An additional link can be drawn between Force, the activities of attraction and repulsion as I have been discussing in Hegel's work, and the form they take in the psychoanalytic realm as they pertain to the processes of judgement. The primary process is seen as "wishful cathexis to the point of hallucination [and] complete generation of unpleasure which involves a complete expenditure of defence."[54] The wishful state, Freud writes, "results in a positive *attraction* towards the object wished for or, more precisely, towards its mnemic image; the experience of pain leads to a repulsion, a disinclination to keeping the mnemic image cathected. Here we have primary *wishful attraction* and primary *defence* [fending off]."[55] At stake, ultimately, is the idea of self-preservation wherein the psyche is attracted to, and will bind itself to, those images, objects, and experience that it believes will fill its lack and bring a sense of wholeness. It avoids, is repulsed by, that which would cause it pain and therefore that in which it would not invest its energy. Up until this point, the consideration of the 'Project' has all implicitly been taking place in the intrapsychic sphere. One significant intersubjective element can be located in the embryonic form of a Freudian "process of recognition," which is intricately related to the processes of judging and, in particular, of perception.

We find that it is "in relation to a fellow human-being that a human-being learns to cognize." This is due to the fact that the object, as fellow human being, resembles the subject's "first satisfying object and further his first hostile object, as well as his sole helping power."[56] In essence, the other, this object, represents the first activities of attraction and repulsion related to its knowing of itself in the world as well as that to which the subject is bound for its existence. This leads to a series of questions: what is the link between cognition and recognition? What does it mean to literally re-know one's self through recognition of the self in the other? What does this imply about the acquisition of the knowledge that we do possess about ourselves? When we "recognise" ourselves in the other, and when for Hegel this recognition is essential to the becoming of self-consciousness, are we simply repeating back to ourselves the information we have already learned? What, then, is the link here to repetition and of retrospective knowledge? Žižek writes, "We can *recognize* the other, *acknowledge* him as a person, only in so far as, in a radical sense, he remains *unknown* to us—*re* cognition implies the absence of *cognition*."[57] I would disagree to the extent that it seems that this "re-knowing" of the self could be seen as a "re-acknowledgement" of information that we already possess about ourselves but do not understand until we "recognise" it in the Other. But perhaps Žižek and I are approaching the same question from opposite sides, where he is looking for the knowledge of the other, and I am exploring the knowledge of the self as reliant upon knowledge of the other. I would argue, however, that these are two sides of the same coin. Hyppolite asserts,

> To fail to recognize is not completely equivalent to not to know; to fail to recognize is to know in order to be able to recognize and say one day: 'I have known this all the time.' He who fails in a certain way to recognize himself knows himself. Thus, whereas natural consciousness

> is fundamentally unconsciousness of self, it is also in a certain manner, by failing to recognize itself, enabled one day to recognize itself.[58]

These questions must be kept constantly in mind, as they lie at the very heart of the question of intersubjectivity.

'Beyond the Pleasure Principle'

Now that the origins of the binding process are in place, I turn here to 'Beyond the Pleasure Principle' to locate the links of this process with the movements of the drives towards life (Eros), on the one hand, and towards destruction/death, on the other. This will allow me to begin to weave such links into my discussion of Green's theories of the tripartite binding process. This paper is perhaps one of the most referenced of Freud's work and is arguably one of the most heavily indebted to the 'Project.' It is, in many ways, a far more palatable read and is, in Freud's own view, a highly speculative text. He begins the paper by stating that he is introducing an economic point of view, which, with the "topographical" and "dynamic" points of view, makes up the "metapsychological" aspects of psychoanalysis. It is partly the seductions of the speculative nature of this work that makes it such a fecund ground for many other speculative projects. For my purposes, I will focus on and discuss not only the notion of bound quantities of pleasure and unpleasure but also Freud's elaboration on the use of the concept of binding and the potential of its agency with further theoretical configurations.[59] For example, he offers the example that "ties of affection" *bind* the child as a rule to the parent of the opposite sex, thus expanding the capacity for binding into the affective dimension.[60]

Most importantly, Freud introduces the idea of binding in the "psychical sense," which is the activity of taking up "an additional stream of fresh inflowing energy and of converting it into quiescent cathexis." Systems can have greater or lesser "binding force" and, depending on this force, will suffer more or less significantly from the "breaching" of the internal world by the external forces.[61] Should the binding process fail, the pleasure principle is hindered. Once the binding process is reinstated then both the pleasure principle, and its modification, the reality principle, can proceed in its movement.[62] A particularly useful formulation he offers is that of the idea of transformation. Although I am not considering the idea of a "pleasure principle" as such in the *Phenomenology*, I am examining the process of becoming and in particular the states of transitions and transformation in consciousness and self-consciousness of which it is comprised. The notion of binding that I am reading back into Hegel, and that I will shortly illuminate via Green, involves and effects a series of conversions and reversions that are all involved with, and aim to keep on track, the movement of becoming. To return to the idea in Freud, we find that:

> while this transformation is taking place no attention can be paid to the development of unpleasure; but this does not imply the suspension of the pleasure principle. On the contrary, the transformation occurs on *behalf* of the pleasure principle; the binding is a preparatory act which introduces and assures the dominance of the pleasure principle.[63]

The binding, therefore, is an activity that effects transformations and thus in some senses cannot be a static designation. It must always hold within it, and Green asserts this, the potential for its unbinding and subsequent rebinding. By designating it as a "preparatory act," Freud elaborates the notion of the transformational process taking place, of which the binding is a key element, as well as being a process unto itself. Furthermore, another aspect of the connection between binding and the affective level is that "there seems to be no doubt whatever that the unbound or primary processes give rise to far more intense feelings in both directions than the bound or secondary ones."[64] Indeed, the definition of the pleasure principle is that it is a tendency to "free the mental apparatus entirely from excitation or to keep the amount of excitation in it constant or to keep it as low as possible."[65] Again, we can recall the unhappy consciousness and its highly charged affective state, where its awareness is focussed on the feeling of its own nothingness, its extreme despair, and can begin to see how the unhappy consciousness can be designated as the Hegelian paradigm of an unbound state. Yet, it is a complicated paradigm. On one hand, it represents an intrapsychic binding, a consciousness bound only to its own play of Force. On the other hand, it is unbound from the external world and thus from an intersubjective binding until it meets the third consciousness. When I consider the state of madness in the "beautiful soul," I will locate a second, powerful illustration of the dangers inherent in the breakdown in the play of Forces that we see causing this state of unboundedness.

The famous introduction of the notion of the death drive comes with Freud's claim that the "aim of all life is death." Simultaneously, he brings into consideration the drive towards life in the form of Eros.[66] Eros is introduced as that which combines "organic substances into ever larger unities."[67] It is the ultimate binding force; it is the "preserver of all things."[68] What Freud is interested in here is not necessarily the substances, the things themselves, but rather the forces that are at play in them.[69] Ultimately, Freud finds that the preserving, attractive, binding forces of Eros are at play with the repulsions inherent in the destructive forces of the drive towards death. This, says Freud, is the basis of our instinctual life. It is in a footnote that Freud cements this formulation that it is, indeed, the life and death instincts that "were struggling with each other from the very first" and discusses that this view has "transformed" the prior distinction that he made between the "ego-instincts" and the "sexual instincts of which the libido is the manifestation."[70] I have asserted that the notion of the attractive and repulsive forces of the drives was prefigured in the 'Project.' Thus the notion of binding and energy can be seen as a model for the notion of "libidinal" energy and a binding that is based on sexual desire. Additionally, although I am making an interpretative choice by reading the language of attraction and repulsion into 'Beyond the Pleasure Principle' and thus into the concepts of the life and death drives, Freud himself was quite aware of the potential for this parallel as is evidenced in his response to the letter from Einstein in the exchange 'Why War.' He writes:

> According to our hypothesis human instincts are only of two kinds: those which seek to preserve and unite—which we call 'erotic,' exactly in the sense in which Plato uses the world 'Eros' in his *Symposium*, or 'sexual,' with a deliberate extension of the popular conception of 'sexuality'—and those which seek to destroy and kill and which we group together as the aggressive or destructive instinct. As you see, this is in fact no more than a theoretical clarification of the universally familiar opposition between Love and Hate which may perhaps have some fundamental relation to the polarity of attraction and repulsion that plays a part in your own field of knowledge [. . .]. The phenomena of life arise from the concurrent or mutually opposing action of both.[71]

This is perhaps the most profoundly simple and striking explanation that Freud gives for these fundamental elements.

Recall that one of the fundamental features of Hegel's concept of Force is that it preserves within it moments of difference; it allows moments to subsist. Through this act of preservation, it facilitates the movement and binding of consciousness, both within and to itself and to the external world. With this in mind, I am building on my earlier claim that we can conceive of Force as operating concurrently with negation in the *Phenomenology* as a sort of drive towards life or at least as a life-supporting element in what we can see as the energetic/economic model at play. I now turn to Green's formulation of the binding process through which we can return to Hegel and the set of questions under consideration.

Green's Tripartite Process

In Chapter Two I used the theoretical concept of binding to articulate the movement of self-consciousness as the play of Forces. It was not yet fully formulated as the binding that we have come to understand in the psychoanalytic realm. A quick summary of how I speculated about the process through the figures of the lord and bondsman, the stoic, sceptic, and finally the unhappy consciousness might be useful at this point. Locating the binding in the realm of self-consciousness as a process initiated by the play of Forces, we found that the activity of mutual recognition lay at its root or was, in other words, the first stage of the intersubjective bind. Within this play we saw that the lord was bound to the world and itself via the bondsman, who in turn was bound to the object that is created through its work. We observed that this object could be seen as the appearance of the bind, and thus, in a manner corresponding to the consideration of Force, was the bind itself. We then witnessed the shift from the activity of externalization to the internalisation of the Stoic, a shift that marked the turn from intersubjectivity to a consideration of the intrasubjective status of consciousness and the designation of the first stage of the unbinding process. Stoical self-consciousness, through its reality as freedom, has released itself from bondage and entered into the universality of thought. Yet it is confined only to the "thought" of this freedom and in order to find the reality of this freedom it must transition into the shape of the Sceptic. We found the Sceptic entirely aware of its agency in the situation, as possessing the knowledge that it holds the power to sever its bonds with the external world; it was Force testing the power of its own Force. This I designated as the second stage of the unbinding process. With the transition into the unhappy consciousness, we encountered both the paradigm of the split self, unbound from the world struggling with its existence as a Force bound only to its feeling of nothingness and to the flux of despair, and we witnessed the rebinding of consciousness to the external world through the work of the "counsellor," my vanishing mediator, my proto-analyst. This "third" unbound the unhappy consciousness from its state of despair in order to rebind it to the movement of becoming and to re-instigate the play of Forces, and so we saw both the dangers of unbinding on an intrapsychic level and its inherent potential for beneficial and generative effects.

One final point should be recalled regarding Hegel's formulation of "Life as a process." In a rather remarkable passage, we saw Hegel positing that not only is life a universal fluid medium, but in its activity of the splitting into individual shapes and then the eventual collapse of the differences that those shapes are, it is a process, it is a "living thing" (*PS*, 107). Furthermore, "the object of immediate desire is a *living thing*." Recall my claim that we can see a form of life drive here, in that the immediate object of desire is a living thing, which is a shape of Life itself. Hegel asks throughout the *Phenomenology* that we bear witness to exquisite tension that is at play between the activity of negation, the destructive tendency towards "utter dismemberment," and the immediate desire for life, for a living thing. By incorporating Green's psychoanalytic theory of binding with my reading of Freud and by combining both with my reading of Hegel, I can now more intricately weave these various threads together.

Green uses the terms *binding* and *unbinding* as "less ideologically loaded" terms for designating the work of Eros and the destructive drives respectively. He uses the terms to refer both to the activity of bindings within the ego and its internal objects as well as the relationship between the ego and its external objects (*KI*, 119).There are various contexts within which he discusses binding throughout his body of work and various modes of the binding process that are at play. Green sees that "Eros consists of a dialectical play in which binding and unbinding alternate and are combined" (*KI*, 121). Moreover, Green emphasises that Eros is a force, an energy, which is "one of a pair of forces" as it is "regularly accompanied by destructivity." Further, he posits that it holds as its fundamental characteristic "binding, unification, preservation" (*CE*, 109–12). Although he acknowledges that the concepts of force and energy are controversial designations in post-Freudian psychoanalysis, at the heart of Green's theorising on the whole is an unwavering belief in the reinsertion of the metabiological aspects of thought. He sees that these concepts are "hardly more imaginary than the metapsychology we employ with no proof of its existence" (*CE*, 57). The theory of the tripartite process he proposes can be seen as having its roots in both the metabiological and metapsychological camps:

> Binding and unbinding are the two main functions that Freud found to be the basic characteristics of life or love instincts on the one hand and of destructive instincts on the other hand [. . .]. Two functions seem to be quite enough to explain the interplay of these basic activities, but I wish to propose a third element: rebinding, which corresponds to reunion after separation. (*Squiggle*, 48)

When I return to the paradigm of the unhappy consciousness, I will illustrate what this state of "reunion" might look like.

One of the purposes of binding is to prepare the way for the pleasure principle. Green elaborates that binding is a sort of "structural suture" that acts to "create an ensemble which acquires meaning by bringing together elements that are insufficiently meaningful in isolation" in order that the subject avoid the "danger of non-meaning and possibly of disorganised chaos" and that this type of bind exists prior to the pleasure principle (*TP*, 94). The rich notion of a "structural suture" can help us to conceptualise the structural importance of the activity of binding for the processes of thought.[72] In Hegel, the "suture" of Force acts to bring together the elements of the external world and the internal world and allows consciousness to become self-consciousness. The "suture" of desire and further of recognition as modelled on Force are structural representatives of the binding process that allow for self-consciousness to know itself and thus create meaning out of its existence. Following the logic of the metaphor, if there were no wounds, no gaps, no fissures, there would be little need for sutures. We can perhaps see the work of Force as that which heals the wounds inflicted by the "tarrying with the negative," by the staring of death in the face and experiencing the terror of existence. Famously, for Hegel, the "wounds of spirit heal, and leave no scars behind" (*PS*, 407). Instead of scars we have in the *Phenomenology* a continuous process of regrowth, of renewal, and the resurgence of Life, forever in the flux of becoming.[73]

Green also discusses the original process of binding that precedes the introduction of the libido. This would be a form of intrapsychic binding that then leads to the binding of the ego and the object. While reading Green's formulation, keep in mind the previous discussion of the 'Project' and the energetic roots of the binding process:

> Eros, the force of bonding, would bind simultaneously the internal world—the psyche—and the object relation situated in the external world, but produced through incorporation into the internal world. We could even add that it will bind the object in its unity and bind together the ego and the object, as far as is allowed by the intervention of the super-ego, which will set the limits of that relation, making sure that it is, so to speak, 'legitimate,' that it maintains the psychical and social organisation which also binds together the generations, as it were. The disposable energy of Eros, the very energy at work in love, is libido [. . .]. Eros brings together all the phenomena formerly given the names of self-preservative drives. (*CE*, 114)

It is important to note that for Green the binding process takes place both *prior* to the functioning of the libido (and here my discussion of the binding power of Force as a model for desire in Hegel can be recalled) and also in the energy/economy of Eros in the form of libido. As we saw in the *Phenomenology*, consciousness began to recognise its binds with the external world in Sense-Certainty and Perception. With the introduction of Force, self-consciousness created for itself the possibilities of internalisation and of a more nuanced and complicated relationship with its objects.

The compulsion to repeat is also designated as a process of binding and is linked to the notion of "self-preservation." Remembering the roots traced in the 'Project' of the binding of quantities of energy, we can see in Green's discussion the same mechanisms at work on another theoretical level. Binding is seen as a "transformation of energy," and further Green posits that the "pleasure-unpleasure principle, which governs the transformations of binding, points us even more surely to what seeks to repeat itself in its binding."[74] The ultimate aim of the repetition compulsion is, in a sense, to save the system from total breakdown. When quantities of energy, and Green also categorises this energy as force, are bound, there is left in reserve a quantity of "uncaptured force from which subsequent bindings will come." Because the points of transformation are made visible by the binding, "change takes on meaning." Taken on the most positive, normally functioning level, binding serves to save the system from itself by giving itself a sense of unity and coherence. As Green writes of the compulsion to repeat: "What is repeated is a set of interdependent elements forming a meaningful whole, even when it presents many difficulties for understanding. Without prior binding, there can be no possibility of repetition; just disorganization with fragmentation and parcelling" (*TP*, 84).

The classic case of the repetition compulsion in Freud, of course, is the "Fort-da" game. There is a wonderful illustration of attraction and repulsion at work in this example and a form of the subject exploring the limits of Force.[75] Henry Sussman writes:

> In 'Beyond the Pleasure Principle,' the repetition-compulsion is the sign of a restorative psychic economy that functions alongside an acquisitive and productive one. This text, then, whose point of departure is an automatic psychic repetition ultimately deriving from the cycles that form within the Hegelian subject, is a major factor in restoring a dualism seemingly lost from the psychoanalytic enterprise.[76]

Sussman is not referring here to the activity of Force as a model for the economy of the Hegelian subject, but the notion of repetition and the way in which he implicitly describes the economy at work in Hegel is very much along the lines of my argument.[77] Green posits that it is through "a lack that force manifests itself, but it only reveals the lack by trying to patch it up" (*DP*, 103). So, too, we find consciousness in the *Phenomenology* exposing the lack at its core in its quest for unity and its movement towards the beyond.

There are two final threads that can be drawn out of Green's work that link directly with consideration of the binding nature of "text." The first posits that the ego is that part of the psychic apparatus which is the "homeostatic binding agent" and that the preconscious can additionally be thought of as a "*binding agency* of mental energy, linking the primary and secondary processes. Indeed, transformation of free energy into bound energy is fundamental to analytical work as it is to the functioning of the psychic apparatus" (*OPM*, 301). Green combines his theory with a literary approach and discusses the role of the analyst as unbinding the "text" of the analysand.[78] The analyst "breaks open the secondarity in order to retrieve, upstream from the binding process, the state of bondlessness [*déliaison*] which the binding process has covered up" (*OPM*, 339). There is something interesting at work here with Green's assertion that the binding process "covers up" the unbound state. We might take from this an implication that this bondlessness needs liberation (to be retrieved) and that to be unbound is to both create new meaning and to expose the original fabric of vulnerability that the binding was set in motion to protect.

Secondly, Green offers us a way of marking the transition from the intrapsychic state into that of the intersubjective, which we can see at work between the shapes and transitions of self-consciousness that I have been tracking in Hegel and that will be elaborated on most fully in the next chapter:

> Thus it is through a displacement of the binding which is initially intrapsychic—which is discharged quasi-automatically so that nothing is preserved or permanently lost—that the possibility of intersubjective binding (that is, linking two intrapsychic situations) emerges, showing that the relationship can be objectalised. It is at this point that the

activity of representation is extended, enriched and diversified; in short, it becomes alive. (*TP*, 134)

I am using Green's transition here as my own, in that this present chapter has been focussed on the intrapsychic realm, but now I am starting the shift into a discussion of the intersubjective relation which will be illustrated in my theorising about the analytic setting. Even in the intersubjective bind there are a series of binds simultaneously occurring in each subject that is part of the relationship. We can make a link with the notion of vanishing here. We see that in the economic system, as Green views it, nothing is "permanently lost" but is translated into new representations, much as I have been arguing for vanishing as a state of transformation. With this in mind, let us return briefly to my consideration of the play of Forces of self-consciousness so that I can continue to flesh out my already-staked claims of the binding process at work.

Kojève offers an entirely compelling formulation of the necessity for the binding of the bondsman to the lord. It is, according to Kojève, only to escape his terror of death that the bondsman allows himself to enter into the relationship with the lord and through his service binds himself to him. "It is by serving another, by externalizing oneself, by binding oneself to others, that one is liberated from the enslaving dread that the idea of death inspires."[79] In the life-and-death struggle that is waged between the lord and the bondsman, the bondsman's drive towards life might be seen as the most powerful drive. His externalization, his labour, is a drive outwards and away from death, or rather, away from the fear that the notion of death engenders. The life-and-death struggle is a perfect encapsulation of what we have seen as the inextricable link between Eros and the death drive. Additionally, what we can see at work in Kojève's formulation is the "affective" element of binding. Much as we saw that for Freud it could be the ties of affection that bind the child to its parents, it is through his "fear" of death that the bondsman finds himself bound to the lord. This state of externalization, however, quickly transforms into the internalised state of *thought* of the Stoic as self-consciousness attempts to understand its freedom and then changes further into the shape of Scepticism as thought is actualised. From the externalization of consciousness which results in a bounded state, both to its own object and to the external world, what looks like a move towards freedom is a consciousness edging slowly towards the unbounded state, seen by Judith Butler as "self-enslavement."

Green defines "subject unbinding" as, "a process of disengagement sustained by a more or less omnipotent fantasy of self-sufficiency on the part of the ego" which "has the aim of escaping the object's control, of asserting the ego's freedom through its quasi all-powerful capacity to undo its ties with the object, and, if necessary, with itself" (*KI*, 217). There is a striking parallel to be found in Hegel's formulation of Scepticism:

> As Scepticism, on the other hand, it is a moment of self-consciousness, to which it does not *happen* that its truth and reality vanish without its knowing how, but which, in the certainty of its freedom, *makes* this 'other' which claims to be real, vanish. What Scepticism causes to vanish is not only objective reality as such, but its own relationship to it. (*PS*, 124)

With full knowledge, consciousness destroys for itself a sense of grounding in its activity *as* this unrest. It has unbound itself.

Green, however, paradoxically argues for the positive role that unbinding might take in the process, as he sees that it "produces discontinuity without which the mechanisms of recombination could not take place" (*OPM*, 249). It seems that Hegel would agree. A great deal of the strength of the unhappy consciousness paradigm is that it offers a complete rupture in the movement of consciousness and through the rupture a space for *active* reflection and renewed activity is opened up. Here we find the reflective gaps to which I have been referring throughout. We saw that the unhappy consciousness is bound only to itself and the *feeling* of its own meaninglessness, its own "nothingness." Despair, Hegel seems to imply, is what awaits a consciousness that cannot recognise the other in itself and itself in this other. In the vanishing mediator/proto-analyst's recognition of the unhappy consciousness, and in the unhappy consciousness recognition of it, a play of Forces recommences, and the movement of its becoming is no longer, to use Green's phrase, "jammed." Self-consciousness is now re-bound to the external world. Green's formulation proposes that rebinding as seen along with the activity of binding and unbinding "corresponds to reunion after separation." Hegel's quite remarkable introduction of this third consciousness facilitates the necessary reunion, this rebinding, of the unhappy consciousness with itself and with the external world. This counsellor, too, is a Force. Yet it is a Force that is brought in from outside the "play" that we have been observing in order to prove that, to put it quite simply, consciousness cannot become on its own. Without being called forth, solicited by another and made to exist in the external world, consciousness remains within its own restricted economy. Through the counsellor as mediator, Hegel offers consciousness a way out of this restriction and out of the pain of purely internalised existence. Self-sufficiency, he seems to say, will only take us so far.

We can also witness the activity of unbinding and eventual rebinding in the figure of the "beautiful soul" as a subsequent form of the unhappy consciousness taken to an even further extreme, where what was "implicit" in the unhappy consciousness is now taking place "explicitly for consciousness within itself." Here we find a self-consciousness "withdrawn into its innermost being, for which all externality has vanished—withdrawn into the contemplation of the 'I' = 'I,' in which this 'I' is the whole of essentiality and existence." Again, we see the activity of vanishing at work in consciousness. In fact, the only thing that self-consciousness possesses, the poverty of its existence, "is itself a vanishing" (*PS*, 398–99).

It is a more advanced shape of spirit that has unbound itself, through its repulsion and renunciation of the other consciousness, and has unbound existence itself as intrinsically bound to the other and the external world. Hegel writes:

> Now, in so far as the self-certain Spirit, as a 'beautiful soul,' does not possess the power to renounce the knowledge of itself which it keeps to itself, it cannot attain to an identity with the consciousness it has repulsed, nor therefore to a vision of the unity of itself in the other, cannot attain to an objective existence. Consequently, the identity comes about only negatively, as a being devoid of spirit. The 'beautiful soul,' lacking an *actual* existence, entangled in the contradiction between its pure self and the necessity of that self to externalize itself and change itself into an actual existence, and dwelling in the *immediacy* of this firmly held antithesis [. . .] this 'beautiful soul,' then, being conscious of this contradiction in its unreconciled immediacy, is disordered to the point of madness, wastes itself in yearning and pines away in consumption. (*PS*, 406–07)

The resolution to the beautiful soul's madness lies within the stages that led it to its state. Consciousness as the beautiful soul perceived itself to be rejected through the act of its confession because the other did not also confess and thus enter into mutual recognition. The other has mutely kept "himself to himself" and the exchange of language, which would have unified the two consciousnesses, has not taken place. The beautiful soul does not realise, however, that it is its own self, its own "hard heart" which "hinders that other's return" (*PS*, 405–06).

Green writes of the figure of the beautiful soul as the perfect example of "moral narcissism" and acknowledges that Hegel did not overlook its narcissistic character (*OPM*, 140).[80] He traces the metapsychology of moral narcissism and relates it to what he sees as the four fundamental aspects of Freudian countercathexes (defensive forms). They are rejection; denial or disavowal ("repression of perception"); repression itself; and negation. (All four of these will also be found grouped together under the umbrella of the "work of the negative." It should be noted that chronologically speaking, *On Private Madness* was published prior to *The Work of the Negative*) Moral narcissism, Green argues, "seems to correspond to an intermediate situation somewhere between rejection and disavowal." Rejection as he writes it here "implies radical refusal of the instinct or instinct presentation" and is the expulsion of these instincts. This refusal involves a refusal of the "world as it is," as well as the refusal of "object cathexis by the ego." Importantly, Green states that "it is not a matter of a repression of reality as in psychosis but more so of a denial, a disavowal of the order of the world and of the personal participation of the subject's desire" (*OPM*, 124–25). I can link this notion of rejection and disavowal to the above discussion to further bolster my claims regarding unbinding and the beautiful soul.

Furthermore, moral narcissism and intellectual narcissism are closely linked. Green understands that intellectual narcissism is that "form of self-sufficiency and solitary valorization which makes up for the lack of human desires with intellectual mastery or intellectual seduction" (*OPM*, 125). This model (the combination of moral and intellectual narcissism) would also seem to fit the movement of the sceptic into the unhappy consciousness. Let us recall that the sceptic, with full knowledge, causes objective reality and its relationship to it to vanish. As noted previously, however, the beautiful soul is a less innocent version of the unhappy consciousness in the sense that it knows, for the most part, what is at stake when it refuses the world. For Hegel, it is only through confession again, through "being enticed into openly confessing itself by the vision of itself in the other" that the hard heart of the beautiful soul is broken and forgiveness, and thus a new form of mutual recognition, can take place (*PS*, 407).[81] Consciousness has renounced itself and reconciled with Spirit, with the universal, and with the other. It is once again re-bound to the external world.

So what do we make of this resolution? How can we think about the rescuing of consciousness from its unbounded state via the introduction of this third consciousness? What are the ramifications of this re-externalization and especially of externalization via language? And what is it that is potentially created in this new configuration? A turn to Green's concept of thirdness might allow for a formulation of a way of gesturing towards a set of responses that I will continue to elaborate upon in Chapter Four.

THE CONCEPT OF THE THIRD AND THIRDNESS: THE BREAKDOWN IN THE PLAY OF FORCES AND THE INTRODUCTION OF THE PROTO-ANALYST

In my discussion of the breakdown in the intersubjective process of recognition, I positioned the unhappy consciousness as a model for the potential dangers of the complete turn to the intrapsychic realm. I offered Hegel's introduction of the "counsellor" as the figure that brought the unhappy consciousness out of its internalised existence and re-bound it to the external world and to the movement of consciousness. In Chapter Two I designated this counsellor as a vanishing mediator, building upon Frederic Jameson's definition that this mediator is "a catalytic agent that permits in the strictest sense of the word an exchange of energies between two otherwise mutually exclusive terms" and "serves in its turn as a kind of overall bracket or framework within which change takes place and which can be dismantled and removed when its usefulness is over."[82] I took this notion of vanishing mediator a step further and posited the birth of a proto-analyst, the figure we saw beginning to come to life in the discussion of binding. In so doing, I set the foundations to envision this "catalytic agent" not only as an abstract "framework" (acting on a structural level) but also as a subject, an other, for consciousness. Shortly, I will posit a complementary and alternative configuration of this concept to be considered in striking parallel with the concept of the analytic third, an object that is created out of the intersubjective work of the analytic pair. With my preliminary discussion of energy, drawn from the 'Project' and translated into the process of binding in place, I am in a much better position to understand how to conceive of Jameson's "exchange of energies." It is important to acknowledge that with this move into the topic of thirdness, we are also shifting, more significantly than we have had occasion to do so previously, into a discussion of the interaction between analyst and analysand and therefore into the more concretely imagined realm of the analytic setting. I will begin by exploring Green's definition of what he sees as a "tertiary process," introduced as an addition to Freud's already existing primary and secondary processes. This concept paves the way for his notion of thirdness and the creation of the analytic third and will lead us to a discussion of "transitional space."[83] The second aim of this section is to examine the concept of the analytic third as found in the work of Thomas Ogden. Ogden's work *The Subjects of Analysis* owes, and acknowledges, a great debt both to Hegel's *Phenomenology* and to Green's work and therefore acts as a binding agent of sorts for various elements and arguments of my own investigation.[84] In this chapter I am simply setting the foundations for the discussion of the third. In Chapter Four I will more fully engage with its various manifestations in psychoanalytic theory and in the work of Christopher Bollas.

Green's Introduction of the "Tertiary Process" or "Analytic Binding"

Quite simply, Green does not think that Freud's dualistic model of the primary and secondary processes is sufficient to explain the full range of intersubjective relations and in particular the potential space of the analytic situation.[85] He sees that Freud is rather limited to a dualistic framework when it comes to explaining basic processes and mechanisms but also notes that Freud modifies his approach to the use of a triadic model when looking at more complex structures such as the psychic apparatus and the Oedipus complex. Green wishes to elaborate upon this triadic model and therefore introduces the concept of "tertiary processes" as "instruments of liaison, or connections" to accompany the primary processes (designated as subjective reason) and the secondary processes (designated as objective reason) (*PM*, 20).[86] Green sees the tertiary process coming into play most significantly in the analytic situation to enable the analysand to both recreate bonds that have been broken (to rebind itself) and create new, significant bonds from which meaning can be drawn: "The silent work of such processes is what enables the analytic process to progress towards insight." The indication of the absence of such a process, Green says, would be the lack of progress in analysis. In other words, this tertiary process in action can be conceived of as the interpretation of thought, as the act of analysing and in so doing of creating new levels of thought and understanding (*Squiggle*, 48, 59).

In light of my discussion of Green's tripartite process of binding, we can consider the tertiary process as illustrating the potential for the rebinding process as encapsulated in the binding process itself and as upholding the necessity for a third to allow the split self to move again in the process of its becoming. Green sees the importance of the tertiary process magnified in cases where "psychotic unbinding gets the upper hand." "It is in these cases," Green writes, "that the analytic binding processes—which I call tertiary processes—should come into play, introduced by the analyst's spoken word" (*OPM*, 248). We are now entering a rather more linguistically based model of binding, one that has been shadowing my theoretical movements thus far and one that I will elaborate on more fully in Chapter Four. What is at stake, however, is just how far and in what manner Green wishes to take the linguistic framework. Importantly, he sees that a form of binding takes place in and through language and that it is very much an element of the economic framework of binding: "Another type of binding occurs through language, and what is maintained here is the instinctual cathexis—I mean the interest, the energy, and the force that can detach itself from the imagery so that the energy is still available and can now invest in new forms of representation, such as words, that also require a great amount of binding" (*Squiggle*, 30). Green seems to be saying that language itself contains Force of its own that can be extracted from words, from imagery, from the trappings of language as we conceive of them. This binding with language is secondary to what Green, as I noted earlier, following Freud, calls an "original binding." I have already stated that Green sees that there are bindings for Freud that take place prior to the bindings that are based on the desire of the object. This original binding acts as the "first form of an organization of material that already belongs to the psyche" (*Squiggle*, 29). The bindings occurring via language, then, are secondary (at least) bindings that then enter into the economic framework on another level. It is extremely difficult to think of the energy of language as a component separate from its forms of representation, but in order to understand Green's later configuration of the analytic third, among other reasons, it is necessary to do so. Such an idea allows for us to conceive of the "exchange of energies" in a linguistic sphere that does not rely solely on a symbolic framework and allows for the creation of an "object" that does not have a "material" basis as such. We will soon see how this relates to the tertiary process as an act of interpretation.

Thirdness and the Analytic Third

In his lecture 'On Thirdness,' Green discusses the considerable influence of American philosopher and semiotician Charles Sanders Peirce on both Lacan's use of linguistic theory and clearly on his own concept of thirdness.[87] On an extremely basic level, Peirce's triadic conception of the sign is that "firstness is associated with qualities of feelings and emotion, secondness with being, and thirdness with generalization such as law, thought processes and so on" (*Squiggle*, 50).[88] The usefulness of Peirce's theory for Green lies in the idea that thought itself, especially the "thought" of interpretation, is a sign, one that, according to Peirce, "mediates between the interpreter and its origin" (*Squiggle*, 52).[89] The leap we need to make for the purposes of the present investigation is to conceive of a sign as an object. In order to move into the idea of this thirdness in terms of the creation of the analytic third, we must think of the creation of a mediating object out of the work that takes place between the analyst (interpreter) and analysand (origin) within the analytic space.

Green states that one of the cornerstones of Freudian theory regarding the psychic apparatus is representation. He is of the opinion that where Lacan's later theory of the signifier goes wrong is in its restriction of the notion of representation as it is found primarily within a linguistic structure. For Green the question also needs to be based around what happens in the process of a non-linguistic structure (in the world of objects, for instance), and thus he wishes to understand the designation of "sign," and the "signified" outside of the Saussurian structuralist model to which he sees Lacan as predominately tied (*Squiggle*, 50). Accordingly, he wants to see thought, and the element of thought that is the activity of interpretation, as a sort of sign itself.

It is important to recall here my previous assertion that for Green the "whole of psychic structure is based on thirdness" and add to it that the triadic structures of child/mother/father, binding/unbinding/rebinding, and primary/secondary/tertiary processes all fall under this rubric (*Squiggle*, 48).[90] Beyond this triadic understanding, Green wishes to explore what the processes *between* the various parts might look like. To this end, he created the concept of the analytic object, also designated as the analytic third, as born out of the tertiary process (which we can now understand as the process which, standing in some senses for interpretation, mediates, connects, binds). Intrinsic to the creation of this analytic object is the activity of "splitting."

As I have noted, a splitting conceived as an unbinding instigates the rebinding process; a sundering of a sense of wholeness, however momentary the state of wholeness might be, calls for an act of reunion. I conceived of the splitting of the unhappy consciousness, the creation of its dual-natured being as the inescapable unbinding of itself from its own process. Help came in the form of the "counsellor" that saved it from its painful state by rebinding it to the external world. I pointed to Green's assertion that, however painful, unbinding held within its process a measure of generative potentiality. So now to an understanding of rebinding I add this notion of the tertiary process as it pertains to the necessity of these acts of diremption. Green writes, "Yet splitting is essential in providing a way out of confusion. Such is the fate of human bondage, that it has to serve two contrary masters—separation and reunion—one or the other, or both" (*OPM*, 83). Undoubtedly, the Hegelian influence can be felt here as, such is the fate, indeed, of consciousness throughout the *Phenomenology*. For Green, the work of symbolization is a form of rebinding, which is the creation of a third element from the two elements that are the products of the splitting (*OPM*, 73). The tertiary process is not materialised as such but is rather a "mode for establishing flexible mental equilibrium." In other words, it is the job of this process to establish new forms of binding in the aftermath of disruptive splitting, fragmented thought, or the rigidity of jammed forces (energy).

Green sees the analytic situation as dialectical and that the analyst and analysand strive to communicate using the language of the other.[91] The aim, and the result of this striving, is the birth of the analytic object, a new form of being that can be taken up by the analysand. This analytic object functions as a sort of vanishing mediator in that it allows the two subjects involved in the dialectical relationship of the analytic setting to exchange energies and generate meaning out of the work of interpretation. The work is done on behalf of the analysand, and the basic material of the object is made up of its conscious and unconscious thought. "But," Green stresses, "in the end the real analytic object is neither on the patient's side nor on the analyst's, but in the meeting of these two communications in the potential space which lies between them, limited by the setting which is broken at each separation and reconstituted at each new meeting" (*OPM*, 48). Recall here Jameson's formulation of the framework of the vanishing mediator as "dismantled and removed," and we can see the parallel fleshing out.

The question arises as to whether or not this vanishing mediator is permanently removed. In the next chapter I will address the matter of the ownership of this mediator in greater detail and will argue that it is potentially incorporated by both of the subjects, both analyst and analysand, where it is reassembled and utilised in their own processes. Effectively I have set up the figure of the vanishing mediator in two significant ways. The first is that the analyst can be seen as working to unite the potentially split self of the analysand through its work with the tertiary process. That is to say, through interpreting, through the making of connections and the creation of meaning out of the parts of the self offered by the analysand, the analyst "permits the exchange of energies," our Hegelian play of Forces, to effect change and to rebind the analysand to its process of becoming. In this regard, the analyst is the third consciousness, is thirdness itself. Secondly, we can see the analytic object, as the third, as binding the two consciousnesses of the analyst and analysand, thus creating new shapes of being, new shapes of knowing, in both. I continue to build upon the structural importance of vanishing in the *Phenomenology*, which we can look now in light of Green's commentary on "transitional space" that he draws out of Winnicott's work: "Let us remember, the transitional space is not just 'in between': it is a space where the future subject is *in transit*, a transit in which he takes possession of a created object in the vicinity of a real external one, before he has reached it" (*Squiggle*, 88). This, too, is how the moments of vanishing as transition, and Force as transition, might be considered; where consciousness is "in transit" towards becoming. These moments mark the progress. A turn to

Ogden's *Subjects of Analysis* will allow for a fuller picture of Green's "analytic object" as an "intersubjective analytic third."[92]

Ogden's Analytic Third

As previously stated, the reason for choosing to touch upon the work of Ogden is that he finds his theoretical basis both in Hegel's *Phenomenology* and in Green's work surrounding the concept of thirdness. On the Hegelian front, Ogden can be located in the intersubjective school, alongside Jessica Benjamin and others, that utilises the dialectic of the master/slave as a model for intersubjectivity, particularly for the aspect of recognition and for what they see as a grounding understanding of the dialectical nature of the theory and practice of psychoanalysis.[93] In his definition of a psychoanalytic "subject" and the process by which it is constituted, we find not only the dialectic but also the notion of becoming via negation that I have been tracing throughout my investigation:

> Central among the contributions of psychoanalysis to a theory of subjectivity is the formulation of a concept of the subject in which neither consciousness nor unconsciousness holds a privileged position in relation to the other. Emanating from a continuous process of dialectical negation, the subject is forever decentred from static self-equivalence. That is, the psychoanalytic subject never simply is; the subject is always *becoming* through a process of creative negation of itself.[94]

Again we see an idea of "creative negation," presumably drawn directly from the Hegelian model. There is not static state of being but only a flux of conscious and unconscious thought assisting in the creation of a subject. Ogden aims to see what the analytic situation then contributes to this process. Building upon Green's concept of the analytic third Ogden writes:

> The analytic process reflects the interplay of three subjectivities: the subjectivity of the analyst, of the analysand, and of the analytic third. The analytic third is a creation of the analyst and analysand, and at the same time the analyst and the analysand (*qua* analyst and analysand) are created by the analytic third. (There is no analyst, no analysand, no analysis in the absence of the third.)[95]

The reciprocal exchange of energies is allowed by the figure of the analytic third, which for Ogden is a third "subject." I locate here the second version of my vanishing mediator. Not only, then, have I figured the analyst, seen in Hegel as the counsellor as third, as a vanishing mediator, but we have also seen that that which is the product of the analytic situation is this third. In turn the creation of this third is that which creates the relationship, that which binds, the analyst and analysand in the first place.

To the question posed earlier regarding what use does the subject of analysis make of the analytic third once the analytic session ends, Ogden would reply: "The termination of a psychoanalytic experience is not the end of the subject of psychoanalysis. The intersubjectivity of the analytic pair is appropriated by the analysand and is transformed into an internal dialogue (a process of mutual interpretation taking place within the context of a single personality system)."[96]

We see this illustrated in the Hegelian context when the unhappy consciousness, having been rescued by the Third, our proto-analyst, turns to Reason. Having incorporated the work of its interaction with the "counsellor," it has created for itself a new shape of being. Recall that it has turned itself into an object and "in this object, in which it finds that its own action and being, as being that of this *particular* consciousness, are being and action *in themselves*, there has arisen the idea of *Reason*, of the certainty that, in its particular individuality, it has being absolutely *in itself*, or is all reality" (*PS*, 138). Thus, the vanishing mediator has performed its task. It has reunited the split self of the unhappy consciousness, allowing for the exchange of energies (the play of Forces) to take place, and silently it vanishes.

CONCLUSION

What remains for me to do now is to see how the concepts of the tertiary process and the analytic third can be seen at work on a structural, not simply episodic, level in the *Phenomenology*. What I will soon argue in the next chapter is that one of the outcomes of the work of thirdness in Hegel's philosophy could be seen as the new shapes of knowing which all move towards new shapes of consciousness. This will take us through a further fleshing out of concepts of the third and binding in psychoanalytic theory, anchored in the work of Christopher Bollas. The foundations built here with the concept of negation and the drawing out of the presence of drive activity (both Eros and destructive) in what Green would call its "internal functioning" have allowed me to combine thinking about Force in Hegel with an economic model drawn from psychoanalysis. I have located the origins of the processes of thought, of judgement, and cognition of objects. In so doing, one of the aims in this chapter was to build a way of thinking about the nature of the *transition* between intrasubjective and intersubjective processes of binding; my next concern is to see what the potential "products" of these binds might be and how the processes of thought and knowing are affected. I will be moving even deeper into considerations of the analytic situation in order to see how notions of alterity might flower there and what the unique intersubjective relationship that is the analytic situation might offer to our wider understanding of the creation of the self in and through intersubjectivity.

4 Thought Structures and Shapes of Knowing

Christopher Bollas, the Elaboration of "The Third," and the Binding Process

> Although all persons form mental representations of the other, in the form of internal objects, psychoanalysis not only favours the representation of such objects, it also facilitates the self's capacity to communicate the aesthetic of one's being to the other. In a sense, it allows self to convey its own otherness.[1]

INTRODUCTION

In Chapter Three I began the move into the more reified realm of the analytic setting with Green. In this chapter, as the second of two "case studies," the aim is to not only evolve the theoretical underpinnings thus far introduced but also to continue locating ourselves in the practical (admittedly still speculative) realm of the analytic space, in which is found a unique illustration of intersubjectivity at work. The reasons for choosing to explore Bollas's work are various. His connection to Hegel's thinking is not as obvious or concrete as is Green's, but the manner in which he thinks through the concepts of binding and the third in particular allow for a move beyond explicit connections and formulate new ways of reading Hegel and psychoanalysis together. The chapter on Green is in many ways the pair for Chapter One, where I endeavoured to work through concepts to be explored in the intrapsychic realm before moving into the interpsychic. Following this dialectical model, this present chapter on Bollas is a dialectical partner for Chapter Two, where I explored notions of intersubjectivity and the play of Forces in Hegel.

Furthermore, if we were judging simply by the fact that André Green dedicated his work *On Private Madness* to Bollas and supplied a ringing endorsement of Bollas and his work on the jacket of Bollas's *Being a Character*, we could, without even considering the content of their work, say that these two thinkers are connected in some way. In turn, Bollas refers to Green throughout his work. This is, in part, a reason that they have become the analytic pair sitting on the other side of the dialectical divide in my reading of Hegel. All of this, however important, is clearly only the superficial indication that the work of these two writers owes something to the other.

Clearly, the resonance must necessarily go deeper than professional use of and acknowledged respect for the other's work. Starting with the above epigraph, Bollas seems to echo Green's assertion that it is psychoanalysis which establishes "favourable conditions for the flowering of [. . .] alterity and for the revelation of its conflictual nature" (*WN*, 42) when he writes that psychoanalysis allows the self to "convey its own otherness" via the presentation and representation of its internal objects to an other (as well as the capacity to form new objects through the interplay—a form of the play of Forces—with this other). Psychoanalysis, Bollas continues, allows for the "deeply meaningful experience" of "conveying one's self to an other" through this otherness (*FA*, 66). The articulation of the sense of one's own "otherness," while simultaneously recognizing the undeniable alterity of the other, is the work of self-consciousness in the *Phenomenology*. Bollas here places a value on this experience in that it is "meaningful." But this does not seem to go far enough. I might add that it is entirely essential. What is key is that which is created in this interaction between self and other, figured as the play of Forces in Hegel and translated into the analytic setting as seen through the work of Bollas.

First, this chapter is an expansion upon the notion of the analytic third (variously referred to as the third) and the process of thirdness. This entails an exploration of the "object" that is created between the analyst and analysand out of articulated language and unconscious interplay. Bollas terms this entity the "analytic genera." I have understood thirdness not only as a way of talking about the third but also as a way of designating the move into the work of interpretation (the tertiary process) and how this work may affect the analytic pair once the third has been generated. Bollas's concept of analytic genera stems, in part, from his theory of "psychic genera" and thus a bit of grounding in a brief examination of this theory is helpful. However, as highlighted in the last chapter, this notion of the third cannot be pinned simply on an object. The discussion of what this object is sits on rather shifting foundations. It must remain fluid enough to encompass the idea of the "space" that is created in the interaction of two subjectivities and to incorporate the work of interpretation and the creation of meaning. I will note further ramifications as the chapter proceeds and will trace Bollas's own slippages and oscillations regarding the concept.

The second aim of this chapter is to elaborate upon the notions of binding and unbinding. Although the terminology might shift, and it does throughout Bollas's work, the activity of binding and unbinding (with rebinding as the third part of the process, taken by now as inherent to the process itself) subsists as a vital function in the formation of thought, meaning, and the development of the subject. These very slippages on Bollas's part, it can be argued, speak to the immense difficulty that comes in writing about what actually occurs and, furthermore, what is produced in the intersubjective realm. I therefore also turn to Bollas as a practicing analyst who writes theoretically about the very complexities of the intersubjective and dialectical relationship between the analyst and the analysand and, moreover, one who is heavily invested in the notion of the analyst as a subject. Although he is obviously not the originator of the reading of this relationship as a dialectic, throughout his work Bollas is consistently attempting to formulate just how this dialectic functions.

The Use of the Term *Object*

There is difficulty in attempting to wrest the notion of the object out of the analytic situation in order to understand it in the context created through and alongside our reading of Hegel. This is difficult for a number of reasons and while the scope of this book does not allow for more than a cursory nod in the direction of this intellectual history, I must acknowledge the particular way in which the term *object* is formulated, especially in Bollas's work. First of all, Bollas is located as a descendent of the "object relations" tradition. Gregorio Kohon writes that object relations "implies a way of relating that is considered as an interrelationship: the individual affects his objects as much as his objects affect him." Kohon further remarks that it is from the work in the clinical space that object relations theory arose and that importantly it is "not only the real relation with others that determines the subject's individual life, but the specific way in which the subject apprehends his relationship with his objects (both internal and external). It always implies an unconscious relationship to these objects."[2] The difference between "real" relations and apprehended relations and between others and objects is crucial for psychoanalysis. Much of Bollas's work is devoted to thinking through what these objects are, how they are given shape, and how they are used in transformations of the individual.

The notion of object (*Gegenstand*) for Hegel slides more easily, conceptually speaking, between the designation of other and object. Object in the *Phenomenology* is used to refer to that which exists outside the self, in both the form of the other and of the things of the physical world. For instance, "the Unchangeable" is an object; "pure thinking" is an object. As I have been tracing, this object, in whatever form it arises, is bound to the self as part of the process of becoming of consciousness. Hyppolite writes:

> Strictly speaking, there is no object which is simply an object, or any subject that is only a subject, one without and the other within. My internal life does not exist as such; rather it exists through my exchange with the world, or in my projects which alone confer a meaning upon what is outside. Hegel returns to this point in connection with the nature of human individuality, of its own body, the world which is its world and is such that one cannot be understood apart from the other.[3]

We can recall that this other/object cannot, for Hegel, be found where it is sought, "for it is supposed to be just a *beyond*." Most importantly, "when sought as a particular individual, it is not a *universal* individuality in the form of thought, not a *Notion*, but an individual in the form of an object, or an *actual* individual; an object of immediate sense-certainty, and for that very reason only something that has already vanished" (*PS*, 131–32). This means that when the other has concrete form, as a particular individual, as a body, it then becomes part of the physical world and does not simply exist in the realm of notions, and thus is apprehended *as* an object. Then, however, it has always already vanished but not disappeared, for it has thus become part of consciousness' knowledge about the world.

There is a way of reading Bollas's theory of the object as it is coming out of object relations theory alongside Hegel as long as we accept the difficulty of taking what is a phenomenon of the clinical setting out of context in order to see how such formulations might be thought about in another theoretical/philosophical frame. It is important to acknowledge that the apprehension of objects for the journeying consciousness of the *Phenomenology of Spirit*, and my analysis of that set of relations, is not necessarily dependent on the work of the unconscious, as it is in psychoanalysis, although I have suggested that a notion of the unconscious could be found in Hegel. Again, it is the deliberate blurring of the lines between the two disciplines and the melding of the ways of thinking about what these objects are and what their purpose is that is the most fruitful approach for our present consideration.

Psychoanalysis as a Dialectic

I have already remarked upon Green's thinking about the dialectic and here can give further background, as the very activity of the analytic encounter as a functioning form of the dialectic will become more important in this chapter. Lacan, at many points, gives us clear language for situating the importance of Hegel's dialectic for psychoanalysis. For example, he tells us, "It is impossible for our technique to ignore the structuring moments of Hegel's phenomenology: first and foremost, the master/slave dialectic, the dialectic of the beautiful soul and the law of the heart, and generally everything that allows us to understand how the constitution of the object is subordinate to the realization of the subject." So for Lacan it is the dialectic that is both at work between subjects and creates "the subject." This subject then has a position of power over the formation of the object. The technique of psychoanalysis, according to Lacan, acknowledges that the subject is something not preformed or given but is created, is "realised," out of the dialectic. He further states:

> Psychoanalysis is a dialectic, what Montaigne, in book III, chapter VIII, calls *an art of conversation*. The art of conversation of Socrates in the *Meno* is to teach the slave to give his own speech its true meaning. And it is the same in Hegel. In other words, the position of the analyst must be that of an *ignorantia docta*, which does not mean knowing [*savante*], but formal, and what is capable of being formative for the subject.[4]

For Lacan, then, this dialectic takes place in language, and it is through speech, through the dialectic of conversation as such, the subject is formed. I am taking Lacan's model of the dialectic and moving in and around it to see, via the concept of Force and with the help of Bollas, what might exist outside of thinking, outside of language, that constitutes the subject. Importantly, I am continuing to speculate on what happens when the dialectic of the subject (in the form of the unhappy consciousness, the precursor to the beautiful soul) ceases to move.

While there is never direct reference to Hegel in Bollas's work, in an interview he acknowledges that the *Phenomenology of Spirit* is one of the seminal texts that influenced his thinking about psychoanalysis. I take the liberty here of assuming that the dialectic to which Bollas refers is that of the Hegelian variety.[5] To begin with, Bollas views the dialectic of the analytic situation as taking place on multiple levels. He writes:

> The analysand's transferences and the analyst's countertransferences, between the patient's narratives and the analyst's associations, between the analysand's linguistic specifications and the clinician's readings, between the patient's declarations and the clinician's questions [. . .] is the labor of two separate yet deeply involved unconscious subjectivities.[6]

Bollas would not, however, align himself with the relational school of psychoanalysis that also takes the view of the analytic situation as dialectical.[7] Bollas is careful to emphasise that the "play of [these] two subjectivities" that are at work in the "formation of psychoanalytic genera" (and I will soon discuss the nuances of Bollas's concept of genera) is not a play between two equal subjectivities, or rather it is not a "relation between equals," as one subject is a patient who has come to the analyst in a state of crisis, and the analyst is a trained subject who "offers a procedure for the investigation into and the possible cure of such suffering" (*BC*, 129). Although he is presumably taking his language of "play" from a Winnicottian perspective, it is a description that fits quite well with my previous discussions of the play of Forces and the subsequent discussion of subjects, self-consciousnesses, as "Forces," and thus I continue to think within this framework. What both senses of "play" indicate are active, living processes that are necessarily generative, and it is with this common base that they can be read together. Furthermore, it must be stated that this disparity of the "unequal" roles of analyst and analysand, while crucial for psychoanalytic practice, does not fundamentally shift the potential outcomes of my investigation. We undoubtedly are obliged to keep it in mind when considering the notion of intersubjectivity in the analytic situation. I argue, however, that it does not shift the outcome because I am primarily examining what it is that is created out of the work of this relationship and, according to both Bollas and Green, that which is created belongs to neither the analyst or analysand but is dependent upon the interaction of both for its existence.

FURTHER THEORETICAL GROUNDING OF THE THIRD

At the centre of this book sit several questions as to the nature of what it is that occurs or is created and what it is that is preserved or subsists in the transitional space between the self and the external world, composed as it is of objects and of other consciousnesses. This line of questioning has led me to interrogate a key set of theoretical concepts both in Hegel's philosophy and in the psychoanalytic realm, including Force, vanishing, the existence of a vanishing mediator, and, most prominently in the last chapter, the concepts of negation and binding (as they related to the activities of Eros and the death drive). While I continue here to conceive of thirdness, the analytic third, as a psychic construct, an object of sorts, that leads to the formation of, or rather becomes part of new psychic structures, the line of argument I started with my discussion of vanishing and negation must be kept in mind. In other words, I am also aiming to think of these structures as the transitional and transformational "space" that emerges out of the activity of self-consciousnesses. I have posited that this space enables the creation of new moments of understanding, of knowing, of self-consciousness.[8] With my reading of Bollas in place, I can then return briefly to an interpretation of Hegel that offers a way of reading the notions of shapes of knowing (*Gestalten des Wissens*) and shapes of consciousness (*Gestalten des Bewußtseins*). Such an interpretation enriches my earlier investigation and gestures towards a way of thinking about the structural significance in the *Phenomenology* of the concepts of thirdness and the third.

I return to the question raised between Lacan and Hyppolite in their conversation following Hyppolite's lecture, 'Hegel's Phenomenology and Psychoanalysis.' Recall that Lacan asked Hyppolite what he meant by his use of the "we" in his talk, and Hyppolite responded by asking Lacan "what psychoanalysis in its practice may contribute to the third term which appears in the interaction of two consciousnesses." Recall, too, that the question for the two thinkers also involved the location of "original speech, a primordial logos."[9] By interrogating the particular situation of the intersubjective, dialectical relation of the analytic setting, I have been attempting to draw out the ontological and epistemological implications of not only posing such a question but also of asking for the combination of Hegelian philosophy and psychoanalytic theory to help formulate an answer. This necessarily calls for thinking not only about the subject, the consciousness as found in the analytic situation, but consciousness as such. It can be argued that both Hyppolite and Lacan (at least at the earlier points in his career) did not seem to wish to think of either of these in isolation but wished to work towards a theory of consciousness that was born out of the resonance between the two fields. It will be, however, only a gesture towards locating the notion of the third in Lacan's work that I will be able to provide. This is also in part because, ultimately, it is not necessarily his model of the third that I will be focussing on. That being said, because he is widely credited with bringing the concept to psychoanalysis, I will briefly address what form his concept of the third takes.

First, Lacan provides us with language for expanding our thinking about the analytic third, the psychic genera as constructed out of language, as a form of binding. He writes:

> Hooking on to the other is not alien, if I can put it that way, to the essence of speech. Without doubt, speech is mediation, mediation between subject and other, and it implicates the coming into being of the other in this very mediation. An essential element of the coming into being of the other is the capacity of speech to unite us to him.[10]

With speech as mediator, the subject and the other are bound to and reliant upon one another for their "coming into being." For Lacan, however, it is not simply a question of whether or not the subject and the other are, in the language of my study, bound, or in his terms "united" or "hooked." This seems to be understood to be essential to the being of the subject. It is more a question of at what level and in what capacity this binding occurs. "The point is to know how, at a given moment, this quite mysterious feeling of presence points to the other."[11] As I have been arguing, however, there are forms of binding that take place outside of language, outside of thought, and which necessarily complicates this "mysterious feeling of presence" that exists in the subject in relation to the other. Lacan's designation of what could be considered the enigma of the bind as an affective state is quite striking, for it seems he is saying that there is something in the notion of the presence of the other that remains unarticulated in the subject. Ultimately, his designation of the third is drawn from considerations of the unconscious in Freud. Shoshana Felman also locates his discussion of this third in *Écrits*. Lacan writes:

> It is therefore in the position of a third term that the Freudian discovery of the unconscious becomes clear as to its true grounding. This discovery may simply be formulated in the following terms: The unconscious is that part of concrete discourse in so far as it is transindividual, that is, not at the disposal of the subject in re-establishing the continuity of his conscious discourse.[12]

What Felman pinpoints here is the connection between the third and Lacan's formulation of the unconscious as "the discourse of the Other." Furthermore, she sees that a "subtle reference to the Oedipus" is implicit. Felman elaborates that this is what helps to define Lacanian psychoanalysis:

> But the Lacanian psychoanalytic story is an altogether different story because the narration happens not between two agents but between three terms, and since it takes place (takes effect) only *through* the

> emergence of this third—this Other; since the subject of the psychoanalytic narration, in all senses of the word (both its speaking subject and what is being spoken of), is neither the analysand nor the analyst, but the discourse of the Other. The psychoanalytic narrative is nothing other, for Lacan, than the story of, precisely, the discovery of the third participant in the structure of the dialogue. And this dramatic, narrative and structural discovery implicitly refers to Oedipus.[13]

As I noted in the last chapter, this Lacanian version of the third is then translated into the realm of the symbolic and resides in the Law of the Father, following as it does from the triangular structure of "the Oedipus."

What is so helpful about Felman's reading is that it offers a wonderful way of encapsulating Lacan's framework that in many ways responds to the Hyppolite-Lacan question about what emerges from the "we" of psychoanalysis. Rather interestingly, this third for Felman, following Lacan, is a "participant" and not simply an inert by-product. This designation aids us in thinking about the third as an active, living entity, another kind of subject. It also necessarily complicates the notion of intersubjectivity and moves it beyond the simple dialectic (of master/slave) and into a realm, in John Muller's words, "beyond the psychoanalytic dyad." Importantly, however, we have to note that a "participant" is not in this sense necessarily an object or a space or indeed another subject and is, instead, a "discourse." Ogden, as we can recall, also designated the third as another "subjectivity" but did not go down the Lacanian route and extend this subject into discourse.

Michele Minolli and Maria Luisa Tricoli argue that it is in the 1950s with the debates regarding the concept of countertransference that the psychoanalytic origins of the concept of the third can be located.[14] Lacan speaks to this very phenomenon, at the time it was occurring: "The growing importance attributed today to countertransference means that it is a recognised fact that in analysis the patient is not alone. There are two of us—and not only two."[15] The third, in the opinion of Minolli and Tricoli, was needed because the phenomenon of countertransference "was a manifestation of the analyst's subjectivity," the emergence of which set in motion a new and vital line of theoretical thinking that took this subjectivity seriously.[16] Bollas is an heir and prominent contributor to this theoretical development, and the processes of transference and countertransference are elements of the analytic encounter that reside at the centre of his work. However, the scope of my book does not allow for an exploration of the development of these concepts or a discussion that would do justice to the complex nature of their functioning.[17] In addition, as we will see with the notion of free association, there is no real equivalent to transference or countertransference in Hegel's *Phenomenology*. (The closest we could come is to try and read a version of transference as existing in "The Unhappy Consciousness" episode, but this would be to turn that episode into a parody of an analytic situation.) That being said, we can follow Bollas's thinking that the transference and countertransference are transformative processes and add that they also are an element of the binding process that takes place between the analyst and analysand.

Minolli and Tricoli's basic argument is that the third was introduced in psychoanalytic theory as an attempt to find a solution to the "problem of establishing and clarifying the relatedness between subject and object" that arose in post-Freudian thought.[18] In their valuable tracing of the historical roots of the concept, they do not discuss the Hyppolite–Lacan exchange, although they do discuss Lacan's general contribution to the history of the idea. What they do provide is crucial support for my reading of the third/thirdness in Hegel in that they locate a concept of the third in the *Phenomenology*. Ultimately, however, I do not entirely agree with their conclusions. They argue that "the third was born as an attempt to recall the human being's capacity to grasp himself reflexively," and their argument is invested in a view of the third that utilises Hegel's concept of self-consciousness as the most apt way of describing this activity in the psychoanalytic realm.[19] In fact, they posit that the third is "self-consciousness" in Hegel's system. Not surprisingly, they restrict their reading of Hegel to the master/slave dialectic. Refreshingly, though, they interrogate the standard use of Hegel's model of intersubjectivity for psychoanalysis, and its dependence on the Kojèvian/Lacanian reading, and push for a rereading of Hegel's own thought rather than understanding Hegel only through the lens of the Kojèvian interpretation.[20]

They point to the use of Hegel in psychoanalytic thinking in the past decade (they are writing in 2004) as arising from the interest in the notion of the psychoanalytic dyad,[21] which predominantly occupies the relational school, and situate their own reading of Hegel:

> Such appreciation of Hegel is consistent with the deeper interest in the dyad that characterizes psychoanalysis today. In the work of these authors, the third is conceptualized as a new dimension or quality of the self that is achieved by analyst and patient together in the ongoing process of analytic interaction. We share this position in our conceptualization of the third as self-consciousness—a quality, according to Hegel, that is reached by the I-subject in an endless dialectical process. It is a process in which the I-subject confronts others in order to recognize the otherness as a denied part of the self, returning back to himself with new awareness.[22]

This return to the self, armed with new moments of understanding, is exactly the moment that we located in Hegel's description of the move from the unhappy consciousness to Reason via the counsellor, or our vanishing mediator. We must note that they designate the third as a new shape of knowing, a new moment of self-consciousness, as self-consciousness itself.

On one level, I am in agreement with their formulation and take it into consideration alongside my reading of Bollas, so that I might further nuance ways of thinking about the concept in Hegelian terms. However, where I part company from Minolli and Tricoli's reading is in the idea that they believe that "if the third had the power to engender self-consciousness in someone else, it would turn that person into a puppet." The crux of their argument is that the third, as self-consciousness, is simply something that we are already equipped with and that does not come about in relation to or is not an external factor in any way. They argue that it is "necessary to stop ascribing a magical power to a third factor—a power viewed as different from what the human being has inside himself."[23] While they do acknowledge that self-consciousness for Hegel is "comprehension of ourselves in our relationship with others," they also insist that the self in this process "cannot be dependent on anything other than itself."[24] Surely, however, as we have seen, Hegel is at great pains to illustrate that self-sufficiency is simply not enough, especially when our process of becoming is "jammed" (to use Green's term). As I have been arguing, this means that we are not this third, nor do we possess thirdness as an inherent part of our consciousness. Neither are we "puppets" if we rely on the interaction with an "other" to draw ourselves out of the danger of stasis. The significance of the third is that it can be incorporated into our process of becoming and serve to elaborate our self-consciousness, not control us, as Minolli and Tricoli seem to suggest.

There is a final note to be made before proceeding. The work of Christopher Bollas, in many ways unlike the work of André Green, has been far more difficult to pin down or, in any way (systematically) map out. This is due, in large part, to Bollas's own refusal to systematise; he is simply neither that kind of thinker or analyst, nor is he invested in the rigorous use of theory as such. Roger Kennedy also writes about the difficulty of locating a "theoretically comprehensive" system in Bollas's work regarding "subject relations theory" (which is Kennedy's primary interest in Bollas and an explanation of which will be given shortly) and chooses, as I do, to read him implicitly, building a theoretical framework from elements that can be found throughout his writing.[25] Green does not construct a system either, but there is a particular stringency to his writing and thinking that enables a more theoretical approach. In and of itself this is not a problem, and it is clearly not simply a system as such that I am after.

What has created difficulty in writing about Bollas's work is what I have seen as an oscillation in the formulation of theoretical frameworks, a near failure of theory as a mode of articulating those elements of existence that perhaps find their very articulation in the failure to capture them entire and alive.[26] However, what Bollas does offer in many of his wonderfully written and thoroughly engaging works is a way of combining thinking about a more economically centred model of consciousness with a linguistic framework that does not ask that we necessarily remain entirely fixed in a symbolic universe. As Malcolm Bowie writes in the preface to *Vitality of Objects*, because for Bollas there is something in the kernel of our being that resists language and resists representation, "language matters, but is not alone in mattering."[27] Bollas himself writes, "There is no reason in Freudian theory why we cannot hold that the energy of the instincts is intrinsic to and inseparable from the economics of ego life" (*FD*, 12). I will shortly show how Bollas considers the concept of "energy" in Freud's thinking and how the metapsychological aspects of his thought should be used. Clearly this present chapter does not aim to perform an exhaustive or comprehensive study of Bollas's work and so, as I did with Green, I will simply mine the particularly rich veins of thought that can be found in his body of work, finding an anchor in them and adding them to the psychoanalytic framework so far in place. I will begin by examining Bollas's concept of psychic genera and the elaboration of the concept into "analytic genera."

BOLLAS AND THE CREATION OF PSYCHIC GENERA AS A FORM OF THE THIRD

> The patient-analyst relationship is inevitably dialectical, as each participant destroys the other's perception and rhetorical rendering of events, to create that third intermediate object, a synthesis, that is owned by neither participant and objectifies the loss of omnipotent wishes to possess truth just as it situates the participants in that collaborative place from which the only analytically usable truth can emerge. (*BC*, 112–13)

Bollas's description here veers extremely close to the activity of *Aufhebung* as it begins to both complicate and complement the notion of intersubjectivity that I am taking out of Hegel and have been reading through and alongside the work of Green. Recall that according to Green,

> In the end the real analytic object is neither on the patient's side nor on the analyst's, but in the meeting of these two communications in the potential space, which lies between them, limited by the setting which is broken at each separation and reconstituted at each new meeting. (*OPM*, 48)

Without getting too far ahead of myself, I read here echoes of the binding and unbinding process in the analytic setting itself. With the work of interpretation binding the patient and the analyst together into this potential space, the end of the session is an unbinding of sorts. Following this logic, there is a new rebinding with each session. What will remain, then, outside of it all, is the new binding to the objects created in that space. I am compelled to stretch even further into the realm of the analytic situation to elaborate upon my discussion of the analytic third. Bollas's development of the concept of psychic genera and its further expansion into the concept of analytic genera will aid in doing so. What we are looking at is that which is not only created but also survives the intersubjective communication that takes place in a theoretical analytic space. Recall here the language of "subsistence" from the discussion of Force in Hegel. What remains, in essence, are forms of psychic structures, entities created through the collaborative work of the analyst and analysand that can then serve as both transitional and more importantly as transformational objects for both subjectivities.

It must be noted, however, that Bollas makes a very clear distinction between the analytic space as a "transitional area" and the "mental objects (association, comment, interpretation, mood, environment, etc.)" that are created in this area through the interaction of the analyst and analysand in the capacity of "an *intermediate object*." A transitional object, he argues, is the product not of the interplay between two subjects but is instead derived from one subject's "development of his own idiom irrespective of the other's desire" (*FD*, 108–09). The analyst is designated as a "transformational object" since he "processes" the analysand's "thoughts, moods, and communications."[28] Recall that for Green, the analytic space is not only transitional but is also potential space that is occupied by what the patient and the analyst bring to it. He writes, "The patient's communication—different from what he lives and feels—is situated in the transitional space between him and us, in the same way as our interpretation is carried by communication" (*OPM*, 47).[29] We must, then, be slightly careful when drawing the distinction between "transitional space" and "transformational space."[30]

Now, the object created out of the collaborative work of the analysis is clearly not a material object as such but one comprised of the traces of interactions with the material world. It is largely, but certainly not solely, an object that is created out of language and, according to Bollas, out of the communications between the unconscious forces at play, as those forces that are at work in and behind language. As can be recalled from the examination of Green's work, the analytic third is that which is created during the analytic session and through, amongst other things, interpretation, or what Green designates as the "tertiary process." This notion can now be enriched with the aid of Bollas.

Although the concept of psychic genera is one that he formally introduces in his third book, *Being a Character*, we can see the embryonic elements of this formulation from the time of his first book, *Shadow of the Object*. There he writes of the patient as being an object in the analytic setting and of the analyst as having the agency to initiate in the patient a new relationship to the self as this object (*SO*, 61). Along these lines, he discusses the idea of "evocation" where an object is created by the analyst's solicitation of the unarticulated content of the patient's unconscious. In his second work, *Forces of Destiny*, Bollas begins to complicate the relationship of the analyst and patient and discusses the "psychic movement that takes place when the analysand is free to use the psychoanalyst as an object through whom to articulate and elaborate his personality idiom" (*FD*, 8).

Bollas defines idiom as the "unique nucleus of each individual, a figuration of being that is like a kernel that can, under favourable circumstances, evolve and articulate. Human idiom is the defining essence of each subject, and, although all of us have some acute sense of the other's idiom, this knowledge is virtually unthinkable" (*FD*, 212). To speak in Hegelian terms, the becoming of the individual for Bollas involves the articulation, the expression, of this inner kernel (which we are born with), and it needs to be called forth or solicited by the external world, be it in the form of an object or another subject (that is then used in the form of an object) (*BC*, 51). The idiom, the life of the "true self," comes about in the experiencing of the world. For Bollas, then, like Hegel, the process of becoming is dependent upon the interaction of the self with the external world of objects and others. When considering the psychoanalytic realm, the self finds its elaboration, it discovers itself, in being called forth by the presence of the analyst, and the process of becoming is intricately tied up with the activities of transference and countertransference, which Bollas sees as transformational processes. In this way, the model of Force I have suggested has purchase in the analytic situation. The solicitation on the part of the analyst as a Force, and expression of the Force of the analysand, compose the play of Forces that takes place. Writing on Bollas's work, and particularly on the notion of the idiom and "grammar" of the self, Frank Summers states,

> The analyst continually identifies the glimmerings of the buried self to show the patient the potential of spontaneous expression, and the patient struggles with ways to use these nascent states. Any creation fashioned from them is a new way of being, and the analyst, as labelling it as such, must help the patient see her self in creation. The self is now being created as it is found.[31]

Summers describes here, without stating it explicitly, the very fashioning of the third that I am exploring. Furthermore, his description finds resonance in my Hegelian framework where the self is a constant process of becoming and each new way of being is an element of this creating of self.

Bollas is particularly invested in the moments of transformation that occur in this process and especially in the transformation of the "lived processes" into "mental representations." Yet, he also allows that the core of our being is a "wordless, imageless solitude" (*FD*, 14, 21). We cannot, he claims, access this core by "insight or introspection" but only through actually living. This inner core is, for Bollas, the "force to become." And here is where Bollas is pushing the boundaries of psychoanalysis in a rather interesting way. The analytic situation, he argues, is not simply a deconstructive process but is rather the place for this calling forth, for the elaboration of this inner core. Clearly he is not only interested in the dialectic between the unconscious and the conscious processes but also claims that it is truly the interpretation of that which emerges between the patient and analyst that is the transformative, generative act. Bollas adheres to Freud's notion of interpretation as "a dialect(ic) of two unconscious systems" and further claims that "each interpretative act acknowledges this movement of patient to analyst, of analyst to patient" (*FD*, 62). We can add this to our understanding of interpretation taken out of Green and think of it not only as action but also as representation of intersubjective work. Crucially, Bollas believes, and especially articulates in his later work, that the interpretive process should not be forced to fit the temporal confines of the analytic session. The danger lies, for Bollas, in attempting to complete an interpretation before it has been fully allowed to elaborate itself over time.

Inherent in our subjectivity is the "urge to articulate the true self," and this is what Bollas terms the "destiny drive," which he designates as a form of the life instinct (*FD*, 3, 211).[32] Crucially, it is the conflict between the forces of the true self and of the external world of objects and others that creates the fabric of psychic life (*FD*, 9). Bollas locates a facet of the role of analyst in his existence as an *object* to whom one can turn as part of this "play of forces" should the destiny drive become jammed or should the patient's elaboration of the self (the becoming of the self) be in any sort of danger or heading towards stasis (*FD*, 97).[33] An essential aspect of this play for Bollas is free association, both on the part of the patient *and* psychoanalyst. Indeed, it is the element of free association that generates much of the material (linguistic and other) out of which the analytic objects are formed. I will approach free association more directly when I discuss Bollas's considerations of the binding and unbinding processes, and we will see that the analyst's own processes of free association are crucial to the analytic process.

Because, as I have noted, he sees the analysis as a "dialectic between two subjectivities," Bollas introduces the idea of subject relations theory to both complement and move beyond object relations theory. This allows him to designate the existence of objects that are the creation of the play of two distinct subjectivities, which he calls "intermediate objects." We can see here how we are inching towards the designation of the third/thirdness in Bollas's work. He writes in *Forces of Destiny*:

> I suggest that we term any mental object (association, comment, interpretation, mood, environment, etc.) derived from patient-analyst interplay, an *intermediate object*. This respects the fact that it derives from the contribution of two subjectivities and that it is part of the transitional dialectics of subject relations. Such objects are not transitional objects, because the transitional object is not derived from interrelating, but reflects the subject's development of his own idiom irrespective of the other's desire. An intermediate object respects the status of an object that is indeed negotiated by two subjectivities, and most analytical objects are therefore intermediate ones. (*FD*, 109)

I have noted the distinctions that Bollas draws between transformational and transitional objects and spaces, but for now let me just focus on locating the seeds of the third in this passage. We have here the existence of an object stemming from the negotiation between the subjectivity of the analyst and that of the patient. We do not yet know, however, what happens to this object once it is created, although we are by now aware that this object has the potential to create new forms of being and aid in the elaboration of the self. We now need to continue fleshing out of the idea of the intermediate object into that of the third.

It is in *Being a Character*, his third book, that Bollas designates the intermediate object as a third. As we saw in the epigraph to this section, Bollas begins to discuss this object as a "synthesis," a product of the dialectical relationship of the analytic pair. Prior to this designation of the third, Bollas introduces the concept of "psychic genera," which he aims to pair with "trauma," but only insofar as the genera are to be the opposite of trauma. These genera are "particular types of psychic organisations of lived experience that will result in creative new envisionings of life, either in psychoanalysis or other walks of life" (*BC*, 68). Interestingly, he sees trauma as binding and accordingly we can argue that in seeing these genera as the "opposite," they are also to be part of an unbinding process, where the self elaborates its being.

At the heart of his thinking about these psychic genera lies Bollas's intention to conceive of a theory or repression, and of the unconscious, that allows for a profound generative potential to be recognised as inherent in the work of the unconscious and in the activity of repression. He thus introduces the "theory of reception," a theory "which designates some ideas as the received rather than the repressed" (*BC*, 73). Bollas offers a view of genera from the topographical perspective. He discusses Freud's theory that repressed ideas hold an "intrinsic energy to find expression." Once banished to the unconscious, they form a "nucleus of interlocking ideas," and it is through the collective force of their energy that they aim to return to consciousness and will do so in some derivative form. Bollas argues that not all of these ideas are unwanted but were perhaps simply received by a consciousness not quite ready to process them (that they are in some senses "invited" into the unconscious), and thus he formulates his theory of reception. The ideas, he argues, are sent by the ego to be "given mental space for development which is not possible in consciousness" (*BC*, 72, 74).

Let us think back to the generative potential of repression that we saw embedded in Hegel's notion of Force. As can be recalled, the movement of Force, in fact the existence of Force in general, was entirely dependent upon it being driven back into itself, the repression of itself (its being-for-self), and then its subsequent expression. We can consider how the play of Forces that is the analyst/analysand relationship can also create a form of mental space for the development of ideas and in so doing fashions a new form of thinking for both subjects. This is precisely what Bollas is aiming for in his introduction of the principle of genera. It would be a form of internal work that could "enable the clinician to see how psychoanalysts and patients unconsciously collaborate to construct psychic structures that change the analysand's view of himself and his world" (*BC*, 75). These new psychic structures are brought about by what he now terms the "analytic genera." He writes:

> An analysis is a creative process involving two subjectivities at work on overlapping tasks, and analytical genera are formed as shared internal structures. The respective significance of such complexes to the two persons will naturally differ; for the analyst such devotions are unconsciously sought after as part of his creative work with a particular patient, while such internal objects become part of the analysand's mental structure. But the psychic structure that will evolve out of psychoanalysis is the result of such a collaborative effort and its desires. (*BC*, 93)

It is important to note that although these genera are "shared internal structures," the significance and use of these structures will be different for each side of the dialectical partnership of analyst and analysand. When considering the ownership, then, Bollas complicates his own theoretical model that we saw in the epigraph to this section, where neither part of the pair owned the "third intermediate object." Why, for instance, are these psychic structures "devotions" for the analyst but become "internal objects" for the analysand? Indeed, what Bollas might mean by "devotions" is extremely puzzling.

Bollas discusses how the work of the analytic situation condenses into a structure, the "network of thinking," that both the analyst and analysand bring to the room and posits that this structure, which has "psychic gravity," now "serves both persons as a shared internal object" (*BC*, 93). On one hand, the notion of something that is "shared" prevents either side of the dialectical/analytic pair from having full ownership of the structure, particularly since the structure is the product of collaborative, and partially unconscious, work. On the other, though, Bollas seems to waver with regards to the implication that the analyst does not really incorporate the object/structure. Again, however, this very instability speaks to the difficulty of articulating the existence of these structures.

It is perhaps telling that these structures are always referred to in the plural, as "genera." Such a designation implies that they will always be shared and never owned, will never be found in the singular. Bollas himself argues that he uses the plural designation to signify its "dynamic origins," its generative strength. He does so by following in the footsteps of Henri Bergson, who linked the concept of genera with his concept of vital energy (*FD*, 67). What this further implies is that there is a certain insistence in Bollas's thinking that we will never be able to truly own, that which generates us. For Hegel this is both the motor of dialectic and the idea that causes the most existential pain. As seen when tracing the movement of self-consciousness in the *Phenomenology*, the other is always already moving beyond us, just out of our grasp, even as it is part of our creation. This is why, according to Hegel, we always feel a constitutive lack at the core of our becoming.

Bollas continues slightly oscillating with this line of argument in his next book, *Cracking Up*. There he points to his argument in *Being a Character* and states:

> The analytical couple unconsciously specify an area of work to which they both contribute and where eventually the analysand develops a new psychic structure. I term this a 'psychic genera' to indicate its generative function, insofar as the newly developed psychic structure offers wide new perspectives on the world of objects and upon the self. (*CU*, 25)

Here we can pause to note the aforementioned difficulty in pinning Bollas's terminology down. We have moved from an initial understanding of psychic genera to the concept of analytic genera and then to a "third intermediate object" and now, by the time of his fourth book, back again to psychic genera. On one level we could posit that the concept of psychic genera in his earlier work, when he is more specifically talking about the creations of artists/scientists/writers, is used to designate the work of the individual, whereas the "analytic genera" are the products of collaborative work. It is clear, however, that in one form or another Bollas is invested in pursuing the notion of what is created out of the work taking place in dialectical analytic setting.

By the time of his fifth book, Bollas seems to imply that this third object is now somehow equivalent to the "analytical process" itself. He states:

> Indeed a part of therapeutic alliance is the mutual recognition and use by the patient and the analyst of the analytical process which precedes, holds and will outlive any specific analytical couple, and which is implicitly present as a third object. It cannot, of course, go without saying that the psychoanalyst—for innumerable reasons—can lose his alliance with the third object such as when he dispenses with requests for free association, or abandons the essential ballast of silence to make interpretations.[34]

So, the question of ownership is somewhat resolved here: if the third object is thought of as the process of and not as the product of this process, then it exists external to both of them and belongs to neither. In order for this process to work, Bollas seems to be saying, not only do both subjects need to make a choice to join the "alliance," and in this way to be bound to one another, but also they must choose to recognise it as a process and particularly as a process that is to be "used." It seems, however, that the analyst has more agency (if not ownership) in the process, in that he can choose to shift the parameters and manipulate the mechanisms of the analysis. However, the analyst seems to be at risk, in a way that the patient is not, of losing this state of being bound to the process when he makes interpretations. In a moment, I will touch upon how Bollas formulates the destructive nature of interpretation, but for now we can see that this is the direction in which he is heading. The fragility of this third, Bollas seems to say, deserves equal recognition. Bollas is making claims for silence as stability and seems to indicate that an interpretation, as destructive, creates an unbinding of the analyst from the process.

On another note, if the nature of subsistence found in my reading of Hegel is considered, then it can be posited that it is the "process" that survives its own movement beyond the space in which it takes place. In fact, it exists in its potentiality before the analytic pair comes together. Clearly, the third object and the analytic genera are not always for Bollas the same thing. Thinking back, then, to Minolli and Tricolli's paper which outlined at least ten ways in which the third can be thought about, we might have to say that Bollas's inconsistency or, more generously, his theoretical oscillation, could strike one as at least faithful to malleable nature of the concept. As a way of supporting my thinking and about the connections being made here, Gabriela Mann helpfully draws a parallel between "what Bollas calls an environment of genera, and what Ogden (1996) calls 'the analytic third,' that is, a space or object dimension in which the patient and the analyst engage together in intersubjective construction of an experiential space for the patient's unconscious."[35] What Mann emphasises is the aspect of the space, the environment, of the analytic setting, as that which emerges from, or is created in, the work of the analytic pair. In a later reflection and rethinking of the concept, Ogden also adds that the analytic third is, by necessity of the very nature of the analytic setting, utilised differently by each member of the analytic pair and that it is, in fact, asymmetrical. He writes: "In short, the analytic third is not a single event experienced identically by two people; it is an unconscious, asymmetrical cocreation of analyst and analysand which has a powerful structuring influence on the analytic relationship."[36] So for Ogden, even though he grants the "cocreation" of this third, the question of ownership is complicated by what he sees as the unevenness of the pair.

If I combine the various ways in which the notion of the third can be read (and we will shortly see how thirdness, as a tertiary process, as interpretation, will manifest itself in Bollas), I can conclude the following: for Bollas, the analytic genera is a third, intermediate object created out of the collaborative (both conscious and unconscious) work between analyst and analysand. This object exists independently of them (even though its origins might partially lie in their respective unconscious) but is most likely to be incorporated by the analysand as part of its psychic structure. It thus forms a new way of understanding and knowing the self and becomes a new level of psychic functioning. It can also be concluded that this third is the analytic space that is created between the two dialectical partners, as well as being the analytic process itself. With all of that in mind, in reading Bollas's work, and in recognising that he does credit Green with certain of the theoretical models with which he is working, it becomes increasingly odd that he does not once mention Green's notion of the third object.

That noted, I move on here to think about the ways in which the process of analysis is seen by Bollas as holding the potential for generative destruction and the importance of this destruction for the creation of new lines of thought, new shapes of knowing. In so doing, new ways of talking about the binding and unbinding processes can be incorporated. Joel Beck writes that Bollas's "hypothesis about generative psychic structures attempts to conceptualize the way in which the mind arrives at a new perspective. When this happens, we begin to think differently about the world and ourselves."[37] This is precisely why Bollas is of such use to my investigation and is the topic that I now pursue.

THE GENERATIVE NATURE OF DESTRUCTION: BOLLAS, FREE ASSOCIATION, AND THE BINDING/UNBINDING PROCESS

With the help of Bollas we can examine what can be looked at as "generative forms of destruction" (*MT*, 27). This will be interwoven with a discussion of the forms of binding and unbinding that can be found in Bollas's work. He links these forms of destruction to the processes of unbinding and thus I am able to loop back to my understanding of unbinding as a generative act. Jessica Benjamin writes of the "breakdown and recreation of the tension between asserting one's own reality and accepting the others" and asserts that it is

> destruction—negation in Hegel's sense—that enables the subject to go beyond relating to the object through identification, projection, and other intrapsychic processes having to do with the subjectively conceived object. It enables the transition from relating (intrapsychic) to using the object, carrying on a relationship with the other who is objectively perceived as existing outside the self, an entity in her own right.[38]

We can interpret "breakdown and recreation" as other terms for the acts of unbinding and rebinding that occur when the self attempts to navigate the boundaries of its own psychic reality in the face of the other. In Benjamin's opinion the danger resides in the "loss of balance between the intrapsychic and the intersubjective," in the breakdown in the process of recognition, which is the very instability whose culmination I located in "The Unhappy Consciousness" episode.[39]

Throughout my discussion of the *Phenomenology* so far, I have traced the generative power of the negative as the "energy of thought" and drawn the links between the negative and the life-and-death drives, both as located structurally in Hegel and in psychoanalytic theory. By weaving together notions of the tertiary process as the process of interpretation that is found in Green, I can begin to gesture towards an understanding, with the help of

Bollas, of interpretation as a form of destruction that then gives rise to new, thicker, richer forms of thought. Bollas writes:

> The psychoanalytic process, however, sustains generative forms of destruction that break disturbances of thought and character. In very differing ways the method of free association and the act of interpretation are forces of destruction that decentre the analysand's psychic hegemony and the repeated sensibleness of the analyst's interpretive grasp [. . .]. Free association, for example, breaks up mental knots, just as it destroys the dream text. By deconstructing its parts into psychological divisions, each a turning point in a movement through differing memories and desires, it fragments the analyst's interpretations. (*MT*, 27)

The breaking up of thought via the work of free association is essential to the movement of both the process of psychoanalysis and of the subject's elaboration of self. The key is that free association and interpretation are, for Bollas, operating in different, almost opposed ways, even if they are both "forces of destruction." These "mental knots" could be seen as the moments that are jammed in consciousness. The crucial work of the unconscious, arising in the activity of free association, can destroy them. Importantly, Bollas sees that it is the collaborative work of the death instinct and the life instinct that "create new combinations of thought." It could be argued that he is rather Hegelian in his thinking that each new moment of thought, each new "psychic intensity," is the "result of the movement of prior lines of thought" (*MT*, 27). By looking at the ways in which Bollas discusses binding and unbinding alongside the notion of free association, we will better be able to understand this process.

I will start by considering in what ways Bollas takes up the terms *binding* and *unbinding*, and these might be used to build upon my existing formulation of these concepts. These terms find their counterparts in at least two aspects of Bollas's theory. On one hand, Bollas's investment in the linguistic elements of psychoanalysis is centred, for the most part, around the activity of free association. There is no simple equivalent to free association in Hegel, and I do not intend to build the case for one here. My interest, then, in spending a brief amount of time with this concept is to see how the terms *binding* and *unbinding* are found at work in Bollas's writings on free association.[40]

On the most basic level he sees that "free association unbinds meaning [. . .] while interpretation creates and binds meaning" (*MT*, 70).[41] How do we reconcile this idea of interpretation as a binding force with a treatment of it as a destructive, yet generative, activity? As we saw with Green, the tertiary process, the process of interpretation, was seen as a rebinding of sorts. Initiated by the spoken word of the analyst, interpretation was a re-creation of bonds that had been broken. Here with Bollas we can see that it is the activity of free association that is breaking the bonds of existing meaning and that it is interpretation that rebinds, thereby creating new meaning. However, what do we make of the fact that Bollas has also posited that interpretation is a "force of destruction"? This should recall the paradoxical bound/unbound condition of the unhappy consciousness; these parallels will be further developed shortly. It is important, however, to briefly address the concept of free association as found in Bollas so that I can more properly contextualise my line of argument.

Bollas sees that free association is a "play of elements" where the unconscious of *both* the analyst and analysand are engaged in, are collaborators in, the creation of "spoken objects." We see, then, that the work of free association is essential to the creation of the analytic genera. Furthermore, the to-ing and fro-ing that occurs in this method "becomes a new form of thinking" (*FA*, 65). We have seen that both free association itself and interpretation are seen by Bollas as forms of destruction. Holding the tension of interpretation as both a destructive (unbinding) and generative (binding) act, we see in Bollas that it is the transformation of the play of forces (linguistic and otherwise) between the analyst and the analysand into new meaning and new thought. Interpretation rests on the use by the analysand of the analyst as an object (this is elemental to the transference) and on the countertransference of the analyst to transform the patient's use of him into "meaning and language" (*FD*, 59).

Keeping in mind that for Bollas destruction is also inherently a generative act, we can draw our thinking back to the place of the life-and-death drives and see how they can now be found in Bollas's theory. He writes:

> This destruction is the joint work of the death instinct, breaking up links in order to reduce excitation, and the life instinct, creating new combinations of thought. If the thrill of consciousness is to create fresh unities and momentarily bind the unconscious in narrative, then the breaking of the texts of consciousness, by a work that endlessly displaces it, defeats that pleasure by a kind of fragmentation [. . .]. The dissemination of thought is destructive. Each psychic intensity is formed as the result of the movement of prior lines of thought conjoined by the evocative power of the object only to be dissolved by the force of displacement, condensation, substitution and symbolisation as constituent elements launch new lines of thought. (*MT*, 27)

Here we can note the shifts in terminology that can be tied back to the notion of unbinding. We see "destruction," "breaking up," "break," "displace[s]," "dissemination," "dissolved." Here, too, I locate traces of my earlier considerations of attraction and repulsion, of introjection and expulsion. Consciousness is thrilled to bind itself and the unconscious into a sense of wholeness. Yet, intrinsic to this binding is the capacity for its own destruction by the counter-force of the death drive. Although Bollas is clearly using the standard translation of *Trieb* as "instinct," and although we saw translations of Lacan and Hyppolite doing the same, it is important to my line of argument to use the translation of "drive." As argued in Chapter Three, this is because there is no use in making an argument for "instincts" in the *Phenomenology*, and my discussion so far of Force and the process of binding/unbinding is dependent on the correlation with the concepts of drive and Force. We find in the above passage an echo of the metapsychological underpinnings to the binding and unbinding process traced in Chapter Three, where the life drive (Eros) was the binding force and the death drive was the force behind unbinding. There is, too, Bollas continues on to say, a pleasure in destruction, the pleasure of opening up a new internal space. In other words, "Liberation comes through destruction" (*MT*, 29). Again, and it is something that once we have made it part of our own structure of knowing after having read Hegel, we can recall that it is only in "looking the negative in the face," that we "win our truth in our utter dismemberment" (*PS*, 19). This is at the heart of the Bacchanalian Revel. We are to be drunk with the pleasure of life and death as part of our struggle to become.

Ultimately, however, we are left with the same conclusion: the introduction of "new lines of thought." These lines of thought are comprised of the movement of previous shapes of knowing (to speak in Hegelian terms) and new shapes of knowing are added to them. Thus arise new shapes of consciousness. Simultaneously, it is the production of thought that allows for these new shapes of knowing to appear. For Bollas, it is the tension, the dialectic, between binding and unbinding, between knowing and unknowing, which creates the environment necessary for the production of thought. He writes:

> Free association is somewhere between knowing and unknowing, binding and unbinding. As words are used to speak one's mind, it is possible to consider this a form of knowing and a binding procedure. But as one is meant to say whatever comes to mind regardless of how silly or senseless it seems, this invokes a different principle: of unknowing and of unbinding. Perhaps the inspired thought, the deep reflection, the de-repression of a memory, emerges from an optimal state of tension between the binding and unbinding process. (*FD*, 66–67)

What we have here is language in the form of a speech act used to bind, and this binding through language is also a way of knowing. The articulation of one's self is a way of connecting to the external world. We can recall here Lacan's idea of "hooking" to the other via the medium of language. To articulate those parts of the self that are unknown, unthought, and unconscious is to surrender to the potential fear of a groundless state of being. It is to unbind one's self from one's self. We must come to grips with the complexity of knowing as a form of binding that is simultaneously an unbinding. What Bollas asserts is the potential for the dialectical tension between knowing and unknowing, between binding and unbinding, to create new forms of being, new shapes of knowing.

On the other hand, and not at all unrelated to the activity of free association, we also find correlative terms in his discussion of the activities of "dissemination" (read through the lens of the present discussion as a form of unbinding) and "cohesion" (read as a form of binding), as they are related to his consideration of interpretation and the search for truth and meaning in the analysis (*MT*, 33). The material of this interpretation is the language, the words expressed (spoken) in free association and in the analytic dialogue. Moreover, Bollas refers to the "dialectic of the unconscious" as constituted by the activities of "bringing together and cracking up" (read as versions of condensation and free association within Freud's language of dream interpretation). Units of meaning (constructed via condensation, cohesion, "bringing together," binding) hold within them the capacity for elaboration into myriad new and separate forms of meaning which will arise due to the generative destruction ("cracking up," dissemination, unbinding) that is inherent in this very search for meaning (*CU*, 53). As noted above, Bollas also relates the concept of binding to trauma. What is interesting about this mode of binding is that it "sponsors a type of psychic pain" and further that the pair of trauma and genera begin as "fundamental ego dispositions towards reality" (*BC*, 68).

Bollas sees the genera, then, as representing the process of generative unbinding, the working of the subject towards the freedom of self-elaboration, self-articulation. By taking into consideration the idea of the binding as trauma bringing with it psychic pain, we are made to add another layer to our understanding of the concept, one which draws attention to the potentially detrimental nature of binding that I will shortly link back to the figure of the unhappy consciousness. As we have been formulating it, binding can be harmful if the state of being bound becomes a permanent state, when the movement of becoming, which necessarily entails unbinding, ceases. It is possible to argue that the unhappy consciousness is a traumatised subject in many ways, even if the trauma is self-inflicted.

We see, most significantly, a direct correlation between Green's theories of binding and unbinding in Bollas with his work *Forces of Destiny*. Such an exact correspondence between the two lines of thought (Bollas's and Green's) allows for the terminological move made above. In *Forces of Destiny* he writes about the fabric of the analytic situation and the activity that he terms the "unknowing process." Bollas sets up the tradition from which he takes his lead regarding the notion of the "psychoanalyst as subject" and states that what is important to him is the "integrity of the analyst's relation to his own subjectivity" (*FD*, 53).[42] In order that new meaning is created, there must be an activity of "unknowing" that occurs in the analytic process. Bollas writes:

> Each analyst who comes to know his patient through a coherent analytical understanding of the patient must unknow him [. . .]. This unknowing process, perhaps akin to the concept of unbinding (see Green, 1987), is

> essential to any further generative knowing, and to any further symbolically complex binding. Unknowing is essential to the creation and (internal) maintenance of the interior analytic screen. That which has been known after a while must be assumed to be still available to both patient and analyst as they rid themselves of such organization of the unconscious in order to receive new unconscious communications, made possible through unknowing. In my view this establishes something of an essential dialectic, one that I think is at the heart of creativity in living, a dialectic between knowing (organizing, seeing, cohering) and unknowing (loosening, not perceiving). (*FD*, 63)

This is an important passage to unpack and see what links can be drawn to both Green and to our reading of Hegel. Bollas asserts that there is a state of unknowing that must be lived through and accepted as part of the dialectic of what he terms "creativity in living" in order that the process of knowing has movement and maintains its generative capability.

As the paradigm of "not knowing," perhaps we can recall the enactment of "unknowing" we witnessed in the figure of the unhappy consciousness. This stage of consciousness was the culmination of a series of bindings and unbindings that led to its pained existence (however temporary) as a consciousness that does not know its own self. It is a dual-natured being that does not know that both parts of its self are its self. Here we can revisit the activity of vanishing as allowing for what has been known to momentarily disappear. However, in Bollas's words, it necessarily "must be assumed to be still available" in the structure(s) of consciousness. I asserted that it was this very state of not knowing, of being unbound, that allowed for the shape of the unhappy consciousness, via the work of the counsellor, to slip into its new form in Reason. From this illustration I drew the conclusion that new states of consciousness, new forms of knowing, came about when there was a reflective gap created, when the unbound state was lived in and through. Here the work of Bollas can be used to further enrich an understanding of Hegel. Can negation, then, be considered as an act of unknowing, and in the psychoanalytic sphere, of a wilful unknowing, albeit perhaps on the level of the unconscious?

One of the differences, however, between the kind of unknowing we find in Bollas and that which we find in Hegel is that Bollas would not see this as forming a sense of "lack" in the subject, whereas for Hegel (and for Lacan at his most Hegelian) consciousness is forever attempting to fill this lack that it finds at its core with that which is "beyond," that which is always already out of reach. For Bollas, the elaboration of the self is not towards a single, unified end, since he does not believe that such a thing does or could possibly exist (and neither does Lacan for that matter). He, like Hegel, sees that the self is a constant process of splitting and that it is through the self's interaction with the outside world, with the world of objects that creates the many selves of which we are composed. He states: "I have hundreds, thousands, by my death millions, of sequential self states arising from the dialectical meetings between my self and the object world, which release me to some conscious knowing of my life" (*BC*, 29). Bollas chooses to not see these selves as part of an integrated whole, as Hegel does, but the action of the self's internal splitting with both itself, and the outside world of other/object might be read in a similar manner.

Bollas does, however, see the self as a "spirit" that is composed by its encounters with the world and additionally sees the objects/others that have been encountered as "spirits" that inhabit the self and become part of it, helping to compose its consciousness. He writes: "Being a character means that one is a spirit, that one conveys something in one's being which is barely identifiable as it moves through objects to create personal effects, but which is more deeply graspable when one's spirit moves through the mental life of the other, to leave its trace" (*BC*, 63). Reading through the lens of Hegel, we note that it is the self's interaction with the consciousness of the other that brings it a fuller understanding of its own being. We haunt and are haunted by objects and others. When he writes of "choosing" the external objects that elaborate the idiom, that all contribute to the development of the psychic genera, what Bollas is describing is the binding of the self to the external world. It is through these binds that the self is then created and sustained in this creation.

Another of the significant aspects of unbinding/unknowing that must take place in the analytic situation is that the analyst must unknow himself. This is part of what Bollas terms the "dialectic of difference," and he asks that along with taking himself as a subject, that the analyst allow for the destruction of his own knowledge. This form of unbinding "checks the binding work of interpretation" and shores the analytic process up against the dangers of interpretation as a form of resistance to the generative potential of the free associative process (*FD*, 66). This implies that it is the timing of the interpretation that is key and that interpretation, as binding, has the potential to hinder the process of development. In *The Freudian Moment* Bollas seems to move even more in favour of the process of free association and become even more stringently critical of interpretation as a potentially dangerous destructive activity. One is increasingly struck when reading through Bollas's body of work by the difficulty of knowing when interpretation as a generative form of destruction gives way to the destruction of the process itself, thus losing its generative, productive capacity.

This is a difficulty that Bollas seems to chart through his texts both explicitly and implicitly. He argues in *The Freudian Moment* that if the analyst is simply poised "on the edge of his seat just waiting to make a here-and-now transference interpretation," then "he will not only never hear the free associations, he will destroy them." If the analyst is not listening with an open mind, but with his interpretation at the ready, then he is interfering with his own process, and will, more damagingly, "prevent the analysand from free thinking." The consequence of this prevention would be that the analyst would not be able to uncover what Bollas terms "a logic of sequence" that lies buried beneath the Freudian "chain of ideas" that is the product of the free association.[43] This is because, Bollas argues, unconscious thinking is revealed in the "links between narrative units," the "caesura" in which "one finds the logical possibilities." Put another way, it is "in and through these gaps that the logic of thought occurs."[44]

If the analyst resists making a "here-and-now" interpretation (to use Bollas's most current language) and leaves himself open to the state of unknowing, what this destruction of established knowledge and what the following of the "caesura" allows is the creation of a "space that now contains not knowing, but recognizes the presence of an unthought knowledge that may find its way to knowing" (*FD*, 65). Again we see here a space being created in which both unknowing and knowing are held in suspension, subsisting together and together forming part of the movement towards new forms of knowing. Thus is introduced one of the key concepts for Bollas, the "unthought known." This comes into thought and is expressed "through the experience and the interpretation of the transference and countertransference" (*SO*, 9). This "unthought known" is simply the knowledge that exists in us (in the primary repressed unconscious) but has yet to be thought/articulated. The analyst must make himself available as a "transformational object" so that this unthought known can come to its expression for "mutual consideration" (*SO*, 234). Free association is, for Bollas, the very movement of the "unthought known." Herein is encapsulated our otherness (*FA*, 28).

If we can follow Minolli and Tricoli's assertion that the notion of the third arose with regards to the problematics of the transference/countertransference and Bollas's placing the emergence of the "unthought known" in the activity of these interactions, then it can be posited that the material of the unthought known is woven into the fabric of the third. John Muller asserts that Bollas's "unthought known" can be likened to the Lacanian category of the Real. In that the unthought known exists outside of language until it comes into its expression, I would agree. But isn't it the point that the Lacanian Real can never exist in the Symbolic? It could be argued, then, and it might seem an obvious point, that once the "unthought known" finds its movement in free association, and thus emerges in language, it necessarily transforms into a new form of knowing.[45]

HEGEL, PSYCHOANALYSIS, AND SHAPES OF KNOWING

Although I have been referring to them throughout this chapter, let me take a moment to address the concept of "shapes of knowing" (*Gestalten des Wissen*) in Hegel. I argued that one of the most important aspects of Hegel's thought for André Green was his investment in describing the "development of the figures of consciousness" (*WN*, 41). Also recall that for Hegel the movement of consciousness involves the shifting, the transitioning, from one shape of knowing to a new, more advanced shape of knowing. This was articulated most specifically in the shift from consciousness to self-consciousness that I traced in Chapter Two. In this transition I argued that moments of otherness, although vanished, subsisted and were preserved in the new shapes that followed. This designation of "shapes" of consciousness is quite striking and crucial to an understanding of how we can read the notions of psychic genera and thirdness together with Hegel's philosophy.

Michael Forster argues that Hegel's designation comes from his view of consciousness taking the form of genus and species. Forster writes, "These different species of consciousness are what Hegel in the *Phenomenology* calls 'shapes of consciousness.'" Further, Forster states, "It is Hegel's idea that what defines a shape of consciousness and sets it apart from other shapes is always a set of distinctive conceptions of self, objectivity, and representation which at the same time amount to distinctive concepts of them" and that the distinctive conceptions are interdependent.[46] Each moment of consciousness, then, has a particular structure that contains within it, "preserved," the structures of all previous shapes of knowing even if the previous moment has itself vanished. Let us quickly revisit this passage in Hegel:

> If we consider this new shape of knowing, the knowing of itself, in relation to that which preceded, viz. the knowing of an other, then we see that though this other has indeed vanished, its moments have at the same time no less been preserved, and the loss consists in this, that here they are present as they are in themselves. (*PS*, 104–05)

What is crucial here is the very notion of preservation. Hegel further writes that all of these moments that seemed abstract, this other to whom consciousness did not yet know how it was related, are no longer simply empty essences but are moments of self-consciousness. They are the structure of self-consciousness itself. Without consciousness' ability to hold these psychic structures (if we might begin to blur the terminological lines between Hegel and psychoanalysis) within itself, new shapes of knowing would have no depth, no richness, no history. The texture of self-consciousness is dependent upon this preservation and on the movement of consciousness through these shapes. Stephen Houlgate also maintains that the new shapes of consciousness do not replace the previous shape but rather that the "later shape of consciousness takes up the *truth* that is disclosed by the previous shape" and that the movement of the *Phenomenology* is not simply "from one form of object to another, but in each new shape of consciousness preserves what has been learned up to that point."[47] It is not only shapes of knowing but also shapes of Spirit and shapes of consciousness that Hegel wishes to describe. It is the task of the *Phenomenology*, on one level, to delineate the movement and describe the fabric of these structures.[48] These transitions are, according to Houlgate, a logical necessity for consciousness, and as it moves through the different shapes, consciousness gains a "richer understanding" of its own truth and process. This is the notion behind Hegel's "education of consciousness" (*PS*, 50).[49]

I am examining within the context of Bollas's work how, through language, the formation of the analytic genera (Green's analytic third) gives rise to new shapes of knowing and how these new shapes, objects without a material form, become psychic structures borne by both the analyst and analysand. It is key to recall here my formulation of the analyst as a vanishing mediator and to add to this understanding this third, this analytic genera, as a vanishing, mediating entity. In a manner of speaking, both the space of the analytic session and the analyst vanish, but part of the work is to accept these vanishings as part of the process, much like the consciousness of the *Phenomenology* had to accept its own set of vanishings.

Let us just pause for a moment to touch again on the importance of the recentring of the unhappy consciousness that was worked towards in Chapter Two and how it relates to the "shapes of knowing" element I have just introduced. In unhappy consciousness we find that it is the shape, the form that gives birth to what is the most important shape of all for Hegel, that of Spirit. The rest of the shapes of consciousness that we have dealt with (stoic, sceptic, lord, and bondsman) stand on the outside, witnesses to this birth, but they are also inhabited by the unhappy consciousness. We can recall here, though, John Burbidge's assertion that "absolute spirit is not a singular entity but a dynamic interplay, as many agents reciprocally interact."[50] In a sense, although the stoic and the sceptic are located on the periphery, their presence, their interaction in this scene, is crucial to the birth of Spirit, even if it is unhappy consciousness that experiences the pain of labour. Hegel writes:

> These forms [. . .], the person as *thought* in Stoicism, and the unstable restlessness of the Sceptical consciousness, constitute the [audience or] periphery of shapes which stands impatiently expectant round the birthplace of Spirit as it becomes self-consciousness [. . .]. The grief and longing of the Unhappy Self-consciousness which permeates them all is their centre and the common birth-pang of its emergence—the simplicity of the pure Notion, which contains those forms as its moments. (*PS*, 456–57)

For Hegel, the state of the unhappy consciousness, in its grief and longing, is essential for Spirit's emergence. Without the reflective gap created in its self-splitting despair, and without the simultaneous preservation of hope and desire for unity that exist in the shape of the unhappy consciousness, Spirit itself would not be born.

Furthermore, recalling two additional moments from "The Unhappy Consciousness" episode will help to illuminate the connections I am attempting to draw between the creation of the self as an object and the formation of new shapes of knowing/thinking. Taking them chronologically is key because the second of the moments, in Hegelian fashion, resolves the first. We can recall that the unhappy consciousness had to "surrender" to the experience of mediation, to the work of the counsellor. In doing so, it "divested itself of its 'I,'" consequently turning its "immediate self-consciousness into a *Thing*, into an *objective* existence" (*PS*, 137). In this chapter I have been attempting, in some senses, to imagine the predicament of the unhappy consciousness finding a resolution in the analytic setting. We can recall that the unhappy consciousness turns itself into an object and recall that Walter Davis sees this as the way out when he writes: "Objectification is a necessary release from inner pain; it prevents a suicidal enclosure of unhappy consciousness in its own inwardness. Unable to master itself, subject can still develop its possibilities by externalising them."[51] This is, then, another way of looking at the "object" that the third potentially is. In the analytic space, it is necessary for the analysand to turn itself into an object, to externalise itself in order to move through and beyond the state of painful "enclosure" that it might find itself in. What becomes important is what this object affords consciousness and how consciousness is able to *use* its existence in the form of this object.

The very last moment of the unhappy consciousness episode is one that was quoted in full in Chapter Two, so let us pause here now to acknowledge that for Hegel, when consciousness has become an object for itself, it creates the perspective it desperately needed in order to see that the power of its reality was in its possession. Hegel writes, "But in this object, in which it finds that its own action and being, as being that of this *particular* consciousness, are being and action *in themselves*, there has arisen for consciousness the idea of *Reason*, of the certainty that, in its particular individuality, it has being absolutely *in itself*, or is all reality" (*PS*, 138). Once consciousness is in the realm of Reason, we see that the fundamental purpose of entering such a state is to reinforce the paradoxical truth that the unhappy consciousness learned: true Freedom comes in being bound to the world and to the other. Self-sufficiency, as attempted by the stoic and the sceptic, is not enough.[52] It is not enough, Hegel says, to know that "*I am I,* my object and my essence is *I.*" We need Reason to "sanction" the "other certainty, viz. that there is for me an 'other'; that an other than 'I' is object and essence for me, or, in that I am object and essence to myself, I am only so by drawing back from the 'other' altogether, and taking my place as an actuality *alongside* it" (*PS*, 141).

It could be read that the true lesson of the *Phenomenology* is not necessarily that Reason reigns supreme but that it supports (cognitively, structurally) the essentiality of intersubjective relations. As Jean-Luc Nancy writes,

> If self-consciousness kept itself within the immediate immobility of an 'I = I,' it would not even be *consciousness*. The simple position of the I is an abstraction. On the contrary, the concrete awakening of the I is its awakening to the world and by the world—the world of alterity in general.[53]

For Hegel, even if this other/object is to vanish (the various possibilities of which we have traced), it is still an "essence," an ontological necessity, for this I. There is a certain peace that comes with this understanding. Although this sense of peace is but a moment, and it, too, will vanish, it does not disappear. Instead it remains a new shape of knowing for consciousness and part of its very being. Hegel also offers that a certain tranquillity comes from the acknowledgement that pure consciousness is a process that is at once "the restless movement to and fro through all its moments, aware of an otherness which is superseded in the act of grasping it" and the paradoxically related knowledge of its own unity (*PS*, 143). Each element holds the other as other, and there is a constant shifting between the two states where each state at its given time is the "object" of consciousness. But crucially, for Hegel,

> consciousness, however, as essence, is this whole process itself, of passing out of itself as simple category into a singular individual, into the object, and of contemplating this process in the object, nullifying the object as distinct [from it], *appropriating* it as its own, and proclaiming itself as this certainty of being all reality, of being both itself and its object. (*PS*, 143–44)

The concept of the third as I have been working through it and the interaction between the subjects in the analytic situation can be thought of alongside this Hegelian notion of consciousness as process.

The ultimate challenge for the consciousness of the *Phenomenology of Spirit* and therefore for us, its readers, is to fully accept the groundlessness of the self. This is also to accept that the very ground of understanding, Force, is groundlessness itself.[54] By this I mean that Force is always movement, it is always expression, it is only alive in being solicited by another Force. Force exists outside of thought, it only knows itself, is only given meaning by being "recognised" by another Force. Thus, groundlessness means that we are dependent on the other for grounding us in the world. In a sense, it is in the moments of crisis, represented in my investigation by the figure of the unhappy consciousness, that we recognise, most profoundly, this dependency. Jean-Luc Nancy articulates the generative potentials of this state of being:

> Right at misfortune, right at my misfortune, I recognize myself separated and finite, shut in, reduced or reducible to the very point of my pain. To know oneself as such a one is not an abstract knowledge; it is to be, concretely, before the insufficiency and incompletion of self and, by this very lack, to be in relation to the other, to all of the other and all the others that I lack; it is to be already in movement, to become.[55]

As Nancy writes, this is a concrete form of being and to condemn the *Phenomenology* to the realm of the abstract is to not fully give credence to this ontological and epistemological reality.

We have also seen that Force gives Understanding its consistency, it provides it with its method of preservation, its medium of survival. Whether consciousness has caused these vanishings or simply must witness them, when faced with the vanishing of certainty, of ground, of moments of knowing, it has no real choice but to know and believe that these vanishings are not disappearances but are moments of transformation. They are invisible, but will be known and recognised in future manifestations as new shapes of knowing and being. We can also think here of Bollas's form of unknowing as a state of groundlessness that must be accepted. The creation or appearance of the third is absolutely necessary to escape the stasis of groundlessness, but the moment of groundlessness itself is essential to the process of becoming. In other words, as Peter Dews notes, "For Hegel the primordial encounter of consciousness is inherently unstable."[56] The third helps in the acceptance of the vanishing moments, in the acceptance that these vanishing moments are vital.

This acceptance of the perpetual state of groundlessness involves, it can be argued, accepting oneself as a "living thing," as Life, as a process. Hans-Georg Gadamer offers a brilliant way of addressing what it would mean to accept this as our reality:

> We have no choice but to admit that the unsensed, supersensible world of the universal represents only an aspect of that which really is. The true reality is that of life, which moves itself within itself [. . .]. In the progression of the forms of knowing which the *Phenomenology* traverses, an enormous step is made here, where the being of what lives is grasped. What lives is not an instance of law or the composite result of laws bearing on each other, rather it is turned towards itself or it relates itself: it behaves. It is a self. There is an enduring truth here. For however far modern physiology might go in unlocking the secrets of organic life, in knowing what lives we will never cease to make a turnabout in our thinking of that which, as the play of forces, lawfully determines organic nature: we will think of it, conversely, as the behavior of the organism and 'understand' this organism as living.[57]

Gadamer has rather succinctly and eloquently tied up the various theoretical threads for me here. Each of these "forms of knowing," a psychoanalytic model for which I have worked through in this chapter, are the ways in which the self knows itself as a living thing. It appears that Gadamer is saying that we are not meant to think of the play of Forces as laws that are to be followed or mysteries that need solving. They are simply what allow us to understand ourselves as a living self.

CONCLUSION

Starting in Green's work and moving through Bollas's, I have argued that in exploring what an element of the third might be, we are pushing our reading of Hegel even further. I am positing that not only is the other necessary but also that not even the relationship between the two is enough. I started out from the premise that self-sufficiency could only take us so far and to this can add that in order for the intersubjective relationship to actually be productive there needs to be a third element created, recognised, and utilised. This is the ultimate power of the third: it makes intersubjectivity a living thing.

Finally, I have argued for a two-pronged understanding of this third. On the one hand, I have been arguing that it is an object, created out of language and out of the interaction between the unconscious of the analyst and analysand and that it belongs in some sense to both but is never fully owned by either of them. This object corresponds to the idea of "shapes" of knowing and of consciousness that we briefly read out of the *Phenomenology*. On the other hand, I have been arguing towards an understanding of this third as a space created in the analytic situation that is created out of the work between the two members of the analytic dialectic. On a spatial level, my exploration of the concept of vanishing in Hegel finds resonance here. Of particular interest to me was the way in which reflective gaps were opened up between moments of knowing. The reflective gaps, caused by the activities of both vanishing and negation, allow consciousness to slip into its new shape while preserving, but not being dominated by, the previous shapes of knowing.

Conclusion

> These are the moments of which the reconciliation of Spirit with its own consciousness proper is composed; by themselves they are single and separate, and it is solely their spiritual unity that constitutes the power of this reconciliation. The last of these moments is, however, necessarily this unity itself, and, as is evident, it binds them all into itself (*PS*, 482).

> The philosophical subject, in effect, can in no case give up the privilege of its transcendental solipsism. Which is why it was necessary to wait for psychoanalysis to establish favourable conditions for the flowering of this alterity and for the revelation of its conflictual nature (*WN*, 42).

André Green suggests that in order to examine how a speculative philosophy of consciousness might be actualised, it is necessary to let it flower in another context. In this book, to follow the metaphor, I have planted the seeds of particular aspects of Hegelian thought and have embarked on an investigation of how they might grow within the context of psychoanalysis. Throughout, I have attempted to show the way in which the process of becoming for Hegel is, at its base, modelled on a play of Forces. Once traced through 'Force and the Understanding,' this play of Forces first manifests itself in the realm of consciousness with the birth of self-consciousness. We find it gives rise to the burgeoning knowledge that consciousness has regarding the relationship between its internal existence and the external world. Starting with this basic assumption, I have argued that at the root of an understanding of intersubjectivity as drawn from the *Phenomenology of Spirit*, there must be an understanding of the role of Force. Ultimately, the model of Force created in this book, and the readings performed via psychoanalytic theory, enable a rereading of the entire *Phenomenology* as an elaboration of how a theory of "relation" plays itself out in the various realms that Hegel moves through. A "relationship" cannot be comprised of a single Force; it is, by its very nature, a play of Forces. It is for this reason that the Force paradigm persists. Although the scope of my study meant that I did not push through Reason and into the second half of the *Phenomenology*, I can say that we are now ready to do so.

I designated Force as a model for the concepts of recognition and desire, thus representing that which is binding and generative in the relation between consciousnesses. Moreover, I argued that its role as both an ontological and epistemological category in the *Phenomenology* is often overlooked. If considered in this light, the further importance of Force lies in the paradigm it offers of the fundamental groundlessness that persists in the *Phenomenology* and in consciousness as Hegel describes it. As a model for relation, Force offers us a way of understanding how it is that that which is other than us, be it an object or another subject, gives us grounding. The "motionless tautology of: 'I am I'" is exploded by Hegel himself if we take Force into account (*PS*, 105). Force allows us to understand on another level what Hegel means by the notion of the "'I' that is 'We' and 'We' that is 'I'" and thus gives us a model for understanding the elaboration of consciousness into self-consciousness (*PS*, 110).

Consciousness, I have interpreted, is structured much like Force in that we are called forth into experience, solicited by the "other" and by the outer world much in the same way that Force is called forth, becomes Force, only by another Force. Only in actively recognising this solicitation and being recognised in turn are we truly living. In the figure of the unhappy consciousness we witnessed an illustration of what the breakdown in this play of Forces would look like and located the remarkable resolution that Hegel offers to remedy, if only momentarily, this collapse. We found the unhappy consciousness as proof of the failure of blind belief in complete self-sufficiency. With the lord and bondsman, we witnessed the root of the binding process, the birth of intersubjectivity. The stoic and the sceptic were each a moment in the experiment of consciousness to see if, indeed, it actually needed this other which caused it so much suffering. Here we witnessed the activity of unbinding, where consciousness attempted to unbind itself both from the external world and from its own process of becoming. Such unbinding culminated in the figure of the unhappy consciousness, and it was only with the intervention of the third consciousness, the "mediator as counsellor" that the unhappy consciousness was able to rebind itself to the other and to its own process. Yet, I also argued that this breakdown was necessary, if utilised, in that it created a reflective gap from which consciousness, when it emerged, was able to gain a new level of understanding. It is essential that we "unknow" ourselves, as we learned with the help of Christopher Bollas. We are to live in and through the caesura, the breaks in our own movement.

Alongside Force I also highlighted the concept of Life and argued that there is very much a movement towards Life, a sort of Eros, that is woven into the *Phenomenology*. It exists along with the movement of negation, which in itself is the "energy of thought" and thus a generative, affirmative action. Essential to this living is the recognition and acceptance of the moments of transition and of transformation, traced in my book as moments of vanishing. I have argued that a transformation occurs in the activity of vanishing that alters the shape of consciousness by giving it a new moment of being, a new form of knowing. Given the scope of my book, I was not able to pursue the concept of Life in a comprehensive way, and it seems there is much still to be discovered in tracing the connections between Hegel's *Phenomenology*, the *Philosophy of Mind*, and *Philosophy of Nature* that will illuminate Hegel's ontology even further.

In Hegel's introduction of the Third (*das Dritte*), the "mediator as counsellor," I located the first designation of the vanishing mediator. Following Frederic Jameson, I posited that this vanishing mediator was responsible for the "exchange of energies" between two entities. Thus, I was able to combine my discussion of an energetics or economy of Force in Hegel with a model drawn from psychoanalytic theory. It did not prove satisfactory, however, to confine this model of the vanishing mediator to the idea of a subject (e.g. an analyst) and thus, in tracing the concept of the third through psychoanalytic literature, beginning with Green and culminating in Christopher Bollas, I located a surprising number of ways in which this vanishing mediator could be understood as the third. The complexities of both the vanishing mediator and the third deserve careful consideration because they both allow us a way of understanding the complexities that reside at the very heart of intersubjective relations. I also argued that, in a sense, we as readers of the *Phenomenology* are vanishing mediators that allow for the text to work and for the enacting of its content.

As the product of the intersubjective analytic situation, the third as vanishing mediator was variously understood as a transformative, transitional *space* and as an "object" that is created by both subjects (and their unconscious) but is not really owned by either. Both a product of language, and of a play of forces, this third, whether consciously or not, is incorporated by both members of the analytic pair and functions to bring new moments of knowledge. In this way, the pair is bound by its mutual creation and by the work of production. In response to one of the questions posed by Lacan and Hyppolite with which I began my book, we might say that neither the philosopher nor the psychoanalyst can be "beyond" the discussion of the "we." In truth, both are bound to the creation of the third term, and both are forms of the vanishing mediator.

This model is not confined to the analytic setting alone but can be used for understanding the way in which all subjects are bound to the other and to their own process of becoming. Our existence, we might say, is dependent upon our intersubjective relations, which draw forth our intrapsychic life. This is not to say that our truth, or our meaning, is solely constituted by the other. Yet, in being recognised and in recognising in return, we are able to elaborate our own process of becoming. More than that, though, I have argued that not only is self-sufficiency not enough but that even the intersubjective relationship is not enough. It requires this third in order to be a truly living, generative interaction.

The resonance between the work of Green and Bollas resides on one level in their commitment to working through and beyond Freudian theory to understand the figure of the analyst as a subject. Thus they have proven to be a suitable pair to sit on the other side of the dialectical divide from my reading of Hegel and have provided the ground for the consideration of intersubjectivity in the analytic setting. Both have also supplied us with theories of interpretation as paradoxically both generative and destructive. They have given us grounding for elaborating upon our theory of binding and for the place of the third, even if it came in a different guise in Bollas's theory. Through the work of André Green, we were able to understand this tripartite process of binding from the angle of psychoanalytic theory. I drew on Freud's 'Project for a Scientific Psychology' in order to provide a foundation for such an economic argument and moved through 'Beyond the Pleasure Principle' and his paper 'Negation' via the guides Hyppolite and Lacan. In so doing, I found resonance in psychoanalytic theory with the theories of the origin of thought and judgement regarding the internal and external world that we were drawing out of Hegel's concept of Force. I was then able to draw the links between the origin of thought structures and shapes of knowing. By looking at this aspect of Hegel's thought via the lens of psychoanalytic theory, my book has opened up a way of seeing the *Phenomenology* in a different light and the process of becoming that it offers. Much more work has yet to be done with studies concentrating on the crossover between Hegel's philosophy and psychoanalytic theory. It is incredibly fruitful territory, and a topic such as temporality, which I hinted at but was not able to tackle, would be a starting place.

For now, the conclusion I have reached that ties my many threads of argument together is that Hegel did not mean that to reach the height of Spirit was to reach the *end* and thus that the attainment of Absolute Knowing was a point at which all work, all process, could cease. Of course, a stage, a *moment*, called Absolute Knowing is possible and is reached in the *Phenomenology*. Yet, to experience this moment is arguably to reach a place where the "movement returns into itself"; it is "the circle that presupposes its beginning and reaches it only at the end" (*PS*, 488). Robert Solomon writes of Absolute Knowing that it does not mean "knowing everything," but, rather, it means "recognizing one's limitations" and that this "itself can be a liberating, even exhilarating vision."[1] It is in this manner that I have been discussing the paradoxical state of finding one's freedom in recognising that we are bound to an other. Our "limitation" is that we are not entirely self-sufficient. Yet, this is not a cause of despair but rather the way out.[2] Jean-Luc Nancy offers another way of viewing the state of "absolute thought" that resonates with our formulation of the binding process. He writes: "It is the moment of the absolute thought as such: as absolution, that is as unbinding, detachment, and laying bare—not as absolutization. It is the absolution of separation and of relation: everything is at the same time separated and in relation, everything is only separated and in relation. It is this absolution that Hegel named 'history.'"[3] The absolute is not a totality, but it is the moment when we are at our most vulnerable. In a sense, it is the moment when we recognise that we are simultaneously bound and unbound, that our existence *is* relation.

In one of the final passages of the *Phenomenology*, Hegel writes of History as the one side of the Becoming of Spirit and the *Subject* as the other side:

> Thus absorbed in itself, it is sunk in the night of its self-consciousness; but in that night its vanished outer existence is preserved and this transformed existence—the former one, but now reborn of Spirit's knowledge—is the new existence, a new world and a new shape of Spirit. In the immediacy of this new existence the Spirit has to start afresh to bring itself to maturity, as if, for it, all that preceded were lost and it had learned nothing from the experience of the earlier Spirits. But recollection, the *inwardizing*, of that experience, has preserved it and is the inner being, and in fact the higher form of the substance. (*PS*, 492)[4]

Now, throughout my study I have taken the option implicitly offered by Hegel to read the *Phenomenology* at the level of consciousness for the way in which the text charts the development of this consciousness, rather than at the level of universal History.[5] Clearly for Hegel, these two levels are not to be seen in isolation, as one does not exist without the other, but a choice can be made to read with a focus on the particular, rather than on the universal in order to first understand how it is that this particular functions. Thus, I am here reading "History" as representative of the history of the individual subject.[6] What Hegel is saying is that all previous shapes of knowing, the moments of existence, are preserved and made of Spirit, of consciousness in its form of Spirit, what it is. When we need to, and if we are able to, we can access these inner states in order to continue on in the process of becoming.

This would be Bollas's stance, too, I think, if we recall his formulation of the evocation of the self and the elaboration of one's life as a constant interaction with the world of others and objects and the notion that the self draws on its inner experiences in order to create the "genera" so important to this elaboration. What the *Phenomenology of Spirit* does, ultimately, is train consciousness, train us as readers; it equips us with the tools we need to accept that there is no end. Yet, this is not a "bad infinity." We simply realise that groundlessness is a perpetual state, that we are simultaneously bound and free. So, too, we could say does the analysand. We reach the end (of analysis, of the text), but we are not finished; we are only more competent to carry on living.

Notes

NOTES TO THE INTRODUCTION

1. Henry Sussman, *The Hegelian Aftermath: Readings in Hegel, Kierkegaard, Freud, Proust, and James* (Baltimore: John Hopkins University, 1982), p. 59.
2. Jean Hyppolite, 'Hegel's Phenomenology and Psychoanalysis,' in *New Studies in Hegel's Philosophy*, trans. by Albert Richer, ed. by Warren E. Steinkraus (New York: Holt, Rinehart & Winston, 1971), pp. 57–70 (p. 70, n. 26).
3. André Green, *The Work of the Negative* (London: Free Association Books, 1999), p. 1. Further references to this edition are given after quotations in the text, abbreviated as *WN*.
4. Although Lacan's relationship with Hegel's philosophy is mentioned in many texts, a handful of which I will soon touch upon, for the most succinct account from the point of view of an intellectual biography, see Elisabeth Roudinesco *Jacques Lacan & Co.: A History of Psychoanalysis in France 1925–1985*, trans. by Jeffrey Melman (Chicago: University of Chicago Press, 1990) and Elisabeth Roudinesco, *Jacques Lacan: An Outline of a Life and a History of a System of Thought*, trans. by Barbara Bray (Cambridge: Polity Press, 1999), pp. 61–107.
5. Aside from his role as translator of the *Phenomenology of Spirit* into French and his highly influential *Genesis and Structure of Hegel's Phenomenology* (Chicago: Northwestern University Press, 1997), Hyppolite wrote what can be considered ground-breaking pieces on the subject of Hegel and psychoanalysis. The first was 'The Human Situation in the Hegelian Phenomenology,' in *G.W.F. Hegel: Critical Assessments*, trans. by John O'Neill, ed. by Robert Stern, 4 vols (London: Routledge, 1993), II, pp. 400–12; also found in Jean Hyppolite, *Studies in Marx and Hegel*, trans. by John O'Neill (London: Heinemann, 1969), pp. 153–68, and the second is the lecture noted.
6. Jacques Derrida, 'Force and Signification,' in *Writing and Difference*, trans. by Alan Bass (Chicago: Chicago University Press, 1978), p. 4.
7. Arkady Plotnitsky, *In the Shadow of Hegel: Complementarity, History, and the Unconscious* (Gainsville: University Press of Florida, 1993), p. 210.
8. *Hegel's Introduction to the Lectures to the History of Philosophy*, trans. T. M. Knox and A. V. Miller (Oxford: Oxford University Press, 1985), pp. 27–28.
9. Robert Stern, *Hegelian Metaphysics* (Oxford: Oxford University Press, 2009), p. 4. Although Stern traces the history of discussion surrounding Hegel and metaphysics throughout his book, his Introduction and the bibliographical references found therein are particularly key for anyone interested in the subject and details the intellectual field as it stands up to the first decade of the twenty-first century. See in particular 'Introduction: How is Hegelian Metaphysics Possible?' pp. 1–45.

10. I am grateful to an anonymous reviewer of the book for the insight that allowed me to craft my argument in such a manner.
11. Plotnitsky, *In the Shadow of Hegel*, p. 210.
12. For a prime example of the way in which theory has tended to ignore Hegel's anticipation of Nietzsche's "play of forces," see Gilles Deleuze, *Nietzsche and Philosophy*, trans. by Hugh Tomlinson (London: Athlone Press, 1983).
13. Herbert Marcuse, *Hegel's Ontology and the Theory of Historicity*, trans. by Seyla Benhabib (Cambridge, MA: MIT Press, 1987), p. 309.
14. Judith Butler, *The Psychic Life of Power* (Stanford: Stanford University Press, 1997), p. 31. In the chapter of her work devoted to a discussion of Hegel and the unhappy consciousness, Butler seeks to reinsert a reading of the body back into the "Lordship and Bondage" episode and further into the unhappy consciousness to discuss the ethical and political implications embedded there. Although my reading is not as specifically oriented to the "body" itself, I will later show how her reading of the "fashioning of an object" out of the self was important to my interpretation. My interest lies more in a linguistic and psychic fashioning than that of a physical body. However, Butler's links amongst Hegel, Freud, and Nietzsche along these lines were very useful.
15. Alexander Kojève, *Introduction to the Reading of Hegel*, trans. by James Nichols, ed. by Allan Bloom, (Ithaca: Cornell University Press, 1980). The influence Kojève's lectures on Hegel of 1933–39 had on thinkers such as Lacan and his contemporaries has been well-documented. See Roudinesco, *Jacques Lacan & Co.*, pp. 134–47; Peter Dews, *Logics of Disintegration* (London: Verso, 2007), pp. 64–66, p. 304, n. 26. See especially works on 'French Hegel' noted below.
16. Robert R. Williams, *Hegel's Ethics of Recognition* (Berkeley: University of California Press, 1997), p. 10. See Chapter Fifteen, pp. 364–412, for his treatment of the impact Kojève's "misleading" and "distorting" interpretation has had on twentieth-century philosophy and theory and the manner in which Kojève's Hegel became the Hegel of "closure" and "anti-life" in a way that was not true to Hegel's own thought.
17. Butler, *Psychic Life*, p. 31.
18. G.W.F. Hegel, *Phenomenology of Spirit*, trans. by A.V. Miller (Oxford: Oxford University Press, 1977), p. 138. Further references to this edition are given after quotations in the text, abbreviated as *PS*. Butler does note the important presence of this mediator but does not develop its full potential as crucial for the liberation of consciousness (*Psychic Life*, p. 51).
19. When I perform a close reading of the "Self-Consciousness" section, I will refer to the "lord" and "bondsman" using Miller's translation. Otherwise, I refer to the "master/slave dialectic," as this is the most common language used to refer to the episode.
20. Bruce Baugh, *French Hegel: From Surrealism to Postmodernism* (New York: Routledge, 2003), p. 4. Unlike Kojève's lectures, Wahl's seminal text has yet to be published in English—bar a short excerpt from *The Unhappy Consciousness in the Philosophy of Hegel*, in *G.W.F. Hegel: Critical Assessments*, trans. by Rodney Northey, II, pp. 284–310— which has curtailed his influence.
21. Judith Butler, *Subjects of Desire: Hegelian Reflections in Twentieth-Century France* (New York: Columbia University Press, 1999).
22. Michael Roth, *Knowing and History: Appropriations of Hegel in Twentieth Century France* (Ithaca: Cornell University Press, 1988), p. 26.
23. Barry Cooper, *The End of History: An Essay on Modern Hegelianism* (Toronto: University of Toronto Press, 1984), p. 4.
24. Robert Sinnerbrink, *Understanding Hegelianism* (Stocksfield: Acumen Press, 2007), pp. 123–70 (pp. 126–27, 130–33).

25. Hyppolite, *Genesis and Structure*, p. 190.
26. Roth, *Knowing and History*, p. 39.
27. Paul Ricoeur, *Freud and Philosophy: An Essay on Interpretation*, trans. by Denis Savage (New Haven, CT: Yale University Press, 1990). See in particular 'Book III: Dialectic,' pp. 344–551. Ricoeur's text was first published in English in 1970, and there are two articles of note that were published in roughly the same era. The first is Darrell Christensen, 'Hegel's Phenomenological Analysis and Freud's Psychoanalysis,' *International Philosophical Quarterly*, 8:3 (1968), 356–78, and the second is Clark Butler's 'Hegel and Freud: A Comparison,' *Philosophy and Phenomenological Research*, 36:4 (1976), 506–22. Butler notes that at the time there is almost no work on the convergence between Hegelian philosophy and psychoanalytic theory, but cites Ricoeur and Christensen as two thinkers engaged with the topic.
28. Ricoeur, *Freud and Philosophy*, p. 62.
29. Malcolm Bowie in *The Vitality of Objects: Exploring the Work of Christopher Bollas*, ed. by Joseph Scalia (London: Continuum, 2002), p. xvi.
30. See in particular Slavoj Žižek, *Tarrying With The Negative: Kant, Hegel And The Critique Of Ideology* (Durham: Duke University Press. 1993); *The Indivisible Remainder: An Essay on Schelling and Related Matters* (London: Verso, 1996); a collection of his essays, *Interrogating the Real*, ed. by Rex Butler and Scott Stephens (London: Continuum, 2005), Sections I and II, pp. 19–246; and 'Lacan as a Reader of Hegel,' *Lacanian Ink*, 27 (2006).
31. At last count there were at least sixteen critical introductions dedicated to his thinking, most recently Sean Sheehan's, *Žižek: A Guide for the Perplexed* (London: Continuum, 2012). See for particularly helpful works Sara Kay's *Žižek: A Critical Introduction* (Cambridge: Polity, 2003) and Tony Myers' *Slavoj Žižek (Routledge Critical Thinkers)* (London: Routledge, 2003). Due to the broad range of material that Žižek's own thinking engages with, from philosophy to psychoanalysis, film studies and pop culture, religion, politics (and so on), I will not here be able to catalogue the breadth of articles and books in which he may be featured or even indeed which he has written, aside from those I directly engage with.
32. Slavoj Žižek, *Less Than Nothing: Hegel and the Shadow of Dialectical Materialism* (London: Verso, 2012). See Part III, Section 8, 'Lacan as a Reader of Hegel' (pp. 507–51) and Section 11, 'Negation of the negation: Lacan Versus Hegel? (pp. 787–94).
33. Alenka Zupančič, *Why Psychoanalysis?: Three Interventions* (Uppsala, Sweden: Aarhus University Press, 2008). See in particular Part 2, 'Freedom and Cause,' pp. 33–59. I was fortunate enough to hear Zupančič give a paper in London in 2007, on which this chapter is, I believe, based and a draft of which she was kind enough to send me. That work was helpful to my thinking on binding in the work of Green, illustrated in Chapter Three.
34. Jon Mills, *The Unconscious Abyss: Hegel's Anticipation of Psychoanalysis* (Albany: SUNY Press, 2002). See also his article 'Hegel on Projective Identification: Implications for Klein, Bion, and Beyond,' *The Psychoanalytic Review*, 87:6 (2000), 841–74, and collections on the confluence of psychoanalysis and philosophy of which he is the editor: *Psychoanalysis at the Limit: Epistemology, Mind, and the Question of Science* (Albany: SUNY Press, 2004) and *Rereading Freud: Psychoanalysis through Philosophy* (Albany: SUNY Press, 2004).
35. Daniel Berthold-Bond, *Hegel's Theory of Madness* (Albany: SUNY Press, 1995). See especially Chapter Five, 'Madness and the Unconscious: Placing Hegel in Dialogue with Nietzsche and Freud,' pp. 95–119.

36. Wilfried Ver Eecke, *Denial, Negation, and the Forces of the Negative: Freud, Hegel, Lacan, Spitz, and Sophocles* (Albany: SUNY Press, 2006), pp. 136–37, n. 2. See also Ver Eecke's article 'Hegel as Lacan's Source for Necessity in Psychoanalytic Theory,' in *Interpreting Lacan*, ed. by Joseph H. Smith and William J. Kerrigan (New Haven, CT: Yale University Press, 1983), pp. 113–38.
37. Richard D. Chessick, *The Future of Psychoanalysis* (Albany: SUNY Press, 2007). See especially pp. 197–212.
38. Rebecca Comay, *Mourning Sickness: Hegel and the French Revolution* (Stanford: Stanford University Press, 2011). She writes, for example, "Hegel repeatedly anticipates Freud's terminology as he investigates Enlightenment's inquisitorial agenda: disavowal (*Verleugnung*), perversion (*Verkehrung*), splitting (*Trennung, Entzweiung*), isolation (*Isolierung*), the stubborn forgetting (*Vergessen*) of the lost object—the catalogue details the defensive apparatus of a subject bent on sustaining itself on what it gives up" (p. 64).
39. Hyppolite, 'The Human Situation in the Hegelian Phenomenology,' *Hegel: Critical Assessments* , Vol. II, p. 408.
40. Robert R. Williams, *Recognition: Fichte and Hegel on the Other* (Albany: SUNY Press, 1992), p. 1. The aforementioned *Hegel's Ethics of Recognition* is a continuation of this earlier work. For a collection of articles that discuss Hegel along similar lines, see John O'Neill, ed., *Hegel's Dialectic of Desire and Recognition* (Albany: SUNY Press, 1996).
41. Michael Theunissen's compelling book *The Other: Studies in the Social Ontology of Husserl, Heidegger, Sartre, and Buber*, trans. by Christopher Macann (Cambridge, MA: MIT Press, 1984) addresses this very "problem of the other." Theunissen charts the concept of intersubjectivity starting with the work of Edmund Husserl and follows its transformation and use in the other three thinkers. He does not, however, include any considerable discussion of Hegel in his study, as he restricts his scope to works of the twentieth century.
42. John McDowell, 'The Apperceptive I and the Empirical Self,' in *Hegel: New Directions*, ed. by Katerina Deligiorgi (Chesham: Acumen Press, 2006), pp. 33–48 (p. 45).
43. Jacques Lacan, *Seminar of Jacques Lacan: Book I, Freud's Papers on Technique 1953–1954*, trans. by John Forrester, ed. by Jacques-Alain Miller (Cambridge: Cambridge University Press, 1988), p. 274, 277. See especially Chapter XVII, 'The Object Relation and the Intersubjective Relation,' pp. 208–19. See also Jacques Lacan, *Seminar of Jacques Lacan: Book II, The Ego in Freud's Theory and in the Technique of Psychoanalysis 1954–1955*, trans. by Sylvana Tomaselli, ed. by Jacques-Alain Miller (New York: Norton, 1991), Chapter XV, 'Odd or Even? Beyond Intersubjectivity,' pp. 175–90.
44. Roger Frie, *Subjectivity and Intersubjectivity in Modern Philosophy and Psychoanalysis: A Study of Sartre, Binswanger, Lacan, and Habermas* (London: Rowman & Littlefield, 1997).
45. See Dews, *Logics of Disintegration*, for a discussion of the rise of intersubjectivity theory in Lacan and Habermas, pp. 55–99 and pp. 287–97.
46. Frie, *Subjectivity and Intersubjectivity*, p. 197. David Ciavatta's *Spirit, the Family and the Unconscious in Hegel's Philosophy* (Albany: SUNY Press, 2009) is a striking work that discusses intersubjectivity in very fruitful ways. He writes of his own project: "Focusing on Hegel's conception of the family thus provides us with a privileged site for engaging with an important, but insufficiently explored, side of Hegel's overall vision of human life and its intersubjective basis: namely the irreducibility of affective, unconscious, and unreflective experience" (p. 7).
47. Arnold H. Modell, *The Private Self* (Cambridge, MA: Harvard University Press, 1993), pp. 98–99. See entirety of Chapter Four, 'The Dialectic of Self

and Other,' for his full treatment of Hegel, again confined to the master and slave dialectic, pp. 97–120.

48. Donna M. Orange, George E. Atwood, and Robert D. Stolorow, *Working Intersubjectively: Contextualism in Psychoanalytic Practice* (Hillsdale, NJ: Analytic Press, 1997), p. 18. See also George E. Atwood and Robert D. Stolorow, *Structures of Subjectivity: Explorations in Psychoanalytic Phenomenology* (Hillsdale, NJ: Analytic Press, 1984); Robert D. Stolorow, George E. Atwood, Bernard Brandschaft, eds., *The Intersubjective Perspective* (Northvale, NJ: Jason Aronson, 1994); and R. D Stolorow, B. Brandchaft, G. E. Atwood, eds. 'Post-Cartesian Psychoanalytic Theory: Commentary of B. E. Reis, "Adventures of the Dialectic,"' *Psychoanalytic Dialogues*, 9:3,(1999) 407–14.
49. See Jessica Benjamin, *Shadow of the Other: Intersubjectivity and Gender in Psychoanalysis* (London: Routledge, 1998) and *The Bonds of Love: Psychoanalysis, Feminism and the Problem of Domination* (London: Virago, 1990).
50. See in particular *Relational Psychoanalysis: the Emergence of a Tradition*, ed. by Stephen A. Mitchell and Lewis Aron (Hillsdale, NJ: Analytic Press, 1999) and *Relational Psychoanalysis Vol. 2: Innovation and Expansion*, ed. by Lewis Aron and Adrienne Harris (Hillsdale, NJ: Analytic Press, 2005).
51. Jon Mills, ed., *Relational and Intersubjective Perspectives in Psychoanalysis: A Critique* (Lanham, MD: Jason Aronson Publishers, 2005), p. xi. This volume is of particular use to situating where a book such as mine might engage with contemporary scholarship, as it is comprised of discussions and/or critiques of the crossover between phenomenology and intersubjectivity. It highlights the contemporary nature of the topic of intersubjectivity amongst psychoanalysts and psychologists. See in particular the chapter by Roger Frie and Bruce Reis, 'Intersubjectivity: From Theory through Practice,' pp. 3–35. In another chapter tracing the philosophical history of the concept, 'Phenomenology of Intersubjectivity: A Historical Overview and Its Clinical Implications,' pp. 35–71, M. Guy Thompson includes Hegel as a source of intersubjectivity theory but credits Husserl as the 'first philosopher to employ the term as a fundamental facet of his philosophy' (pp. 35–36). His article is a good introduction to the concept and draws out two philosophical traditions from which intersubjectivity originates.
52. Although first published in 1957, Max Jammer's *Concepts of Force: A Study in the Foundations of Dynamics* (Mineola, NY: Dover Publications, 1999) is the text most commonly cited in the discussions of force I have come across and is widely credited as the first work to compile a "history" of force. Jammer traces this concept from Ancient Egypt through Newton, Leibniz, and Kant, to the "contemporary science" of his time. However, he does not give more than a paragraph of space to Hegel's treatment.
53. Martin Heidegger, *Hegel's Phenomenology of Spirit*, trans. by Parvis Emad and Kenneth Maly (Bloomington: Indiana University Press, 1988), p. 103. See Heidegger's full and invaluable treatment of the concept of Force, pp. 97–126.
54. Wolfgang Neuser, 'The Concept of Force in Eighteenth-Century Mechanics' and Karl-Norbert Ihmig, 'Hegel's Rejection of the Concept of Force,' in *Hegel and Newtonianism*, ed. by Michael John Petry (Dordrecht: Kluwer Academic Publishers, 1993), Neuser, pp. 383–97, and Ihmig, pp. 399–414. This is a valuable compendium of papers given at a conference of the same title. See also Stephen Houlgate, *An Introduction to Hegel: Freedom, Truth and History* (Oxford: Blackwell Publishing, 2005), pp. 122–60, for a discussion of Hegel's response to Newtonian science, especially on concepts of attraction and repulsion.

55. Peter Kalkavage, *The Logic of Desire: An Introduction to Hegel's Phenomenology of Spirit* (Philadelphia: Paul Dry Books, 2007). For studies that are particularly helpful regarding Hegel's response to Kant (as well as Newton and Leibniz), see Charles Taylor, 'The Opening Arguments of the Phenomenology,' in *Hegel: A Collection of Critical Essays*, ed. by Alasdair MacIntyre (Garden City: Doubleday, 1972) pp. 151–88; Julian Roberts, *German Philosophy: An Introduction* (Cambridge: Polity Press, 1988), pp. 89–95; Robert Pippin, *Hegel's Idealism: The Satisfactions of Self-Consciousness*. (Cambridge: Cambridge University Press, 1989), pp. 131–43; Joseph Flay, 'Hegel's Inverted World,' in *G.W.F. Hegel: Critical Assessments*, III, pp. 149–61; Terry Pinkard, *Hegel's Phenomenology: The Sociality of Reason* (Cambridge: Cambridge University Press, 1994), pp. 34–45; Tom Rockmore in *Cognition: An Introduction to Hegel's Phenomenology of Spirit* (Berkley: University of California Press, 1997); and Robert Stern, *Hegel and the Phenomenology of Spirit* (London: Routledge, 2002), pp. 59–65.
56. For a comprehensive and illuminating reading of Kant's treatment of the concept of Force, see Jeffrey Edwards, *Substance, Force and the Possibility of Knowledge: On Kant's Philosophy of Material Nature* (Berkeley: University of California Press, 2000). Edwards discusses the intellectual heritage of the eighteenth-century philosophy of Force via Leibniz, Newton, Boscovich, and J. B. Priestly. If mine were a different project, it would have been very interesting to trace back to Kant's concept of physical ether, which Edwards argues by the 1770s Kant has "explicitly deemed to be the *universal* source of all physical bodies and all corporeal formations involving property of cohesion." Furthermore, Edwards posits, Kant saw it as the "generative source [*Gebährmutter*] of all bodies and the grounds of all cohesion" (p. 125). Clearly there is a connection to be made in a further study between this idea of the "grounds of all cohesion" and the argument that my book makes about the nature of Force as a binding entity.
57. Michael Forster, *Hegel's Idea of a Phenomenology of Spirit* (Chicago: University of Chicago Press, 1998), pp. 64–67, 307–11.
58. Robert C. Solomon, *In the Spirit of Hegel: A Study of G.W.F. Hegel's Phenomenology of Spirit* (Oxford: Oxford University Press, 1983), pp. 353–75.
59. Hans-Georg Gadamer, *Hegel's Dialectic: Five Hermeneutical Studies* (New Haven, CT: Yale University Press, 1976), pp. 35–53 (pp. 35, 38). For other examples of this second approach, see Hyppolite, *Genesis and Structure*; Quentin Lauer, *A Reading of Hegel's Phenomenology of Spirit* (New York: Fordham University Press, 1993), pp. 74–95; and Donald Phillip Verene, *Hegel's Recollection: A Study of Images in the Phenomenology of Spirit* (Albany: SUNY Press, 1985).
60. Sussman, *The Hegelian Aftermath*, p. 39.
61. Butler, *Subjects of Desire*, pp. 26–33.
62. Sigmund Freud, *The Standard Edition of the Complete Psychological Works of Sigmund Freud*, trans. and ed. by James Strachey in collaboration with Anna Freud, 24 vols (London: Hogarth Press, 1999), vol. 19, pp.235-243.
63. Roudinesco, *Jacques Lacan: An Outline of a Life*, p. 254. Roudinesco also discusses this exchange in her history of the psychoanalytic movement in France, *Jacques Lacan & Co.* She writes:

    Lacan came to an awareness of a divergence between Hegelianism and Freudianism, based on their common reference to dialectics. In other words, it was a question for him, through the intercession of Hyppolite, of 'stepping out' of Hegelian philosophy, and indeed of philosophy itself, in order to gain access to structuralism. That operation did not lead to a break with the reading of Hegel's work. It was simply that once it had occurred, Lacan no longer read the same Hegel. In between, Heideggarianism had worked its effects, allowing for a translation of the unconscious as a discourse and a language. (p. 300)

64. Freud, *Standard Edition*, vol. 1, pp. 283–346; vol. 18, pp. 7–66.
65. Karen Feldman, *Binding Words: Conscience and Rhetoric in Hobbes, Hegel, and Heidegger* (Evanston, IL: Northwestern University Press, 2006), p. 49, 17. Although Feldman is concerned with the binding nature of language and of conscience, her discussion of the term *binding* can be seen to give a good deal of support to my own use. See in particular pp. 3–18 and 48–79. See also Catherine Malabou's conclusion in *The Future of Hegel* (London: Routledge, 2005) where she discusses 'the event of reading' Hegel, pp. 184–85. Malabou's book is of great importance to readers of Hegel and offers exciting directions that Hegel studies can follow.

NOTES TO CHAPTER 1

1. G. W. F. Hegel, *The Jena System, 1804-5: Logic and Meaphysics,* ed. and intro by H. S. Harris, trans. by John W. Burbidge and George di Giovanni (Montreal: McGill-Queen's University Press, 1986), p. 63.
2. Butler, *Subjects of Desire*, p. 26.
3. John W. Burbidge, *Hegel's Systematic Contingency* (London: Palgrave, 2007), pp. 73, 153. Burbidge does not explicate the "Force and the Understanding" chapter to the degree that some of the introductions to the *Phenomenology* do, but it is clear in his work that he reads Hegel's use of the concept of Force as key to the understanding of how Spirit emerges and of what it is comprised, and thus his work is of more substantial use for my work.
4. Jean Wahl, 'The Unhappy Consciousness in the Philosophy of Hegel,' in *Hegel: Critical Assessments*, II, p. 285.
5. Ibid., *Hegel: Critical Assessments* II, p. 284.
6. Kalkavage, *The Logic of Desire*, p. 61.
7. See also H. S. Harris's work, *Hegel's Development: Night Thoughts (Jena 1801–1806)* (Oxford: Clarendon Press, 1983) for a detailed discussion of the *Jena System* and the place of Force in it. He posits that the "obvious targets of criticism in the discussion of 'force' are Newton's theory of gravitation (on the natural side) and Fichte's theory of the Ego, and the *Anstoss* (on the transcendental side)" as well as Kant's 'Transcendental Deduction,' (p. 347). See also pp. 74–101 and pp. 340–96.
8. See Herbert Marcuse, *Reason and Revolution: Hegel and the Rise of Social Theory* (London: Routledge, 2000), p. 109, for a reading of Force as 'relation' in the *Phenomenology* and Marcuse's tracing of the concept back to the *Jena System*. See his Chapter Four, pp. 91–120, for his reading of the *Phenomenology*. In addition, as noted by Harris, Hegel's dismissal of "the categories of modality as principles of the nonidentity of subject and object" in *The Difference between Fichte's and Schelling's System of Philosophy* can allow me to consider categories of "relation" and make use of the theory of relations for my subsequent theory of binding. See Harris, *Jena System*, xvi.
9. Harris, *Hegel's Development: Night Thoughts*, p. 368.
10. A clear and pared down discussion of Force (specifically as "relation") is also found in Hegel's *Science of Logic*, trans. by A. V. Miller (London: Allen & Unwin, 1969), pp. 518–23. Further references to this edition are given after quotations in the text, abbreviated as *SL*. Because my book cannot be an exploration of the concept of Force throughout Hegel's entire body of work,

I will not deal in any detail with its presence in the *Science of Logic* or the three volumes of the *Encyclopaedia*; in *Encyclopaedia Logic*, trans. William Wallace (Oxford: Clarendon Press, 1975), pp. 192–96, Hegel argues that there is no "one common primary force" but that a multiplicity of forces exists (including in the realm of empirical psychology, the forces of memory, imagination, will, and all the other faculties in addition to those found in empirical physics). Here the length of Hegel's own commentary (*Zusatze*) on his thoughts regarding God as a force ("though we may consent to let the world be called a manifestation of divine forces, we should object to have God himself viewed as a mere force," p. 195) and the bearing of scientific investigation of force on this assertion (and Herder is the main offender here) surpasses the main body of the argument itself.

11. Solomon, *In the Spirit of Hegel*, p. 370.
12. G.W.F. Hegel, *The Philosophical Propaedeutic*, trans. by A. V. Miller, ed. by Michael George and Andrew Vincent (Oxford: Basil Blackwell, 1986), pp. 58–59. Further references to this edition are given after quotations in the text, abbreviated as *PP*.
13. Hegel, *The Philosophical Propaedeutic*, From Logic [For the Middle Class] (1810–11).
14. Hegel, *The Philosophical Propaedeutic*, From The Philosophical Encylopaedia [For the Higher Class] (1808).
15. Hegel, *The Philosophical Propaedeutic*, From Logic [For the Middle Class] (1810–11).
16. Hyppolite, *Genesis and Structure*, p. 120.
17. Sussman, *The Hegelian Aftermath*, p. 35.
18. Plotnitsky, *In the Shadow of Hegel*, p. 211. Plotnitsky does not, however, perform a close reading of the mechanisms of Hegel's concept of Force, nor does he make suggestions as to the nature of Force and binding in Hegel and psychoanalysis.
19. Stephen Houlgate, *The Opening of Hegel's Logic* (West Lafayette, IN: Purdue University Press, 2006), p. 290. Further references to this edition are given as *OHL* after quotations in the text. (The meat of Houlgate's discussion of vanishing is mostly to be found on these pages, but he does explore the concept briefly at other points in his book; see pp. 277–79, where Houlgate specifically asks: "How are we to understand this vanishing?" and "Why does it occur?") Although other works on Hegel might mention the activity of vanishing briefly, there is no particular attention paid to it as an important concept, and thus Houlgate's work stands out. The only other work on Hegel of note in this regard is Herbert Marcuse's *Hegel's Ontology and the Theory of Historicity*. Marcuse gives attention to "the process of vanishing" as it relates to the creation of objects of work which consciousness "transcends," thus making "all reality a 'vanishing moment.'" Helpfully for our purposes, he writes that "precisely in this process of vanishing, consciousness retains *itself* as reality and as the reality of its moments" (p. 283). I find resonance with the ideas of preservation of self and of moments of knowing that I see as arising from the activity of vanishing; see pp. 276–91. I will return to Marcuse's incredibly rich text in the next chapter when I discuss the concept of Life.
20. For reprinted section of the *Logic* see *OHL*, p. 199.
21. See David M. Parry, *Hegel's Phenomenology of the 'We'* (Frankfurt am Main: Peter Lang, 1988). See also Kenley R. Dove, 'Hegel's Phenomenological Method,' *Review of Metaphysics*, 23 (1970), pp. 627–41.
22. Here, discussing the collapse of difference, Hegel uses the example of electricity where "simple electricity is Force" and the expression of the difference of positive and negative electricity "falls within the law."

23. For particularly helpful discussions on the "inverted world," see Solomon, *In the Spirit of Hegel*, pp. 376–84; Joseph Flay, 'Hegel's Inverted World,' in *Hegel: Critical Assessments*, III, pp. 148–61; Donald Verene, *Hegel's Recollection: A Study of the Images in the Phenomenology of Spirit*, Chapter Four, 'The Topsy-Turvy World,' pp. 39–58; and Hans-Georg Gadamer, *Hegel's Dialectic*. Gadamer contends that Hegel argues that the real world *is* in itself contradictory so that the inverted world is, in a sense, an exaggerated version *of* this real world in order to prove that these contradictions, these distinctions, are what make the world what it is. Solomon sees this as a profound move both for the *Phenomenology* and for "philosophy in general". However, Solomon combines Gadamer's suggestion with an alternative offered by Flay that what Hegel is offering is "an intentionally ridiculous counter-example to Kant's notion of the 'thing-in-itself.'"(p. 382).
24. Gadamer argues that one could think about what he translates as "peering" into the inner realm as anticipating the activity of the unhappy consciousness. However, the difference, he says, is that the "beyond" of this inner realm is not empty, for it is the truth of appearance (*Hegel's Dialectic*, p. 41). I agree that the inner is not empty but neither is the inner world that the unhappy consciousness faces. We will see what this "inner" is for self-consciousness in the shape of the unhappy consciousness in the next chapter and note that far from being empty, it is filled with its own self-truth, which it does not yet recognise, since it is too filled with its own split being and with its longing for unification. The "beyond" is, however, filled with the hope of overcoming this despair and therefore is equally not empty.
25. The discussion of "solicitation" in the *Science of Logic* uses slightly different language. There, Hegel discusses force as an "impulse" (*Anstoss*) for "the other force against which it is active." This impulse "solicits it," and, furthermore, "in the expression of force we start from the soliciting impulse." The key action here is the sublating of the "externality of this impulse" and thus arises force's own expression. Ultimately, "the sublating of the impulse is the positing of the externality." Furthermore, "what force in truth expresses is that its relation to other is relation to itself, that its passivity consists in its own activity" (*SL*, pp. 521–23). Tom Rockmore sees Hegel's discussion of solicitation in the *Phenomenology* as a response to Newton's Third Law of motion, which posits the equivalence of action and reaction (*Cognition*, p. 51). See Derrida, 'Force and Signification,' p. 5, for an interesting discussion of solicitation, although he is referring specifically to structuralism.
26. Roberts, *German Philosophy*, p. 91.
27. I will note in the next chapter the way in which Henry Sussman also argues this formulation. Peter Kalkavage additionally posits this formulation but does not refer specifically to "recognition": "The splitting or *Entzweiung* of force prefigures the doubling of self-consciousness in Hegel's next chapter" (*Logic of Desire*, p. 66). Like Rockmore, he refers back to Newton's Third Law as the basis for Hegel's thinking.
28. See Clair May, 'Hegel, Kristeva, and the Language of Revolution,' in *Hegel and Language*, ed. by Jere O'Neill Surber (Albany: SUNY Press, 2006), pp. 219–32, for her discussion of Kristeva's view that negativity is inherent in language itself. I will be working with Julia Kristeva's *Revolution in Poetic Language*, trans. by Margaret Waller (New York: Columbia University Press, 1984) regarding negativity, Hegel, and psychoanalysis in Chapter Three. Further references to this edition are given after quotations in the text, abbreviated as *RPL*.
29. See Jacques Derrida, 'The Pit and the Pyramid: Introduction to Hegel's Semiology,' in *Margins of Philosophy*, trans. by Alan Bass (Brighton: Harvester Press, 1982), pp. 69–108, and 'Force and Signification' in *Writing*

and Difference, pp. 3–30. In 'Force and Signification,' Derrida is specifically addressing Hegel's 'Force and the Understanding' but does not read Hegel in the way that I do. Indeed, there and elsewhere he argues for Hegel's "closed economy," a notion against which I am arguing. Georgio Agamben offers an interesting meditation in *Language and Death: The Place of Negativity*, trans. by Karen E. Pinkus and Michael Hardt (Minneapolis: University of Minnesota Press, 1991). For the most recent studies dedicated solely to the subject, see Jeffrey Reid, *Real Words: Language and System in Hegel* (Toronto: London University of Toronto Press, 2007); Jim Veron, *Hegel's Philosophy of Language* (London: Continuum, 2007); *Hegel and Language*, ed. by Jere O'Neill Surber; and John McCumber, *The Company of Words: Hegel, Language and Systematic Philosophy* (Evanston, IL: Northwestern University Press, 1993).

30. Butler, *Subjects of Desire*, p. 33.
31. Ibid., p. 28.
32. I am saying nothing new when I underscore the importance of the concept of infinity for Hegel's system. My aim here is only to gesture towards an understanding of its introduction in the "Force and the Understanding" chapter. For other facets of Hegel's thinking on the concept in the *Phenomenology* and elsewhere, see Terry Pinkard, as he writes that "infinity," for Hegel, is "a structure that sets its own conditions." See, *Sociality of Reason*, p. 43. Quentin Lauer remarks that "reason" is the infinite and that "it is the universal vitalizing force which animates the whole of reality"; see, *A Reading of Hegel's Phenomenology of Spirit*, p. 92. See also Houlgate, *OHL*, especially pp. 394–436.
33. Butler, *Subjects of Desire*, p. 29.
34. Again, like discussions of Hegel's "we," there are many commentaries on the position of "the reader." See Houlgate, *An Introduction to Hegel*, p. 63, for a lucid and concise discussion of the reader's position.
35. Butler, *Subjects of Desire*, p. 26. Tom Rockmore writes that Desire is Hegel's version of Spinoza's *conatus* (*Cognition*, p. 62). I find support in my claim for Force as a model of Desire if I read both Rockmore's and Butler's interpretations together.
36. See Jon Mills for a comprehensive discussion of the topic of the unconscious in Hegel. Mills sees Hegel's discussions of the "seemingly featureless void that lies *beyond* or *behind* the conscious operations of spirit" as "indeed responsible for its dynamic operative force" (*The Unconscious Abyss*, p. 119).
37. Herbert Marcuse's critique of modern culture in *One Dimensional Man* offers a brilliant way of thinking about what I am calling a reflective gap and the necessity of alienation (also using the figure of the unhappy consciousness as a model) on both an individual and cultural level; see *One Dimensional Man: Studies in the Ideology of Advanced Industrial Society* (London: Routledge, 2002). See in particular Chapter Three, 'The Conquest of the Unhappy Consciousness: Repressive Desublimation,' pp. 59–86.

NOTES TO CHAPTER 2

1. Although the theoretical move into the intersubjective realm from the "Force and the Understanding" chapter is a logical move to make, emphasis is not often given to this shift unless it is to discuss the "Lordship and Bondage" episode. This manner of discussion, however, seems to neglect the essential foundation that the move is an elaboration of the play of Forces and thus of the concept of Force itself. Henry Sussman discusses this move from the abstract world of "Force and the Understanding" into the intersubjective

world of "Self-Consciousness" in a compelling manner essential to my own reading (*Hegelian Aftermath*, pp. 15–62).

2. Ricoeur, *Freud and Philosophy*, p. 463.
3. I encountered the concept of the "vanishing mediator" in the work of Slavoj Žižek, most specifically in *For They Know Not What They Do: Enjoyment as a Political Factor* (London: Verso, 1991), pp. 182–209, and *The Indivisible Remainder: An Essay on Schelling and Related Matters*, Chapter Two, 'Schelling for Hegel: The 'Vanishing Mediator,' pp. 92–186. I then traced it back to Fredric Jameson (to whom, I believe, its originality can be attributed and from whom Žižek took the phrase) in his work *The Ideologies of Theory: Essays 1971–1986. Vol. 2: Syntax of History* (London: Routledge, 1988), pp. 3–34. In his work, Jameson discusses the concept in relation to modern capitalism and to the work of Max Weber in particular. At points he uses the example of religion to illustrate the role of a vanishing mediator in the process. He sees the vanishing mediator as "in the strictest sense of the word a catalytic agent that permits an exchange of energies between two otherwise mutually exclusive terms" and "that serves in its turn as a kind of overall bracket or framework within which change takes place and which can be dismantled and removed when its usefulness is over" (p. 25). This formulation of a framework that "permits an exchange of energies" is of the most use to the present investigation and will come to fruition in Chapters Three and Four. Žižek, as far as I am aware, does not examine Hegel's use of the word *vanishing* in his work, but in *For They Know Not What They Do* he does posit that the vanishing mediator can be found in the mechanisms of the Hegelian "negation of negation" and further that "the vanishing mediator emerges because of the way, in the dialectical process, form stays behind content" (p. 185). My use of the term *vanishing mediator* is a contribution to the discussion begun by Jameson and Žižek but clearly one more specifically suited to my own argument. In Chapter Three I will discuss further the "negation of negation" as a way of reading the notion of a death drive in the *Phenomenology*.
4. Sussman, *Hegelian Aftermath*, p. 52.
5. Hyppolite, *Genesis and Structure*, p. 156.
6. Wahl, quoted in Cooper, *The End of History*, p. 51; see p. 358 for reference to Wahl's text.
7. Wahl, quoted in Baugh, *French Hegel*, p. 22.
8. Wahl, *Hegel: Critical Assessments*, II, p. 288.
9. Again, the literature on the *Phenomenology* is vast and most works include a discussion of the unhappy consciousness, to various extents and levels of interpretation. Amongst the best standard readings, see Verene, *Hegel's Recollection*, pp. 70–79; Charles Taylor, *Hegel* (Cambridge: Cambridge University Press, 1975), pp. 57–64; Rockmore, *Cognition*, pp. 72–79; and Roberts, *German Philosophy*, pp. 103–06. Roberts goes so far as to state that "this section is incomprehensible unless the theological motifs underlying it are made explicit" (p. 103).
10. Tilottama Rajan argues that because Wahl sees the unhappy consciousness through a religious lens, he sees it only as a "darkened happy consciousness" and thus his reading was only an attempt to positivize Hegel's negativity; see *Deconstruction and the Remainders of Phenomenology: Sartre, Derrida, Foucault, Baudrillard* (Stanford: Stanford University Press, 2002), p. 297, n. 57. I highlight this kind of reading, represented here by Rajan but certainly not unique to her, in order to argue that it does not allow for the other facets of Wahl's interpretation to illuminate the episode. Rajan's work, however, does include an interesting tracing of the legacy of Hegel's thought on

twentieth-century French theory and focuses on the impact of the difference between Hyppolite's and Kojève's readings (pp. 1–55).

11. Cooper, *The End of History*, p. 53.
12. Hyppolite, *Genesis and Structure*, p. 196.
13. This is a position held by those readers of Hegel who wish to read the more "existentialist" argument imbedded in the *Phenomenology*. See, for example, John Burbidge's argument that "The Unhappy Consciousness" episode is more about the individual searching for self-knowledge and that suggestions that Hegel is only concerned with the Catholic Church are not sufficient. He also posits that Hegel "avoided specific historical reference" in "The Unhappy Consciousness" episode "lest he direct his reader's attention away from the more universal relevance of his analysis"; see *Hegel's Logic and Religion: The Reasonableness of Christianity* (Albany: SUNY Press, 1992), pp. 108, 117. Additionally, Maurice Merleau-Ponty writes in his powerful essay 'Hegel's Existentialism' that all consciousness is unhappy and further that "Hegel's thought is existentialist in that it views man not as being from the start a consciousness in full possession of its own clear thoughts but as a life which is its own responsibility and which tries to understand itself"; see *Sense and Non-Sense*, trans. by Hubert L. Dreyfus and Patrician Allen Dreyfus (Evanston, IL: Northwestern University Press, 1964), pp. 63–70 (p. 65). See also two chapters in Hyppolite's *Studies on Marx and Hegel*. In Chapter Two, 'The Concept of Existence in the Hegelian Phenomenology,' pp. 22–34, he explores the concept of existence that is "kin to certain contemporary existentialist notions" (p. 23), and in Chapter Eight, 'The Human Situation in the Hegelian Phenomenology,' pp. 153–68, he argues that the chapter on self-consciousness has nothing to do with a history, as such, but that Hegel "wanted to analyse the very *foundations* of historical action. He inquired into the general conditions of *human existence* that constitute the possibility of the human act as such" (p. 154).
14. Hegel's concept of desire is one of the most examined and elaborated upon of the entire *Phenomenology*, and so my interest here is not in duplicating the work already done or recounting the various lines of argument but rather lies in setting forth my thoughts on desire as based on the model of Force. As is well-known, predominantly Kojève's and additionally Hyppolite's reading of the concept paved the way for the substantial impact it had on twentieth-century theory and philosophy. Amongst the best works that discuss the concept and to which we have already referred are Butler's *Subjects of Desire*, Baugh's *French Hegel*, Peter Kalkavage's *The Logic of Desire*, and Roth's *Knowing and History*. See also John O'Neill, ed. *Hegel's Dialectic of Desire and Recognition* and Robert Williams, *Recognition: Fichte and Hegel on the Other*.
15. Butler, *Subjects of Desire*, p. 42.
16. Songsuk Susan Hahn, *Contradiction in Motion: Hegel's Organic Concept of Life and Value* (Ithaca: Cornell University Press, 2007), p. 48. Hahn's work is incredibly valuable as a contemporary attempt to give a place to a more "holistic and organic" view of Hegel's thinking. Although she does not spend much time with the *Phenomenology*, and oddly omits a discussion of Force as it is found in it from her overall discussion of Force in Hegel, her thoughts on the concept of Life and organic holism, and the philosophical background out of which Hegel emerged, are very useful. See also Stephen Houlgate, *An Introduction to Hegel*, Chapter Seven, 'Life and Embodied Spirit,' pp. 161–80, for a discussion of Hegel's concept of Life, centred predominantly, however, on his *Philosophy of Nature*.
17. Judith Shklar writes on forms of Eros as found in Hegel's early writings as well as in the *Phenomenology of Spirit*. Not only was philosophy for

Hegel (as it was for Plato) an "intense striving" a "force of Eros" (p. 53) but Shklar also locates in Hegel a way of thinking about the "erotic energies" (p. 67) that drive consciousness and that helped me to flesh out my own reading of his concept of Life as found in the *Phenomenology*. See *Freedom and Independence: A Study of Hegel's Phenomenology of Mind* (Cambridge: Cambridge University Press, 1976), pp. 1–95.

18. Williams, *Recognition: Fichte and Hegel on the Other*, p. 144. The translation of *Verbindung* as "union" here is not as satisfying as other translations of *Verbindung* as "binding." See for instance Alain Badiou's translation of Kant. Badiou discusses the concept of binding in Kant, particularly in the *Critique of Pure Reason*, and argues that one of Kant's most "radical insights" was to firmly distinguish between binding (*Verbindung*) and unity (*Einheit*); see Alain Badiou, *Theoretical Writings*, trans. and ed. by Ray Brassier and Alberto Toscano (London: Continuum, 2004), pp. 135–37. For the purposes of my own work, Badiou's translation is clearly more fitting, and thus in my interpretation I choose to substitute "binding" for "union." Had the scope of my investigation allowed it, it would have been very interesting to pursue Badiou's discussion of Kant and binding in relation to my own argument about Hegel; see Chapter Eleven, 'Kant's Subtractive Ontology,' pp. 137–44.
19. Benhabib, in Marcuse, *Hegel's Ontology*, xxiii–xxiv. Further references to this edition are given as *HO* after quotations in the text.
20. See Seyla Benhabib's discussion of Marcuse's relationship with Heidegger and his impact on this work, *HO*, ix–xl. See also Andrew Feenburg, *Heidegger and Marcuse: The Catastrophe and Redemption of History* (London: Routledge, 2005), Chapter Three, 'The Dialectic of Life: Marcuse's Hegel,' pp. 47–70. Feenberg considers Marcuse's reading of Hegel (especially his use of Aristotle) as implicitly influenced by Heidegger and Lukács and argues that as Marcuse reads it, "there is a striking similarity between Hegel's concept of Life [. . .] and Heidegger's concept of *Dasein* as being-in-the-world" (p. 53).
21. This is potentially a distinction made by Miller's translation. In the realm of Force, the German for what is translated as "flux" (*Wechselnde*) seems to indicate constant change. In the realm of self-consciousness, Miller also translates *Flüssigkeit* as "flux," yet this seems to express more a state of flow, liquidity. This is consistent with the notion of pure movement rather than the vacillation of Force, which involves the collapse of difference.
22. Gadamer, *Hegel's Dialectic*, p. 58.
23. Hyppolite, *Genesis and Structure*, p. 161. See also Hyppolite, *Studies on Marx and Hegel*, Part 1, 'The Concept of Life and Existence in Hegel,' especially Chapter One, 'The Concept of Life and Consciousness of Life in Hegel's Jena Philosophy,' pp. 3–34. Although I used a reading of the *Jena Logic* to expand an understanding of Force, the scope of this chapter does not allow for me to do the same with the concept of Life.
24. Taylor, *Hegel*, p. 151.
25. Butler, *Subjects of Desire*, p. 31.
26. Ibid., p. 69. Butler then uses a reading of Sartre's work to "trace the gradual embodiment of consciousness, the phenomenological fulfillment of Hegel's early contention that desire both constitutes and reveals the relations that bind the self with its world" (p. 93). Understanding Force as a model for desire is important for grasping this double action of constitution and revelation on the part of desire. We have come to understand that Force is only truly known in its appearance. Therefore, we can say that it is only "made" when observed, revealed.
27. Sussman, *The Hegelian Aftermath*, p. 37.

28. Hyppolite designates "self-consciousness as a mirror play" and further discusses the "mirror play" of judging and judged consciousness that gives rise to the "we," which is no longer abstract but is now the "movement of history." He used this title as a direct reference to Lacan's "mirror phase"; see Hyppolite, 'Hegel's Phenomenology and Psychoanalysis,' p. 61, p. 70.
29. Butler, *Subjects of Desire*, p. 89.
30. Merleau-Ponty, *Sense and Non-Sense*, p. 68.
31. Butler, *Psychic Life*, p. 40.
32. Shklar, *Freedom and Independence*, p. 64.
33. Berthold-Bond, *Hegel's Theory of Madness*, p. 47. Berthold-Bond and Jon Mills each position a reading of the figure of the Unhappy Consciousness as "despairing" consciousness within their respective discussions of Hegel's work; see Berthold-Bond, pp. 47–70, and Mills, *Unconscious Abyss*, pp. 149–59. While I follow their lead, my approach is primarily interested in the implications of the figure of the unhappy consciousness and the mechanisms of the movement that are at work as pertains to the concept of Force, and in the theoretical implications of such an understanding. Additionally, although my interest does not lie in "diagnosing" Hegel's shapes of consciousness as such, I note Judith Butler's comparison between the unhappy consciousness and the neurotic as seen "in the various forms of self-beratement and self-mortification" that the unhappy consciousness displays (Butler, *Psychic Life of Power*, p. 54).
34. Verene, *Hegel's Recollection*, p. 78.
35. Simon Jarvis, 'The "Unhappy Consciousness" and Conscious Unhappiness: On Adorno's Critique of Hegel and the Idea of an Hegelian Critique of Adorno,' in *Hegel's Phenomenology of Spirit: A Reappraisal*, ed. by G. K. Browning (London: Kluwer Academic Publishers, 1997), p. 57.
36. Dews, *Logics of Disintegration*, p. 71.
37. Walter A. Davis, *Inwardness and Existence: Subjectivity in Hegel, Heidegger, Marx, and Freud* (Madison: University of Wisconsin Press, 1989), p. 71.
38. Ibid, p. 89.
39. Jameson, *The Ideologies of Theory*, p. 25.

NOTES TO CHAPTER 3

1. See the Preface to *WN* for Green's brief history of the concept in philosophy and post–Second World War French Psychoanalysis. Also, amongst the studies on the concept of the negative that were of particular help to the aims of this thesis, see Slavoj Žižek's *Tarrying with the Negative: Kant, Hegel and the Critique Of Ideology*; Jean-Luc Nancy's *Hegel: The Restlessness of the Negative*, trans. by Jason Smith and Steven Miller (Minneapolis: University of Minnesota Press, 2002); and two works of Wilfried Ver Eecke: *Negativity and Subjectivity: A Study of the Function of Negation in Freud, Linguistics, Child Psychology and Hegel* (Brussels: Wetenschappen, Letteren, en Schone Kunsten/Paleis Der Academien, 1977) and *Denial, Negation, and the Forces of the Negative: Freud, Hegel, Lacan, Spitz, and Sophocles*. The line of inquiry of our present chapter is Ver Eecke's interest as well, but he does not discuss the relation between Hyppolite, Lacan, and Hegel on the subject of the negative. Jacqueline Rose's *Why War? Psychoanalysis, Politics, and the Return to Melanie Klein* (Oxford: Blackwell, 1993) has an extremely helpful, brief reading of the Hyppolite/Lacan exchange on *Verneinung* embedded within her larger argument on the concept of negativity in Klein's work (pp. 154–56). Julia Kristeva's *Revolution in Poetic Language* has an essential

discussion of the concept of negation and how it relates to "negativity" in Hegel and psychoanalysis. (Further references to this edition are given after quotations in the text, abbreviated as *RPL*.) Kristeva, as we soon will see, also makes a crucial connection between Force and negativity in Hegel and notions of energy.

2. André Green, *The Chains of Eros: The Sexual in Psychoanalysis*, trans. by Luke Thurston (London: Karnac, 2001), p. 53. Further references to this edition are given after quotations in the text, abbreviated as *RE*.
3. André Green, *On Private Madness* (London: Hogarth Press, 1986), p. 203. Further references to this edition are given after quotations in the text, abbreviated as *OPM*.
4. Green's relation to Lacan and to Lacanian thought and the reasons behind his gradual split from Lacan are discussed by Green himself in the foreword to his work *Key Ideas for a Contemporary Psychoanalysis: Misrecognition and Recognition of the Unconscious* (London: Routledge, 2005), pp. 11–14. Further references to this edition are given after quotations in the text, abbreviated as *KI*. Also see the Preface to *The Dead Mother*, ed. by Gregorio Kohon (London: Routledge, 1999), pp. xi–xii, for a potted bio-history of Green and of his final break with Lacan in 1970. Based on interviews with Green, Elisabeth Roudinesco not only gives a short biographical sketch of Green, but she also briefly traces the origins of Green's interactions with Lacan in *Lacan & Co.*, pp. 317–18.
5. *André Green at the Squiggle Foundation: Winnicott Studies Monograph Series*, ed. by Jan Abram (London: Karnac Books, 2000), p. 20. Further references to this edition are given after quotations in the text, abbreviated as *Squiggle*.
6. See also Jon Mills's *The Unconscious Abyss* for his proposal of a "process psychology" based on Hegel's idea of process (pp. 187–202).
7. Mills's compelling argument for locating in Hegel a discussion of the 'unconscious' finds its roots in Hegel's *Philosophy of Mind: Being Part Three of the Encyclopaedia of Philosophical Sciences*, trans. William Wallace, (Oxford: Clarendon Press, 1971).
   It is in the sub-section 'C. Psychology. Mind' that Hegel writes of the "night-like mine or pit in which is stored a world of infinitely many images and representations, yet without being in consciousness" (p. 204). Importantly, Mills sees the unconscious for Hegel as "pure process, a changing, flexible, and purposeful activity of becoming" (p. 4).
8. Hyppolite, 'Hegel's Phenomenology and Psychoanalysis,' p. 59. Whether Green was aware of Hyppolite's formulation from this paper is unclear, as there is only reference to Hyppolite's work *Genesis and Structure*, and Hyppolite does not make such an explicit statement there.
9. Ricoeur, *Freud and Philosophy*, p. 468.
10. Hahn, *Contradiction in Motion*, p. 127.
11. Hyppolite's remarks on Freud's *Verneinung* were added as an appendix to Lacan's 1966 edition of *Écrits* (Paris: Seuil), where Lacan's response was also found (along with Freud's original paper), and both (but not Freud's paper) are reprinted in *Seminar I*. The translator's note to *Seminar I* adds that this is "the one passage in the Seminar with annotations supplied by Lacan and by the editor of *Écrits*, Jacques-Alain Miller" (*Seminar I*, p. 289). Lacan's interjections into the written version of what was a spoken commentary via his footnotes, as well as his one recorded interjection into the commentary itself, will be noted in the following where appropriate and serve to add to the already rich texture of this important exchange.
12. Lacan, *Seminar I*, p. 55

13. Lacan, *Seminar I*, p. 291. (This is Hyppolite's word choice.)
14. As is well-known, but specifically noted by Jon Mills, however, the word *Aufhebung* had common usage in German both in Hegel's (and according to Mills he was borrowing its usage from Schiller) and Freud's era, so I must again make clear that it was not as though Freud was taking a Hegelian concept and utilizing it for his own theory; see *Unconscious Abyss*, p. 194.
15. Freud, 'Negation,' *Standard Edition*, vol. 19, pp. 235–36. Here I am reading together Hyppolite's use of the original German text and the English translation of the *Standard Edition*.
16. Freud, 'Negation,' p. 236.
17. Lacan, *Seminar I*, p. 292.
18. Ibid.
19. Ibid.
20. Ibid., p. 293.
21. Butler, *Subjects of Desire*, p.251, n. 12. Depending on context, *Vereinigung* could be translated as "uniting," "combining," or "merging."
22. Freud, 'Negation,' p. 239.
23. Ibid. It should be noted that *Bejahung* in Freud [affirmation] is not the affirmation of the Hegelian "negation of negation." For Freud it would appear that affirmation is the surface opposite of negation, whereas in Hegel this outcome of affirmation is simply part of the work of the negative. Jacqueline Rose notes that Hyppolite's reading of the term *successor* "opens up a gap between negation and destruction; they are precisely not equivalents, not the same thing" (*Why War?* p. 154). I believe that this is what I am also attempting to argue, in a slightly more circuitous manner, by emphasising the generative nature of negation as it arises from a Hegelian reading of Freud.
24. See also, Žižek, *Tarrying with the Negative*, for his treatment and elaboration of this influential passage.
25. *Hegel's Theory of Madness*, pp. 47, 80, 83, 84. See in its entirety Berthold-Bond's chapter, 'Madness and the Second Face of Desire,' pp. 71–94. Žižek posits the "negation of negation," as the "Hegelian version" of "death drive" but does not seem to have a formulation of a "life drive" (*Interrogating the Real*, p. 34).
26. Lacan, *Seminar I*, pp. 293–94.
27. Ibid., p. 294. The footnote inserted after this passage reads: "The seminar in which J.L gave a commentary on *Beyond the pleasure principle* took place in 1954–55." This is a year after Hyppolite's own commentary was given.
28. Lacan, *Seminar I*, p. 296.
29. Ibid., n. 21.
30. Jean-Francoise Lyotard links Hegel and Freud in a similar manner when he writes that "*death*, which, for Hegel, is the element in which the life of the mind swims, the same thing indeed to which Freud will dedicate what is without doubt his most frenzied, emotional text, *Beyond the Pleasure Principle*." Much of what I will argue in this chapter differs, however, from Lyotard's reading, which states that because Freud "thematize[s] it under the name of the death drives" it does not enter into a "dialectical relation with Eros-Logos" but simply "compels repetition"; see *Libidinal Economy* (London: Continuum, 2004), p. 124.
31. Lacan, *Seminar I*, p. 297.
32. Ibid.
33. Rose, *Why War?* p. 155.
34. Lacan, *Seminar I*, p. 61.
35. The concept of the negative occupies a place Green's work most heavily, as the title would indicate, in *The Work of the Negative* (*WN*; 1999e/f).

Therefore, most of my discussion of Green's take on the concept is based on this densely packed text. That book was born out of a paper of the same name (1986) wherein Green stated that the expression (of the negative) "no longer owes anything to its Hegelian origins" (*WN*, p. 269). Clearly, by the time he came to write his book-length study he had reconsidered the importance of Hegelian links, and it is for that reason that I begin my chapter on Green with a discussion of his book rather than his other writings on the subject. *The Chains of Eros* (2001e/1997f) includes the "work of the negative" under the umbrella of Freud's "metabiology" yet elaborates no further, only referring readers back to his 1986 paper for more detail. In his work *Time in Psychoanalysis*, trans. Andrew Weller (London: Free Association Books, 2002), Green's remarks on the negative are sparse but fruitful. Further references to this edition are given after quotations in the text, abbreviated as *TP*. *Key Ideas for a Contemporary Psychoanalysis* is an indispensable volume of Green's thoughts on the state of contemporary psychoanalysis as well as a summary of his main theories (including the work of the negative) and an outline for the history of psychoanalysis post-Freud. I must be clear, therefore, that it is really only in the book-length *The Work of the Negative* that Green draws the parallels between Hegel and Freud. The other connections I am drawing between Hegel's philosophy and psychoanalytic theory (e.g. binding, thirdness) through the lens of Green, I am making alone, giving myself license to do so based on the philosophical and theoretical ethos with which Green infuses all of his work and which serves to make his work such a fitting case study. In contrast, there is not a specific text dedicated to either the topic of binding or of thirdness, and the fleshing out of these concepts is performed throughout Green's body of work. Thus I will be referring, in those sections, to his body of work as the whole and to specific references when required.

36. Žižek, *Less than Nothing*, pp. 546–47. (He notes that he owes this reference to Force to Benjamin Bliumis, NYU, p. 546.)
37. Žižek, *Less than Nothing*, p. 547. Žižek goes on to characterize the drive as 'not a psychic (or biological) striving for death and destruction' and agrees with Lacan that the death drive 'is an ontological concept' (ibid.). The manner in which he agrees with Freud, that *Trieb* is a 'limit concept situated between biology and psychology, or nature and culture—a natural force known only through its psychic representatives' (ibid.) can illuminate the way in which I read Hegel's concept of Force alongside psychoanalytic theory.
38. James Strachey, in his Introduction to this text in the *Standard Edition* states: "The *Project* must remain a torso, disavowed by its creator"; see 'Project for Scientific Psychology,' *Standard Edition*, vol. 1, p. 293. One cannot help but recall *Frankenstein* and the potential danger and failure contained in such a disavowal by a "creator." It might be argued, and my return to a reading of the *Project* is in a sense doing so, that while Freud could never explicitly acknowledge this creation, and, as Strachey points out, he "threw over the whole neurological framework," (Standard Edition 1, p. 293) there are elements of the economic model, this mind composed of currents of energy, that still pursued him, and its traces are to be found throughout his body of work. Strachey's footnotes to the *Project* indicate where the most obvious of the other traces of the paper can be found in Freud's work. While they do indicate the link with 'Negation' and judgement that we will touch upon (p. 328, n. 1), there is no indication as to the legacy of the concepts of binding.
39. One of the most difficult aspects of writing about the intersection between philosophical and psychoanalytic theory is one of distinguishing which designation of the "mind" to use. Because each term is loaded in either discipline,

the mis-designation at any time can inadvertently shift levels of meaning and further complicate the epistemological and ontological questions at hand. When discussing Freud's *Project*, I will use his language and refer to "psychical processes."

40. Teresa Brennan, *The Interpretation of the Flesh: Freud and Femininity* (London: Routledge, 1992), pp. 19–22, 108–16; Dews, p. 56.
41. Richard Wollheim, *Freud* (London: Harper Collins, Fontana, 1991), p. 63, and Ricoeur, *Freud and Philosophy*, p. 62. See also, Derrida, 'Freud and the Scene of Writing,' in *Writing and Difference*, where he asserts that the *Project* should be taken as a "metaphorical model and not a neurological description" (p. 200). Of note, from an anecdotal perspective, the original text of that chapter "is the fragment of a lecture given at the *Institut de psychanlyse* (Dr. Green's seminar)" (p. 196).
42. It should be noted, however, that "energy" is a notion that is somewhat implicit in the *Project* in the language of "cathexes" and that a notion of "psychical energy" arises later. See, Appendix C, 'The Nature of Q,' *Standard Edition*, vol. 1, pp. 392–97, for James Strachey's expanded discussion on the concept of energy. Ricoeur points out that we arrive at an understanding of energy and thus of an economics in Freud by way of *interpretation* of his texts and that it is an extremely necessary undertaking for, Ricoeur says, Freudianism only exists on the basis of our adamant refusal of the "disjunction" between an energy discourse and a phenomenological discourse. See *Freud and Philosophy*, p. 66. Unfortunately, the scope of my study does not allow for a detailed tracing of Freud's concept of energy, and I can permit myself only our designated anchors for my discussion of Green's work.
43. Freud, 'Project,' *Standard Edition*, vol. 1, p. 295.
44. Ricoeur, *Freud and Philosophy*, p. 65.
45. Strachey remarks that: "This theory of the economics of thought is another basic idea running through all of Freud's later writings." The paper 'Negation' is given in the list of references that are found in another footnote to which we are directed; see Lecture XXXII of the 'New Introductory Lectures,' *Standard Edition*, vol. 22, p. 89 (p. 334, n. 3).
46. Freud, 'Project,' *Standard Edition*, vol. 1, p. 334.
47. Ibid., p. 328.
48. Ibid., p. 333.
49. Ibid., pp. 334–35.
50. See Berthold-Bond's discussion of the "inverted world" (discussed in Chapter One) and "reality" for a similar and persuasive line of argument, although he is discussing the decentring of reason/reality in its most extreme form of madness. (*Hegel's Theory*, pp. 164–68).
51. Freud, 'Project,' p. 368.
52. Ibid., p. 369.
53. Ibid., p. 381.
54. Ibid., p. 326.
55. Ibid., p. 322.
56. Ibid., p. 331.
57. Žižek, *For They Know Not What They Do*, pp. 198–99.
58. Hyppolite, 'Hegel's Phenomenology and Psychoanalysis,' p. 59.
59. Freud, 'Beyond the Pleasure Principle,' *Standard Edition*, vol. 18, p. 8, 27.
60. Ibid., p. 21.
61. Ibid., p. 30.
62. Ibid., p. 35.
63. Ibid., p. 62
64. Ibid., p. 63.

65. Ibid., p. 62.
66. Ibid., p. 38.
67. Ibid., p. 43.
68. Ibid., p. 52.
69. Ibid., p. 46.
70. Ibid., pp. 60–61, n. 1.
71. Freud, 'Why War?' *Standard Edition*, vol. 22, p. 209.
72. It should be noted here that the context for Green's discussion of binding as a "structural suture" is perhaps indebted to the realm of the Lacanian signifier. Green discusses the notion of suture as it pertains to Lacan's theory in the context of Frege's mathematics in *Time and Psychoanalysis* (p. 23). Roudinesco also discusses the concept of suture in the context of Lacanian thought (*Lacan & Co.*, pp. 398–405). See also Žižek, *Less than Nothing*, Chapter 9, 'Suture and Pure Difference,' pp. 581–623.
73. Comparing Hegel and Freud's notions of freedom, Michael Roth argues that the idea of the wounds leaving no scars is part of Hegel's commitment to the "reconciling affirmation" of Spirit. Such reconciliation is dependent upon mutual forgiveness between two individuals and ultimately results in the full consciousness of freedom and the end of history and thus a "full redemption of the past in the Absolute." It is with this notion that he sees the major split between Hegel and Freud, as conversely for Freud, it is the very scars of the "struggle of spirit" that are the material of psychoanalysis and are to be examined and read for meaning. Roth goes on to posit that in Freud "knowing is not resolution" and that the "freedom of the analysand" is the "opportunity to act self-consciously on the basis of this knowing." I would argue that this is the freedom that Hegel offers if only his readers stop insisting on an artificial and totalizing "end of history"; see *Psycho-Analysis as History: Negation and Freedom in Freud* (Ithaca: Cornell University Press, 1995), pp. 131–32. See also his discussion of transference in Chapter Four, pp. 99–136. Missing from his account of Freud's 'Negation,' however, is the crucial exchange between Lacan and Hyppolite, which seems a rather strange omission from such a book on the crossover between Hegelian and Freudian thinking. For compelling contemporary discussions of this passage, see Rebecca Comay, *Mourning Sickness*, pp. 130–31. Comay provocatively comments: "As Karl Krause once said of psychoanalysis (although he meant it as a criticism), absolute knowing is the illness for which it presents the cure; the *Phenomenology* is the perfect case study of interminable analysis." See also Žižek, *Tarrying with the Negative*, pp. 165–99, and Catherine Malabou, *Changing Difference*, trans. Carolyn Shread (Cambridge: Polity Press, 2011) pp. 73–80.
74. André Green, *Diachrony in Psychoanalysis*, trans. by Andrew Weller (London: Free Association Books, 2003), p. 100. Further references to this edition are given after quotations in the text, abbreviated as *DP*.
75. Similarly, Hyppolite sees the "abstract dialectic" of Hegel's self-consciousness to be structured similar to the "absent-present" play that Freud talks about. (He also refers to the paper given by Lacan at the 1953 Rome Convention.) Although Hyppolite does not refer to the movement of Force, my reading finds elements for its continuation in his. See, Hyppolite, 'Hegel's Phenomenology and Psychoanalysis,' p. 63, n. 9.
76. Sussman, *Hegelian Aftermath*, p. 61.
77. Can we conceive of the *Phenomenology* itself as a series of repetitions, whose forward movement saves it from collapse? Anthony Wilden sees that there is a certain "diachronic repetition" at work in the *Phenomenology* and that such similar structures "beg to be considered in the light of the psychoanalytic compulsion to repeat"; see Jacques Lacan, *The Language of the Self: The*

Function of Language in Psychoanalysis, trans. and with notes and commentary by Anthony Wilden (Baltimore: John Hopkins Press, 1968), pp. 286–87.
78. See Zupančič, *Why Psychoanalysis?* pp. 50–56, where she discusses "interpretation as de-interpretation and unbinding" in the work of analysis, which she also characterizes as 'the untying of symptomatic ties.' It is slightly surprising that her astute discussion doesn't mention the work of Green, considering her Lacanian background.
79. Kojève, *Introduction to the Reading of Hegel*, pp. 27–28.
80. See *OPM*, pp. 115–41, for full discussion, as I can only make these brief remarks here.
81. Robert Williams remarks that this is a key moment in that it introduces "reciprocal" recognition and, like Roth, argues that forgiveness is the reason the wounds of Spirit leave no scars; see *Recognition: Hegel and Fichte on the Other*, pp. 207–09.
82. Jameson, *The Ideologies of Theory*, p. 25.
83. Green is elaborating upon the Winnicottian concept of transitional space. Due to the scope of my book, there will not be time to fully explore Winnicott's work itself, and thus I will only be able to approach the topic from Green's point of view. In Chapter Four I will show the usefulness of the idea of this transitional space to my discussion of vanishing. Clearly, however, Winnicott is in many ways a predominate figure behind Green and Bollas to whom full credit of influence must be given.
84. Thomas H. Ogden, *Subjects of Analysis* (Northvale, New Jersey: Jason Aronson, 1994).
85. As far as my theoretical approach goes, I use Green's own justification to shore up the crucial role of theoretical work: "Every psychoanalyst knows that clinical experience is the source of our knowledge, but it only takes on true meaning if it is illustrated by the theory that takes it into account" (*OPM*, p. 13). See also, *Squiggle*, p. 47, for a slightly more in depth discussion of Freud's use of the dualistic model.
86. The concept was first introduced in French in 1972, but the first English publication was not until 1986 with the arrival of *On Private Madness* (*Squiggle*, p. 48).
87. For a discussion of the influence of Peirce on Lacan (especially regarding the categories of the symbolic, imaginary, and real) see John P. Muller, *Beyond the Psychoanalytic Dyad: Developmental Semiotics in Freud, Peirce, and Lacan* (London: Routledge, 1996), p. 31. As I will show in the next chapter, Muller's work offers a reading of the third and Peirce's concept of thirdness within the framework of semiotics.
88. The aim here is clearly not to explore Peirce's theory in depth but is to simply sketch the origins of Green's thought. Green himself works through a close reading of Peirce in this text and sees strong links between Peirce's theory and Freud's paper 'Negation'; see *Squiggle*, pp. 39–68.
89. John Burbidge uses Peirce's language of "firstness, secondness and thirdness" to discuss Hegel's project in the *Phenomenology*. He writes that thirdness, as mediation, works to integrate what in Peirce's language is the "pervasive immediacy" (firstness) and the "brute fact" (secondness) that consciousness experiences as it comes to know itself and the world. Burbidge translates this in Hegel's terms to mean that thirdness works to integrate "essential truths about reality" with "experience," (p. 50). For a full discussion, see Burbidge, *Hegel's Systematic Contingency*, pp. 50–55. Robert Stern translates these categories into philosophical terms to be read alongside Peirce's critique of Hegel: firstness involves elements of individuality; secondness involves particularity and thirdness, universality; see Stern, *Hegelian Metaphysics*, p.40. Stern spends a good deal of time with the concept of 'Thirdness' in Hegel, but

it is in Peirce's terms (and Sterns discussion of Peirce's claims that Hegel was 'overcommitted to Thirdness,' i.e. universality, p. 240), not in the terms that I ascribe to the third, or thirdness; for a full discussion see, Stern, *Hegelian Metaphysics*, pp. 239–99.

90. The interest of my own work does not centre on the notion of thirdness as found in the child/mother/father model but rather as it is found in the latter two models.
91. As we will explore in more detail in the following chapter, when we elaborate on the notion of the dialectic, Lacan clearly viewed the analytic situation as a dialectical process, and it is safe to assume that Green is following suit. Throughout his work, Green (and see *WN* where he sees Freud's reasoning as Hegelian) uses the dialectic model to explore processes of psychoanalysis, and we can only assume he is using the Hegelian rather than the Greek or more strictly Kantian model.
92. Ogden, *Subjects of Analysis*, p. 64. He asks in a footnote on the same page that his concept of the third (a term he sees as completely interchangeable with "the analytic third" and the "intersubjective analytic third") not be confused with the Lacanian oedipal/symbolic third (name of the father). He writes, "The latter concept refers to a 'middle term' that stands between symbol and symbolized, between oneself and one's immediate lived sensory experience, thereby creating a space in which the interpreting, self-reflective, symbolizing subject is generated."
93. The majority of the theory found in Ogden's *Subjects of Analysis* is shot through with the model of dialectical tension (subject and object, analyst and analysand) that he sees as inherent in subjectivity. His Chapters Three and Four, however, are in particular devoted to the discussion of dialectical nature of intersubjectivity. Ogden also often uses (a version of) the activity of *Aufhebung* for his discussion of the analytic setting. He states, for instance: "The intersubjective and the individually subjective each create, negate, and preserve the other" (p. 64). See p. 21 for brief discussion of Freud's paper 'Negation' and the use of *Aufhebung.*
94. Ogden, *Subjects of Analysis*, p. 60.
95. Ibid., p. 93.
96. Ibid., p. 47.

NOTES TO CHAPTER 4

1. Christopher Bollas, *Free Association* (Cambridge: Icon Books, 2002), pp. 65–66. Further references to this edition are given after quotations in the text, abbreviated as *FA*.
2. Gregorio Kohon, *The British School of Psychoanalysis: The Independent Tradition*, ed. by Gregorio Kohon (London: Free Association Books, 1986), p. 20.
3. Hyppolite, 'The Human Situation in the Hegelian Phenomenology,' in *Hegel: Critical Assessments*, II, p. 407; also found in *Studies in Marx and Hegel*, p. 161.
4. Jacques Lacan, *Écrits: A Selection*, trans. by Alan Sheridan (London: Tavistock Publication, 1977), p. 78; *Seminar I*, p. 278. Also recall that it is Paul Ricoeur's project in *Freud and Philosophy* to show that analysis is "inherently dialectical" (see especially p. 460). Furthermore, as mentioned in Chapter Three, Thomas Ogden, Jon Mills, and Jessica Benjamin see the analytic situation as dialectical and use Hegel's model of intersubjectivity and dialectic as the basis for such theoretical moves. See not only Ogden's *Subjects of Analysis* but also *The Matrix of the Mind* (London: Karnac,

1992), pp. 208–14. Since this book is not an investigation of the concept of the dialectic as such, what I am interested in are those thinkers that are consciously utilising an interpretation of Hegelian thought, although I will not be able to touch on all of their works. Moreover, as we can recall, the issue that I take with those that *do* use the master/slave dialectic and the elaboration in the model of recognition is that they do not take into consideration the continuation of subjectivity/intersubjectivity into the later stages of self-consciousness that Hegel describes. In addition, it might be considered that it sets up a power dynamic of the analytic pair that ties it too closely to problematic hierarchical structures.

5. 'A Conversation with Christopher Bollas,' in *The Vitality of Objects*, ed. by Joseph Scalia, pp. 179–222 (p. 207).
6. Christopher Bollas, *Being a Character: Psychoanalysis and Self Experience*, (London: Routledge, 1992), p. 99. Further references to this edition are given after quotations in the text, abbreviated as *BC*.
7. In fact, as an analyst of the Independent Group, Bollas does not wish to claim allegiance to any particular psychoanalytic "school" and sees that each school would profit significantly from crossing its own theoretical boundaries. He writes, in a passage that is illustrative of his stance: "It is clear, I am sure, that my view of what constitutes the analytic is not a classical or a Kleinian position. I think that each of the schools in some respects polemicizes a single feature of analytic life. Each Freudian should also be a potential Kohutian, Kleinian, Winnicottian, Lacanian, and Bionian, as each of these schools only reflects a certain limited analytic experience"; see Christopher Bollas, *Forces of Destiny: Psychoanalysis and Human Idiom* (London: Free Association Books, 1991), p. 99. Further references to this edition are given after quotations in the text, abbreviated as *FD*. It is this open way of approaching the theory (and practice) of psychoanalysis that allows Bollas to be a suitable and crucial "case study" for a book such as the present one. See Gregorio Kohon's *The British School of Psychoanalysis*, pp. 24–50, for his extremely helpful introduction explaining the origins of the Independent Tradition and Bollas's place in it.
8. See Christine C. Kieffer, 'Emergence and the Analytic Third: Working at the Edge of Chaos,' *Psychoanalytic Dialogues: The International Journal of Relational Perspectives*, 17:5 (2007), 683–704. Kieffer's paper is an attempt to think about the "analytic third" as "something that is created that is more than the sum of its parts" (p. 683) and discusses it as an "emergent phenomenon" (p. 684), and she credits Green's work on the concept (p. 690). Also see Jill Gentile, 'Close But No Cigar: Perversion of Agency and the Absence of Thirdness,' *Contemporary Psychoanalysis*, 37 (2001), 623–54. Quite helpfully, Gentile discusses the function of the third as "articulation" and further that it is the breakdown of twoness that brings the emergence of thirdness. Strangely, in all of the material regarding thirdness, Ogden is most heavily credited with the concept. Aside from Kieffer, it is only in a paper by Samuel Gerson that I have been able to locate in the literature on the subject a tracing of the early formations of the concept back to Green. He writes of Green's (1975) contribution of the "intersubjective processes as constituting an *analytic object*." Importantly, he also locates in Bollas (1992) a "similar notion of a relational third in his description of a *third intermediate object*"; see 'The Relational Unconscious: A Core Element,' *Psychoanalytic Quarterly* (2004) Vol. 73, 63–98 (p. 79).
9. Steinkraus, *New Studies in Hegel's Philosophy*, p. 70, n. 26.
10. Lacan, *Seminar I*, p. 48.
11. Ibid., p. 49.

12. Lacan, *Écrits*, p. 258, n. 49.
13. Shoshana Felman, *Jacques Lacan and the Adventure of Insight: Psychoanalysis in Contemporary Culture* (Cambridge: Harvard University Press, 1987), p. 127. In what I find to be a rather liberating reading, Felman appreciates Lacan's use of the Oedipus on a "structural level" and does not tie it down to simply "a question addressing analysands' desire for parents" and further sees it is instead "a question addressing analysands' misapphrension, misrecognition (*méconnaissance*) of their own history" (p. 129).
14. Michele Minolli and Maria Luisa Tricoli, 'Solving the Problems of Duality: The Third and Self-Consciousness,' *Psychoanalytic Quarterly*, 73 (2004), 137–65. See especially p. 142 where they outline ten different ways in which the concept of the third has been used and developed. They list Ogden's theory of "intersubjectively generated experience of the analytic pair" but include no mention of Green. As well, they list the use by certain thinkers of Lacan's "Name of the Father" as an unconscious structure. It is not important at this point to explore each of the ten approaches, but I will be referring again to this contextualisation of the concept as I proceed. See also C.M.T. Hanly, on the history of the concept in both philosophy and psychoanalysis. Hanly highlights, amongst other factors, the importance of C. S. Peirce's philosophy for Lacan and for the concept of thirdness in psychoanalytic theory. See 'A Brief Historical Analysis of an Idea,' *Psychoanalytic Quarterly*, 73 (2004), 267–90 (p. 268). However, his treatment of Hegel is cursory and unsatisfactory, and it is hoped that my study gestures towards an expansion of the understanding of how we can situate Hegel's philosophy in a discussion of the concept. In addition, see Michael Theunissen's *The Other* for his location of the concept of the third in the work of Sartre and his argument that Sartre drew his understanding of the concept from the work of George Simmel (1908) (p. 401, n. 24).
15. Lacan, *Seminar I*, p.2.
16. Minolli and Tricoli, 'Solving the Problems of Duality', p. 140.
17. The concept of countertransference has been the subject of much debate in psychoanalytic theory. Kleinians might argue, for example, that its causes and effects lie in the patient's projections on to the analyst. See *Melanie Klein Today: Developments in Theory and Practice*, ed. by Elizabeth Bott Spillius (London: Routledge, 1988), especially Roger Money-Kyrle's paper 'Normal Counter-Transference and Some of Its Deviations (1956), pp. 22–33, and Irma Brenman Pick's 'Working through in the Counter-Transference (1985), pp. 34–47. See also *The British School of Psychoanalysis*, ed. by Kohon, pp. 51–73. For a very recent collection of papers on the concept, fittingly for my purposes edited by André Green, see *Resonance of Suffering: Countertransference in Non-Neurotic Structures* (London: International Psychoanalytic Association, 2007). See Green's paper 'The Central Phobic Position: with a Model of the Free-Association Method' (pp. 41–74) and a paper by Fernando Urribarri entitled 'The Analyst's Psychic Work and the Three Concepts of Countertransference' (pp. 165–88). Urribarri, in giving an extremely helpful summary of the history of the concept, directly addresses both Green's and Bollas's contribution to the theory and discusses "the psychoanalyst's mental functioning" in the session, the concept of "thirdness"/"third object" (p. 178–80) and the tertiary and binding processes in Green (p. 184).
18. Minolli and Tricoli, 'Solving the Problems of Duality', p. 140.
19. Ibid., p. 143.
20. Jessica Benjamin also posits that it is with Lacan and his Hegelian (via Kojève) views of intersubjectivity that "the idea of the third passed in to

psychoanalysis" but seems content to leave it at that, which is unsurprising given her own heavy investment in the master/slave paradigm; see 'Beyond Doer and Done To: An Intersubjective View of Thirdness,' *Psychoanalytic Quarterly*, 73 (2004), 5–46. That being said, Benjamin offers an illuminating reading of the concept of thirdness in the intersubjective clinical situation and proposes a way of thinking beyond Lacan's notion of the third as having as its primary model the Oedipus and thus later that of the "Law of the Father," the symbolic law (p. 12). Interestingly, she believes that Ogden's concept of the analytic third, which I discussed in the previous chapter and which I am pursuing here in another form with Bollas, is actually a "negative third" because she reads it as "sucking space" rather than creating it (pp. 9–10). I do not entirely agree with her reading due to my view that this third, this "object" that is created out of the work of the two subjects, can be seen to be creating space as well as to be a structure *in* space itself. It is clearly important to acknowledge the number of ways in which the concept is used in psychoanalytic theory and that we are taking elements from certain lines in order to understand the concept in light of Hegel's philosophy.

21. For an in depth discussion of the notion of the dyad and its relationship to the third, see again John P. Muller's *Beyond the Psychoanalytic Dyad: Developmental Semiotics in Freud, Peirce, and Lacan*. There he discusses the third as the semiotic code that exists outside of the dyad of the psychoanalytic situation and, crucially for my discussion, as that which binds them together. Furthermore he sees that it is representative of "culture and semiotics that grounds the positions of each member of the dyad and makes possible a relationship between them" (pp. 61–74 [p. 71]). So the third is for Muller a mediating structural system.
22. Minolli and Tricoli, 'Solving the Problems of Duality', p. 149.
23. Ibid., p. 144.
24. Ibid., p. 144.
25. Roger Kennedy, *The Elusive Human Subject* (London: Free Association Books, 1998), pp. 10–11. Kennedy asserts that it was Bollas who introduced the concept of "subject relations theory" to the psychoanalytic community.
26. See Leo Bersani, *The Freudian Body* (New York: Columbia University Press, 1986), particularly 'Theory and Violence' (pp. 7–27), for a discussion of the "collapse of theory" that he sees as a "constitutive fact of both Freudian theory and esthetic practice." Bersani claims that the "moments of theoretical collapse in Freud are inseparable from what" he "risk[s] calling psychoanalytic truth" (p. 7, 10).
27. Bowie, in *Vitality of Objects*, xvi.
28. Bollas, *The Shadow of the Object: Psychoanalysis of the Unthought Known* (London: Free Association Books, 1987), p. 247. Further references to this edition are given after quotations in the text, abbreviated as *SO*.
29. See also Bollas, *Cracking Up: The Work of Unconscious Experience* (London: Routledge, 1995), 'Communications of the Unconscious,' pp. 9–30. Further references to this edition are given after quotations in the text, abbreviated as *CU*. Here Bollas discusses the way in which the unconscious of both the analyst and analysand communicate with each other.
30. Because Bollas himself admits his debt to Winnicott, there is inevitably a bit of a crossover of theory here with Winnicott's notion of "potential space." We must be careful to distinguish between formulations of this "transitional/transformational" space and "potential space." As argued in Chapter Three, I am not discussing the space that lies between fantasy and reality but am, following Green (who is also following Winnicott), using the notion to think about the "space where the future subject is *in transit*" (*Squiggle,* 88). For an accessible and

informative discussion of Winnicott's notion of "potential space," see Thomas Ogden's *The Matrix of the Mind*, pp. 203–32. One of the key elements that can be taken from the Winnicottian model is that potential space both joins and separates the infant (child or adult) and the mother (object.) We can utilise this to understand how the thirdness, seen in terms of "space," can be seen to both bind and unbind the subject(s). Helpfully, and as aforementioned, Ogden uses the idea of Hegel's dialectical process as "a possible paradigm for understanding the form or mode of the psychological activity generating potential space" (p. 204, 208). I, too, take this route. See Frank Summers, 'Creation and Discovery in the Psychoanalytic Process,' in *Relational and Intersubjective Perspectives in Psychoanalysis*, ed. by Jon Mills, pp. 131–51, for a discussion of the way in which Bollas elaborates Winnicott's model of transitional space.

31. Summers, 'Creation and Discovery in the Psychoanalytic Process,' pp. 138–39.
32. The concept of the "true self" is directly inherited from Winnicott, but Bollas wishes in his work to push the understanding of it further, beyond Winnicott's idea that the true self was simply "aliveness itself" (*FD*, 8).
33. For the origins of Bollas's use of "object," see Winnicott, 'The Use of an Object and Relating through Identifications,' in D.W. Winnicott, *Playing and Reality* (London: Routledge, 2005), pp. 115–27. This chapter is based on a paper, 'The Use of an Object,' given in 1968 and also published in the *International Journal of Psycho-Analysis*, 50 (1969), pp. 711-716. One of the main tenets of his article is the "patient's ability to use the analyst" and the analyst's "survival" of this use.
34. Bollas, *The Mystery of Things* (London: Routledge, 1999), p. 6. Further references to this edition are given after quotations in the text, abbreviated as *MT*.
35. Gabriella Mann, 'Transformational, Conservative and Terminal Objects: The Application of Bollas's Concepts to Practice,' in *Vitality of Objects*, pp. 58–77 (p. 73).
36. Thomas Ogden, 'The Analytic Third: Working with Intersubjective Clinical Facts,' in *Relational Psychoanalysis*, ed. by Mitchell and Lewis, (1994), pp. 459–92 (p. 487). This rethinking on Ogden's part takes place five years after he published the material I considered in the previous chapter. Significantly, he shifts slightly in this rethinking to a consideration of the analytic third as a "third subject" in the room, "which seems to take on a life of its own in the interpersonal field" between the analyst and analysand, thus giving it a more human, embodied dimension than he seemed to grant it in his first formulations (p. 487). The idea of this third as another subject is not necessarily the line I want to follow, although it is important to acknowledge it.
37. Joel Beck, 'Lost in Thought: The Receptive Unconscious,' in *Vitality of Objects*, ed. by Scalia, pp. 9–36 (p. 10). His topic is Bollas's concept of "psychic genera."
38. Jessica Benjamin, 'Recognition and Destruction: An Outline of Intersubjectivity' in *Relational Psychoanalysis*, ed. by Mitchell and Lewis, (1990), pp. 181–210 (pp. 191–92). In spite of the fact that I took issue with Benjamin in the previous chapters for restricting her model of the struggle for recognition to the master/slave episode, she is still of great use to my investigation as a practicing analyst and theorist who incorporates Hegelian philosophy into her work in interesting and fruitful ways. She traces her thinking on intersubjectivity back to Hegel via Habermas in that the shift in thinking of the "primacy of a subject who knows or transforms the object to a subject who communicates with other subjects" started with Hegel and is focussed on the act of recognition. She thus differentiates herself from others in the intersubjective school, "whose definition of intersubjectivity refers to all interplay between different subject worlds" (p. 201). See again Winnicott, 'The Use of an Object,' as the

likely origin of Benjamin's understanding of the transition from "relating" to an object to "using" an object (*Playing and Reality*, pp. 115–27).

39. Benjamin, 'Recognition and Destruction,' p. 192.
40. Clark Butler, however, makes a case for a comparison in 'Hegel and Freud: A Comparison,' that the method of Freudian free association bears a resemblance to Hegel's phenomenological method of charting the appearance of the mind by "empathetically reliving the course of human development" (p. 507). The difference being, Butler notes, that Freud's method is regressive whereas Hegel's is a progressive method. For Freud, Butler argues, "free association aims at unearthing the buried past, while empathetic reliving aims at articulating the meaning of the present by following its development out of the past" (ibid.). For his full discussion of what he sees as the comparison between Hegel and Freud and how they can be used to illuminate the other, see the article 'Hegel and Freud: A Comparison,' pp. 506–22.
41. Although it is discussed most prominently in *The Mystery of Things*, Bollas also refers to interpretation as a binding process in *Forces of Destiny*, which was published ten years earlier.
42. He writes that he is most heavily indebted to Winnicott, Bion, Marion Milner, Theador Reik, and Harold Searles. See *FD*, pp. 51–53, for further history.
43. Christopher Bollas, *The Freudian Moment* (London: Karnac, 2007), p. 9.
44. Ibid., p. 91. Bollas also argues that one of the dangers of the transference interpretation is that the analyst reads the analysand's communications as "hidden references to the analyst's self" and that this can eventually alienate the analysand. Here Bollas states that the analysis could potentially "become a realisation of what André Green terms the 'work of the negative'" (p. 97). It seems, however, that Bollas does not acknowledge the positive potential Green also attributes to the work of the negative as a "moment of transformation."
45. Muller, *Beyond Psychoanalytic Dyad*, p. 98.
46. Forster, *Hegel's Idea*, pp. 119–20.
47. Houlgate, *An Introduction to Hegel*, p. 61–62.
48. Kenneth R. Westphal explains why Hegel uses the designations of "shapes" or "forms" of consciousness in order to encapsulate both of these levels: "Hegel adopts the 'form of consciousness' as a unit of analysis in order to have a general rubric for conceptual schemes that is neutral on some issues, flexible on some others, and committed on still others"; see *Hegel's Epistemological Realism: A Study of the Aim and Method of Hegel's Phenomenology of Spirit* (Dordrecht: Kluwer Academic Publishers, 1989), p. 92.
49. Houlgate, *An Introduction to Hegel*, p. 62.
50. Burbidge, *Systematic Contingency*, p. 73.
51. Davis, *Inwardness and Existence*, p. 71.
52. For a wonderful discussion of such a claim as I see Hegel making regarding the necessity of true freedom arising only in being bound to the other, see Robert Pippin, 'Recognition and Reconciliation: Actualized Agency in Hegel's Jena *Phenomenology*,' in *Hegel: New Directions*, ed. by Katerina Deligiorgi, pp. 125–42. There Pippin claims that "Hegel's argument for a particular sort of original dependence necessary for the possibility of individuality" is a "distinctly philosophical claim, a shift in our understanding of individuality" (p. 129). Pippin extends this argument into a discussion of various strains and complexities of liberal political thought. See also Peter Osborne's *The Politics of Time* (London: Verso, 1995), p. 79, where he argues that "freedom comes, phenomenologically, from the other, and it is the ambivalence of this relationship which is the true source of existential anxiety." Had I the scope, there is potential for a link to be made between the frenzied state leading up to and culminating in the unhappy consciousness with this concept of anxiety.

53. Nancy, *Restlessness of the Negative*, p. 60.
54. This idea of groundlessness, for Robert Williams, also applies to the project of philosophy as such. He argues, "Hegel's phenomenology begins at the abyss where Husserl's ends, namely the discovery of the groundlessness of the philosophical enterprise"; see *Recognition: Fichte and Hegel on the Other*, p. 15. Williams also argues, and I agree, that absolute knowing is an intersubjective, social process. See especially Chapter Eleven, 'Recognition and Absolute Knowledge,' p. 253–84.
55. Nancy, *Restlessness of the Negative*, p. 41.
56. Dews, *Logics of Disintegration*, p. 65.
57. Gadamer, *Hegel's Dialectic*, p. 52.

NOTES TO CONCLUSION

1. Solomon, *In the Spirit of Hegel*, p. 639.
2. On a more technically argued level, John Burbidge discusses absolute knowing as a *way* of "knowing that can be exercised universally." He argues that those who find Hegel's claims to absolute knowing to be absurd are responding to what he sees as a mistranslation of "Das absolute wissen." Based on his own translation, he writes that the noun is an "infinitive, with verbal force." This indicates to him that it does not "name a simple state of affairs" but instead talks about how we know, and thus absolute knowing is not a static and final level that is reached but a way of being "certain of getting at the truth of things." Further he sees that at each stage of consciousness, there is absolute knowing, a momentary certainty that it knows all there is to know, until, that is, it is moved by experience to the next shape of knowing; see *Hegel's Systematic Contingency*, pp. 49, 54, 73. See in particular Chapter Five, "Absolute Knowing," pp. 70–80, for a history of Hegel's use of the term.
3. Nancy, *Restlessness of the Negative*, p. 28.
4. In addition to his thoughts on the "scars" of Spirit discussed in Chapter Three, Michael Roth argues that it is with the notion of forgiveness that forgetting occurs for Hegel, and thus the wounds of spirit *cannot* leave scars because "some wounds cut too deeply [. . .]. Some scars must simply vanish if we are to go on believing in the meaning and direction of our action"; see Roth, *Knowing and History*, pp. 42–43. So this would be Roth's argument for "losing all that preceded" in allowing the scars to vanish. Keeping my thoughts on vanishing in mind, however, it might be argued that transitioning into a new form of being is a way of "believing in the meaning," not losing old meaning.
5. Derrida states that in Hegel, "the philosophical, critical, reflective, consciousness is not only contained in the scrutiny given to the operations and works of history. What is first in question is the history of this consciousness *itself*"; see Derrida, 'Force and Signification,' pp. 22–23.
6. As noted in Chapter Two, I am following the lead of readers of Hegel who read in the vein of Wahl and Hyppolite, thus understanding the *Phenomenology* on the level of consciousness first and via the historical examples it draws from second. One such critic, Kenneth Westphal, takes similar stance and offers as succinct an explanation of this way of reading as can be found: "If Hegel's account is correct, historical epochs and extant philosophies are variations on, if not instances of, the forms of consciousness he recounts in the *Phenomenology*. This is because both forms of consciousness, as well as historically identifiable positions, devolve from the real characteristics of consciousness; see *Hegel's Epistemological Realism*, p. 92.

References

PRIMARY SOURCES

Christopher Bollas

Being a Character: Psychoanalysis and Self Experience (London: Routledge, 1992)
The Christopher Bollas Reader (London: Routledge, 2011)
Cracking Up: The Work of Unconscious Experience (London: Routledge, 1995)
The Evocative Object World (London: Routledge, 2008)
Forces of Destiny: Psychoanalysis and human idiom (London: Free Association Books, 1991)
Free Association (Cambridge: Icon Books, 2002)
The Freudian Moment (London: Karnac, 2007)
The Infinite Question (2009, London: Routledge, 2009)
The Mystery of Things (London: Routledge, 1999)
The Shadow of the Object: Psychoanalysis of the Unthought Known (London: Free Association Books, 1987)

André Green

The Chains of Eros: The Sexual in Psychoanalysis, trans. by Luke Thurston (London: Karnac, 2001)
Diachrony in Psychoanalysis, trans. by Andrew Weller (London: Free Association Books, 2003)
The Fabric of Affect in the Psychoanalytic Discourse, trans. by Alan Sheridan (London: Routledge, 1999)
'The Intrapsychic and Intersubjective in Psychoanalysis,' *Psychoanalytic Quarterly*, 69 (2000), 1–39
Key Ideas for a Contemporary Psychoanalysis: Misrecognition and Recognition of the Unconscious (London: Routledge, 2005)
On Private Madness (London: Hogarth Press, 1986)
Resonance of Suffering: Countertransference in Non-neurotic Structures (London: International Psychoanalytic Association, 2007)
Time in Psychoanalysis, trans. by Andrew Weller (London: Free Association Books, 2002)
The Work of the Negative (London: Free Association Books, 1999)

G.W.F Hegel

Encyclopaedia Logic, trans. by William Wallace (Oxford: Clarendon Press, 1975)
Hegel's Introduction to the Lectures to the History of Philosophy, trans. T. M. Knox and A. V. Miller (Oxford: Oxford University Press, 1985)

Hegel's Philosophy of Mind, trans. by William Wallace, (Oxford: Clarendon Press, 1971)
Hegel's Philosophy of Nature, trans by. A. V. Miller (Oxford: Oxford University Press, 2004)
The Jena System, 1804–5; Logic and Metaphysics, ed. and intro by H. S. Harris, trans. by John W. Burbidge and George di Giovanni (Kingston: McGill-Queen's University Press, 1986)
Phenomenology of Spirit, trans. by A. V. Miller (Oxford: Oxford University Press, 1977)
The Philosophical Propaedeutic, trans. by A. V. Miller, ed. by Michael George and Andrew Vincent (Oxford: Blackwell, 1986)
Science of Logic, trans. by A. V. Miller (London: Allen and Unwin, 1969)

Secondary Works

Abram, Jan, ed., *André Green at the* Squiggle *Foundation: Winnicott Studies Monograph Series* (London: Karnac Books, 2000)
Adkins, Brent, *Death and Desire in Hegel, Heidegger and Deleuze* (Edinburgh: Edinburgh University Press, 2007)
Adorno, Theodor W., *Hegel: Three Studies*, trans. by Shierry Weber Nicholsen (London: MIT Press, 1993)
Agamben, Georgio, *Language and Death: The Place of Negativity*, trans. by Karen E. Pinkus and Michael Hardt (Minneapolis: University of Minnesota Press, 1991)
Altieri, Charles, 'The Concept of Force as Modernist Response to the Authority of Science,' *Modernism/modernity*, 5:2 (1998), 77–93
Aron, Lewis and Harris, Adrienne, eds., *Relational Psychoanalysis Vol. 2: Innovation and Expansion* (Hillsdale, NJ: Analytic Press, 2005)
Atwood, George. E., and Stolorow, Robert D., *Structures of Subjectivity: Explorations in Psychoanalytic Phenomenology* (Hillsdale, NJ: Analytic Press, 1984)
Bachelard, Gaston, *The Psychoanalysis of Fire*, trans. by Alan Ross (London: Quartet Encounters, 1987)
Badiou, Alain, *Theoretical Writings*, trans. and ed. by Ray Brassier and Alberto Toscano (London: Continuum, 2004)
Barnett, Stuart, ed., *Hegel After Derrida* (London: Routledge, 1998)
Baugh, Bruce, *French Hegel: From Surrealism to Postmodernism* (London: Routledge, 2003)
Beardsworth, Richard, 'Freud, Energy and Chance: A Conversation with Jean-Francois Lyotard,' *Tekhnema*, 5 (1999), tekhnema.free.fr/5Beardsworth.html [accessed 3 June 2013]
Benjamin, Jessica, 'Beyond Doer and Done To: An Intersubjective View of Thirdness,' *Psychoanalytic Quarterly*, 73 (2004), 5–46
——— *The Bonds of Love: Psychoanalysis, Feminism and the Problem of Domination* (London: Virago, 1990)
——— *Shadow of the Other: Intersubjectivity and Gender in Psychoanalysis* (London: Routledge, 1998)
Bersani, Leo, *The Freudian Body* (New York: Columbia University Press, 1986)
Berthold-Bond, Daniel, *Hegel's Grand Synthesis: A Study of Being, Thought, and History* (Albany: SUNY Press, 1989)
——— *Hegel's Theory of Madness* (Albany: SUNY Press, 1995)
Binswanger, Ludwig, *Being in the World: Selected Papers*, trans. by Jacob Needleman (London: Souvenir Press, 1975)
Bion, W. R., *Attention and Interpretation* (New York: Jason Aronson, 1983)
——— *Elements of Psychoanalysis* (London: Karnac Books, 1984)
Blanchot, Maurice, *The Infinite Conversation,* trans. by Susan Hanson (Minneapolis: University of Minnesota Press, 1993)
Boothby, Richard, *Death and Desire: Psychoanalytic Theory in Lacan's Return to Freud* (London: Routledge, 1991)

——— *Freud as Philosopher: Metapsychology After Lacan* (London: Routledge, 2001)
Bott Spillius, Elizabeth, ed., *Melanie Klein Today: Developments in Theory and Practice* (London: Routledge, 1988)
Bowie, Malcolm, *Lacan* (London: Fontana Press, 1991)
——— *Psychoanalysis and the Future of Theory* (London: Blackwell, 1993)
Brazill, William J., *The Young Hegelians* (New Haven, CT: Yale University Press, 1970)
Brennan, Teresa, *The Interpretation of the Flesh: Freud and Femininity* (London: Routledge, 1992)
Browning, Gary K., ed., *Hegel's Phenomenology of Spirit: A Reappraisal* (London: Kluwer Academic Publishers, 1997)
Buber, Martin, *I and Thou*, trans. by Ronald Gregor Smith (London: Continuum, 2004)
Burbidge, John W., *Hegel's Logic and Religion: The Reasonableness of Christianity* (Albany: SUNY Press, 1992)
——— *Hegel's Systematic Contingency* (London: Palgrave, 2007)
Butler, Clark, 'Hegel and Freud: A Comparison,' *Philosophy and Phenomenological Research*, 36:4 (1976), pp. 506–22
Butler, Judith, *The Psychic Life of Power* (Stanford: Stanford University Press, 1997)
——— *Subjects of Desire. Hegelian Reflections in Twentieth-Century France* (New York: Columbia University Press, 1999)
Chessick, Richard D., *The Future of Psychoanalysis* (Albany: SUNY Press, 2007)
Christensen, Darrel E., 'Hegel's Phenomenological Analysis and Freud's Psychoanalysis,' *International Philosophical Quarterly*, 8:3 (1968), 356–78
Ciavatta, David V., *Spirit, the Family and the Unconscious in Hegel's Philosophy* (Albany: SUNY Press, 2009)
Comay, Rebecca, *Mourning Sickness: Hegel and the French Revolution* (Stanford: Stanford University Press, 2011)
Coole, Diana, *Negativity and Politics: Dionysus and Dialectics from Kant to Poststructuralism* (London: Routledge, 2007)
Cooper, Barry, *The End of History: An Essay on Modern Hegelianism* (Toronto: University of Toronto Press, 1984)
Croce, Benedetto, *What is Living and What is Dead of the Philosophy of Hegel*, trans from the Original Text of the Third Italian edition, 1912, by Douglas Ainslie (New York: Garland, 1984)
Crossley, Nick, *Intersubjectivity: The Fabric of Social Becoming* (London: Sage Publications, 1996)
Davis, Walter A., *Inwardness and Existence: Subjectivity in/and Hegel, Heidegger, Marx and Freud* (Madison: University of Wisconsin Press, 1989)
Deleuze, Gilles, *Nietzsche and Philosophy*, trans. by Hugh Tomlinson (London: Athlone Press, 1983)
Deligiorgi, Katerina, ed., *Hegel: New Directions* (Chesham: Acumen Press, 2006)
Denker, Alfred and Vater, Michael, eds., *Hegel's Phenomenology of Spirit: New Critical Essays* (Amherst: Humanity Books/ Prometheus Books, 2003)
Derrida, Jacques, *Glas*, trans. by John P. Leavey, Jr. and Richard Rand (Lincoln: University of Nebraska Press, 1986)
——— *Margins of Philosophy*, trans. by Alan Bass (Brighton: Harvester Press, 1982)
——— *The Work of Mourning*, ed. by Pascale-Anne Brault and Michael Naas (Chicago: University of Chicago Press, 2001)
——— *Writing and Difference*, trans. by Alan Bass (Chicago: Chicago University Press, 1978)
DeVries, Willem A., *Hegel's Theory of Mental Activity: An Introduction to Theoretical Spirit* (Ithaca: Cornell University Press, 1988)
Dews, Peter, *Logics of Disintegration* (London: Verso, 2007)
Di Giovanni, George and Harris, H. S., *Between Kant and Hegel: Texts in Development of Post-Kantian Idealism* (Albany: SUNY Press, 1985)

Dove, Kenley R., 'Hegel's Phenomenological Method,' *Review of Metaphysics*, 23 (1970), 627–41
Dow Magnus, Kathleen, *Hegel and the Symbolic Mediation of Spirit* (Albany: SUNY Press, 2001)
Edelman, Gerald, *Bright Air, Brilliant Fire: On the Matter of the Mind* (London: Basic Books, 1992)
Edwards, Jeffrey, *Substance, Force, and the Possibility of Knowledge: On Kant's Philosophy of Material Nature* (Berkley: University of California Press, 2000)
Feenberg, Andrew, *Heidegger and Marcuse: The Catastrophe and Redemption of History* (London: Routledge, 2005)
Feldman, Karen S., *Binding Words: Conscience and Rhetoric in Hobbes, Hegel, and Heidegger* (Evanston, IL: Northwestern University Press, 2006)
Feldstein, Richard, Fink, Bruce, and Jaanus, Maire, eds., *Reading Seminars I and II: Lacan's Return to Freud* (Albany: SUNY Press, 1996)
Felman, Shoshana, *Jacques Lacan and the Adventure of Insight* (Cambridge, MA: Harvard University Press, 1987)
Fichte, J. G., *Science of Knowledge*, trans. by Peter Heath and John Lachs (Cambridge: Cambridge University Press, 1982)
Findlay, J. N., *Hegel, A Re-Examination* (London: George Allen & Unwin, 1958)
Finlay, Marike, 'Post-Modernising Psychoanalysis /Psychoanalysing Post-Modernity: Reontologising the Subject in Discourse,' *Free Assns*, 16 (1989), 43–80
Forrester, John, *The Seductions of Psychoanalysis: Freud, Lacan and Derrida* (Cambridge: Cambridge University Press, 1990)
Forster, Michael, *Hegel's Idea of a Phenomenology of Spirit* (Chicago: University of Chicago Press, 1998)
Freud, Sigmund, 'Negation,' *The Standard Edition of the Complete Psychological Works of Sigmund Freud*, trans. and ed. by James Strachey in collaboration with Anna Freud, 24 vols (London: Hogarth Press, 1999), Vol. 19.
——— *The Standard Edition of the Complete Psychological Works of Sigmund Freud*, 24 vols, trans. and ed. by James Strachey in collaboration with Anna Freud, assisted by Alix Strachey and Alan Tyson (London: Vintage, 2001)
——— 'Beyond the Pleasure Principle,' *Standard Edition*, vol. 18
——— 'Project for a Scientific Psychology,' *Standard Edition*, vol. 1
——— 'The Unconscious,' *Standard Edition*, vol. 4
——— 'Why War?,' *Standard Edition*, vol. 22
Frie, Roger, *Subjectivity and Intersubjectivity in Modern Philosophy and Psychoanalysis: A Study of Sartre, Binswanger, Lacan, and Habermas* (London: Rowman & Littlefield, 1997)
Gadamer, Hans-Georg, *Hegel's Dialectic: Five Hermeneutical Studies*, trans. by P. Christopher Smith (New Haven, CT: Yale University Press, 1976)
Gellner, Ernest, *The Psychoanalytic Movement: The Cunning of Unreason* (Oxford: Blackwell, 2003)
Gentile, Jill, 'Close But No Cigar: Perversion of Agency and the Absence of Thirdness,' *Contemporary Psychoanalysis*, 37 (2001), 623–54
Gerson, Samuel, 'The Relational Unconscious: A Core Element,' *Psychoanalytic Quarterly* (2004) 73, 63–98
Gill, Merton and Pribram, Karl, *Freud's 'Project' Reassessed* (London: Hutchinson & Co., 1976)
Greene, Murray, 'Hegel's "Unhappy Consciousness" and Nietzsche's "Slave Morality,"' in *Hegel and the Philosophy of Religion: The Wofford Symposium*, ed. by Darrel E. Christensen (The Hague: Martinus Nijhoff, 1970).
Habermas, Jurgen, *Knowledge and Human Interests*, trans. by Jeremy J. Shapiro (London: Heinemann, 1972)
_______ *The Philosophical Discourse of Modernity* (Cambridge: Polity Press, 1987)

Hahn, Songsuk Susan, *Contradiction in Motion: Hegel's Organic Concept of Life and Value* (Ithaca: Cornell University Press, 2007)
Hanly, C.M.T., 'A Brief Historical Analysis of an Idea,' *Psychoanalytic Quarterly*, 73 (2004), 267–90
Hannay, Alastair, *Kierkegaard* (London: Routledge, 1982)
Harris, Errol, *The Spirit of Hegel* (Atlantic Highlands, New Jersey: Humanities Press, 1993)
Harris, H. S., *Hegel: Phenomenology and System* (Indianapolis: Hackett Publishing, 1995)
——— *Hegel's Development: Night Thoughts 1801–1806* (Oxford: Clarendon Press, 1983)
——— *Hegel's Development: Toward the Sunlight 1770–1801* (Oxford: Clarendon Press, 1972)
Heidegger, Martin, *Hegel's Phenomenology of Spirit*, trans. by Parvis Emad and Kenneth Maly (Bloomington: Indiana University Press: 1988)
Helm, Georg, *The Historical Development of Energetics*, trans. by Robert J. Deltete (London: Kluwer Academic Publishers, 2000)
Henrich, Dieter, *Between Kant and Hegel: Lectures on German Idealism*, ed. by David S. Pacini (Cambridge, MA: Harvard University Press, 2003)
Henry, Michel, *The Genealogy of Psychoanalysis*, trans. by Douglas Brick (Standford: Stanford University Press, 1993)
Hinchman, Lewis P., *Hegel's Critique of the Enlightenment* (Gainesville: University Presses of Florida, 1984)
Houlgate, Stephen, ed., *Hegel and the Philosophy of Nature* (Albany: SUNY Press, 1998)
——— *An Introduction to Hegel: Freedom, Truth and History* (Oxford: Blackwell Publishing, 2005)
——— *The Opening of Hegel's Logic* (West Lafayette, IN: Purdue University Press, 2006)
Hyppolite, Jean, *Genesis and Structure of Hegel's Phenomenology* (Chicago: Northwestern University Press, 1997)
——— *Logic and Existence*, trans. Leonard Lawlor and Amit Sen (Albany: SUNY Press, 1997)
——— *Studies in Marx and Hegel* (London: Heinemann, 1969)
Inwood, Michael, *Hegel* (Oxford: Oxford University Press, 1983)
——— *A Hegel Dictionary* (Oxford: Blackwell Publishers, 1997)
Iragaray, Luce, *Sexes and Genealogies*, trans. Gillian C. Gill (New York: Columbia University Press, 1993)
Jameson, Fredric, *The Ideologies of Theory: Essays 1971–1986, Vol. 2: Syntax of History* (London: Routledge, 1988)
——— *Postmodernism: Or, The Cultural Logic of Late Capitalism* (London: Verso, 1991)
Jammer, Max, *Concepts of Force: A Study in the Foundations of Dynamics* (Mineola, NY: Dover Publications, 1999)
Kain, Philip J., *Hegel and the Other: A Study of the Phenomenology of Spirit* (Albany: SUNY Press, 2005)
Kainz, Howard, *Hegel's Phenomenology, Part 1: Text and Commentary* (Athens: Ohio University Press, 1998)
Kalkavage, Peter, *The Logic of Desire: An Introduction to Hegel's Phenomenology of Spirit* (Philadelphia: Paul Dry Books, 2007)
Kant, Immanuel, *Critique of Pure Reason*, trans. by Norman Kemp Smith (Basingstoke: Palgrave Macmillan, 2003)
——— *Opus postumum*, trans. by Eckart Förster and Michael Rosen, ed. by. Eckart Förster (Cambridge: Cambridge University Press, 1993)

Kaufmann, Walter, *Hegel: A Reinterpretation* (Garden City: Anchor Books, 1965)
Kelly, Sean M., *Individuation and the Absolute: Hegel, Jung and the Path toward Wholeness* (New York: Paulist Press, 1993)
Kennedy, Roger, *The Elusive Human Subject* (London: Free Association Books, 1998)
Kieffer, Christine C., 'Emergence and the Analytic Third: Working at the Edge of Chaos,' *Psychoanalytic Dialogues: The International Journal of Relational Perspectives*, 17:5 (2007), 683–704
Kirshner, Lewis A. 'The Concept of the Self in Psychoanalytic Theory and its Philosophical Foundations,' *Journal of the American Psychoanalytic Association*, 39 (1991), 157–82
——— *Having a Life: Self Pathology After Lacan* (Hillsdale, NJ: Analytic Press, 2004)
Klein, Melanie, *Love, Guilt and Reparation (1921–1945)* (London: Hogarth Press and the Institute of Psychoanalysis, 1981)
Kohon, Gregorio, ed., *The British School of Psychoanalysis: The Independent Tradition* (London: Free Association Books, 1986)
——— ed., *The Dead Mother: The Work of André Green* (London: Routledge, 1999)
Kojève, Alexander, *Introduction to the Reading of Hegel*, trans. by James Nichols, ed. by Allan Bloom (Ithaca: Cornell University Press, 1980)
Kolb, David, *The Critique of Pure Modernity: Hegel, Heidegger and After* (Chicago: University of Chicago Press, 1986)
Kristeva, Julia, *In the Beginning Was Love: Psychoanalysis and Faith*, trans. by Arthur Goldhammer (New York: Columbia University Press, 1987)
——— *Intimate Revolt: The Powers and Limits of Psychoanalysis*, trans. by Jeanine Herman (New York: Columbia University Press, 2002)
——— *New Maladies of the Soul*, trans. by Ross Guberman (New York: Columbia University Press, 1995)
——— *Revolution in Poetic Language*, trans. by Margaret Waller (New York: Columbia University Press, 1984)
——— *Strangers to Ourselves* (London: Harvester/Wheatsheaf, 1991)
Kurrik, Maire Jaanus, *Literature and Negation* (New York: Columbia University Press, 1979)
Lacan, Jacques, *Écrits: A Selection*, trans. by Alan Sheridan (London: Tavistock Publication, 1977)
——— *The Language of the Self: The Function of Language in Psychoanalysis*, trans. by Anthony Wilden (Baltimore: John Hopkins Press, 1968)
——— *The Seminar of Jacques Lacan: Book I, Freud's Papers on Technique 1953–1954*, trans. by John Forrester, ed. by Miller, Jacques-Alain Miller (Cambridge: Cambridge University Press, 1988)
——— *The Seminar of Jacques Lacan: Book II, The Ego in Freud's Theory and in the Technique of Psychoanalysis 1954–1955*, trans. by Sylvana Tomaselli, ed. by Jacques-Alain Miller (New York: Norton, 1991)
——— *The Seminar of Jacques Lacan: Seminar VII; The Ethics of Psychoanalysis 1959–60*, trans. by Dennis Porter, ed. by Jacques-Alain Miller (New York: W.W. Norton, 1992)
Laing, R. D., *Self and Others* (London: Routledge, 1999)
Lang, Hermann, *Language and the Unconscious: Jacques Lacan's Hermeneutics of Psychoanalysis*, trans. by Thomas Brockelman (Atlantic Highlands, NJ: Humanities Press, 1997)
Laplanche, Jean, *Life and Death in Psychoanalysis*, trans. by Jeffrey Mehlman (London: Johns Hopkins University Press, 1976)
Lauer, Quentin, *A Reading of Hegel's Phenomenology of Spirit* (New York: Fordham University Press, 1993)
Lecercle, Jean-Jacques and Riley, Denise, *The Force of Language* (Basingstoke: Palgrave Macmillan, 2004)

Lukacs, Georg. *The Young Hegel: Studies in the Relations between Dialectics and Economics*, trans. by Rodney Livingstone (Cambridge, MA: MIT Press, 1976)

Lyotard, Jean-Francois, *Libidinal Economy* (London: Continuum, 2004)

——— *Phenomenology*, trans. by Brian Beakley (Albany: SUNY Press, 1991)

MacCabe, Colin, ed., *The Talking Cure: Essays in Psychoanalysis and Language* (London: Macmillan, 1981)

MacIntyre, Alasdair, ed., *Hegel: A Collection of Critical Essays* (Garden City: Doubleday, 1972)

Malabou, Catherine, *Changing Difference,* trans. by Carolyn Shread (Cambridge: Polity Press, 2011)

——— *The Future of Hegel: Plasticity, Temporality and Dialectic*, trans. by Lisabeth During (London: Routledge, 2005)

Marcuse, Herbert, *Eros & Civilisation: A Philosophical Inquiry into Freud* (London: Abacus, 1972)

——— *Hegel's Ontology and the Theory of Historicity*, trans. by. Seyla Benhabib (Cambridge, MA: MIT Press, 1987)

——— *Negations: Essays in Critical Theory* (London: Free Association Books, 1988)

——— *One Dimensional Man. Studies in the Ideology of Advanced Industrial Society* (London: Routledge, 2002)

——— *Reason and Revolution: Hegel and the Rise of Social Theory* (London: Routledge, 2000)

McCumber, John, *The Company of Words: Hegel, Language and Systematic Philosophy* (Evanston, IL: Northwestern University Press, 1993)

Merleau-Ponty, Maurice, *Sense and Non-Sense,* trans. by Hubert L. Dreyfus and Patrician Allen Dreyfus (Evanston, IL: Northwestern University Press, 1964)

Mills, Jon, 'Hegel on Projective Identification: Implications for Klein, Bion, and Beyond,' *The Psychoanalytic Review*, 87:6 (2000), 841–74

——— ed., *Psychoanalysis at the Limit: Epistemology, Mind, and the Question of Science* (Albany: SUNY Press, 2004)

——— ed., *Relational and Intersubjective Perspectives in Psychoanalysis: A Critique* (New York: Rowman & Littlefield Publishers, 2005)

——— ed., *Rereading Freud: Psychoanalysis through Philosophy* (Albany: SUNY Press, 2004)

——— *The Unconscious Abyss: Hegel's Anticipation of Psychoanalysis* (Albany: SUNY Press, 2002)

Minolli, Michele and Tricoli, Maria Luisa, 'Solving the Problems of Duality: The Third and Self-Consciousness,' *Psychoanalytic Quarterly*, 73 (2004), 137–65

Mitchell, Stephen, *Relationality: From Attachment to Intersubjectivity* (Hillsdale, NJ: Analytic Press, 2000)

Mitchell, Stephen A. and Aron, Lewis, eds., *Relational Psychoanalysis: The Emergence of a Tradition* (Hillsdale, NJ: Analytic Press, 1999)

Modell, Arnold H., *The Private Self* (Cambridge, MA: Harvard University Press, 1993)

Muller, John P., *Beyond the Psychoanalytic Dyad: Developmental Semiotics in Freud, Peirce, and Lacan* (London: Routledge, 1996)

Nancy, Jean-Luc, *The Birth to Presence*, trans. Brian Holmes et al (Stanford: Stanford University Press, 1993)

——— *Hegel: The Restlessness of the Negative*, trans. by Jason Smith and Steven Miller (Minneapolis: University of Minnesota Press, 2002)

——— *The Speculative Remark: (One of Hegel's Bon Mots)*, trans. by Celine Surprenant (Stanford: Stanford University Press, 2001)

Navickas, Joseph L., *Consciousness and Reality: Hegel's Philosophy of Subjectivity* (The Hague: Martinus Nijhoff, 1976)

Ogden, Thomas H., *The Matrix of the Mind: Object Relations and the Psychoanalytic Dialogue* (London: Karnac, 1992)

——— *Subjects of Analysis* (Northvale, NJ: Jason Aronson, 1994)
O'Neill, John, ed., *Hegel's Dialectic of Desire and Recognition* (Albany: SUNY Press, 1996)
Orange, Donna M., Atwood, George E., Stolorow, Robert D., *Working Intersubjectively: Contextualism in Psychoanalytic Practice* (Hillsdale, NJ: Analytic Press, 1997)
Osborne, Peter, *The Politics of Time: Modernity and Avant-Garde* (London: Verso, 1995)
Parry, David M., *Hegel's Phenomenology of the 'We'* (Frankfurt am Main: Peter Lang, 1988)
Petry, Michael John, *Hegel and Newtonianism: Proceedings of the Cambridge Conference Hegel and Newtonianism* (Dordrecht: Kluwer Academic Publishers, 1993)
Pinkard, Terry, *Hegel: A Biography* (Cambridge: Cambridge University Press, 2000)
——— *Hegel's Phenomenology: The Sociality of Reason* (Cambridge: Cambridge University Press, 1994)
Pippin, Robert, *Hegel's Idealism: The Satisfactions of Self-Consciousness* (Cambridge: Cambridge University Press, 1989)
——— *Idealism as Modernism: Hegelian Variations* (Cambridge: Cambridge University Press, 1997)
——— *Modernism as a Philosophical Problem* (Oxford: Basil Blackwell, 1991)
——— *The Persistence of Subjectivity: On the Kantian Aftermath* (Cambridge: Cambridge University Press, 2005)
Plotnitsky, Arkady, *In the Shadow of Hegel: Complementarity, History, and the Unconscious* (Gainsville: University Press of Florida, 1993)
——— *Reconfigurations: Critical Theory and General Economy* (Gainsville: University Press of Florida, 1993)
Pribram, Karl, Inaugural Lecture: Energy and Entropy in Psychology: UCL Freud Memorial Inaugural Lectures, 'Psychoanalysis and the Natural Sciences,' Delivered May 1981
Rauch, Leo, *Hegel and the Human Spirit: A Translation of the Jena Lectures on the Philosophy of Spirit 1805–6, with Commentary* (Detroit: Wayne State University, 1983)
Rauch, Leo and Sherman, David, eds., *Hegel's Phenomenology of Self-Consciousness* (Albany: SUNY Press, 1999)
Rajan, Tilottama, *Deconstruction and the Remainders of Phenomenology: Sartre, Derrida, Foucault, Baudrillard* (Standford: Stanford University Press, 2002)
Redding, Paul, *Analytic Philosophy and the Return of Hegelian Thought* (Cambridge: Cambridge University Press, 2007)
Reid, Jeffrey, *Real Words: Language and System in Hegel* (Toronto: University of Toronto Press, 2007)
Ricoeur Paul, *Freud and Philosophy: An Essay on Interpretation*, trans. by Denis Savage (New Haven, CT: Yale University Press, 1990)
——— *Oneself as Another* (Chicago: University of Chicago Press, 1992)
Riley, Denise, *The Words of Selves: Identification, Solidarity, Irony* (Stanford: Stanford University Press, 2000)
Roberts, Julian, *German Philosophy: An Introduction* (Oxford: Polity Press, 1988)
——— *The Logic of Reflection: German Philosophy in the 20th Century* (New Haven, CT: Yale University Press, 1992)
Rockmore, Tom, *Before and After Hegel: A Historical Introduction to Hegel's Thought* (Berkeley: University of California Press, 1993)
——— *Cognition: An Introduction to Hegel's Phenomenology of Spirit* (Berkeley: University of California Press, 1997)

——— *Hegel, Idealism, and Analytic Philosophy* (New Haven, CT: Yale University Press, 2005)

Rome, Sidney and Rome, Beatrice, eds., *Philosophical Interrogations: Interrogation of Jean Wahl, conducted by Newton P. Stallknecht* (New York: Holt, Rinehart and Winston, 1964)

Rose, Gillian, *The Broken Middle: Out of our Ancient Society* (Oxford: Blackwell Publishers, 1992)

——— *Hegel Contra Sociology* (London: Athlone, 1981)

Rose, Jacqueline, *Why War? Psychoanalysis, Politics, and the Return to Melanie Klein* (Oxford: Blackwell, 1993)

Rosen, Stanley, *G.W.F Hegel: An Introduction to the Science of Wisdom*, (New Haven, CT: Yale University Press, 1974)

Roth, Michael S., *Knowing and History: Appropriations of Hegel in Twentieth-Century France* (Ithaca: Cornell University Press, 1988)

——— *Psycho-Analysis as History: Negation and Freedom in Freud* (Ithaca: Cornell University Press, 1987)

Roudinesco, Elisabeth, *Jacques Lacan & Co.: A History of Psychoanalysis in France 1925–1985*, trans. by Jeffrey Melman (Chicago: University of Chicago Press, 1990)

——— *Jacques Lacan: An Outline of a Life and a History of a System of Thought*, trans. by Barbara Bray (Cambridge: Polity Press, 1999)

Rudnytsky, Peter, *Transitional Objects and Potential Spaces: Literary Uses of D.W. Winnicott* (New York: Columbia University Press, 1993)

Russon, John, *The Self and Its Body in Hegel's Phenomenology of Spirit* (Toronto: University of Toronto Press: 1997)

Samuels, Robert, *Between Philosophy and Psychoanalysis: Lacan's Reconstruction of Freud* (London: Routledge, 1993)

Scalia, Joseph, ed., *The Vitality of Objects: Exploring the Work of Christopher Bollas* (London: Continuum, 2002)

Shamdasani, Sonu and Munchow, Michael, eds., *Speculations After Freud: Psychoanalysis, Philosophy and Culture* (London: Routledge, 1994)

Shklar, Judith, *Freedom and Independence: A Study of Hegel's Phenomenology of Mind* (Cambridge: Cambridge University Press, 1976)

Simms, Karl, *Ricoeur and Lacan* (London: Continuum, 2007)

Sinnerbrink, Robert, *Understanding Hegelianism* (Stocksfield: Acumen Press, 2007)

Smith, Joseph H., and Kerrigan, William J., eds., *Interpreting Lacan* (New Haven, CT: Yale University Press, 1983)

Solomon, Robert C., *From Hegel to Existentialism* (New York: Oxford University Press, 1987)

——— *In the Spirit of Hegel: A Study of G.W.F. Hegel's Phenomenology of Spirit* (Oxford: Oxford University Press, 1983)

Steinkraus W., ed., *New Studies in Hegel's Philosophy* (New York: Holt, Rinehart & Winston, 1971)

Stern, Robert, ed., *G.W.F. Hegel: Critical Assessments*, 4 vols (London: Routledge, 1993)

——— *Hegel and the Phenomenology of Spirit* (London: Routledge, 2002)

——— *Hegelian Metaphysics* (Oxford: Oxford University Press, 2009)

Stewart, Jon, ed., *The Hegel Myths and Legends* (Evanston, IL: Northwestern University Press, 1996)

Stolorow, Robert D., Atwood, George E., and Brandschaft, Bernard, eds., *The Intersubjective Perspective* (Northvale, NJ: Jason Aronson Inc., 1994)

Stolorow, Robert D., Brandchaft, B., Atwood, G. E., eds. 'Post-Cartesian Psychoanalytic Theory: Commentary of B.E. Reis, 'Adventures of the Dialectic,"' in *Psychoanalytic Dialogues*, 9(3): 407–14

Strauss, Jonathan, *Subjects of Terror: Nerval, Hegel, and the Modern Self* (Stanford: Stanford University Press, 1998)
Sulloway, Frank J., *Freud, Biologist of the Mind: Beyond the Psychoanalytic Legend* (Cambridge, MA: Harvard University Press, 1992)
Surber, Jere O'Neill, ed., *Hegel and Language* (Albany: SUNY Press, 2006)
Sussman, Henry, *The Hegelian Aftermath: Readings in Hegel, Kierkegaard, Freud, Proust, and James* (Baltimore: John Hopkins University, 1982)
Taylor, Charles, *Hegel* (Cambridge: Cambridge University Press, 1975)
——— *Hegel and Modern Society* (Cambridge: Cambridge University Press, 1985)
——— *Sources of the Self: The Making of Modern Identity* (Cambridge, MA: Harvard University Press, 1992)
Taylor, Mark C., *Journeys to Selfhood: Hegel and Kierkegaard* (New York: Fordham University Press, 2000)
Theunissen, Michael, *The Other: Studies in the Social Ontology of Husserl, Heidegger, Sartre, and Buber*, trans. by Christopher Macann (Cambridge, MA: MIT Press, 1984)
Toews, John Edward, *Hegelianism: The Path Toward Dialectical Humanism, 1805–1841* (Cambridge: Cambridge University Press, 1980)
Ver Eecke, Wilfried, *Denial, Negation, and the Forces of the Negative: Freud, Hegel, Lacan, Spitz, and Sophocles* (Albany: SUNY Press, 2006)
——— *Negativity and Subjectivity: A Study of the Function of Negation in Freud, Linguistics, Child Psychology and Hegel* (Brussels: Paleis Der Academien, 1977)
Verene, Donald Phillip, *Hegel's Absolute: An Introduction to Reading the Phenomenology of Spirit* (Albany: SUNY Press, 2007)
——— *Hegel's Recollection: a study of images in the Phenomenology of Spirit* (Albany: SUNY Press, 1985)
Vernon, Jim., *Hegel's Philosophy of Language* (London: Continuum, 2007)
Wagenbaur, Thomas, *The Moment: A History, Typology, and Theory of the Moment in Philosophy and Literature* (Frankfurt am Main: Peter Lang, 1993)
Wahl, Jean, *A Short History of Existentialism*, trans. by Forrest Williams and Stanley Maron (New York: Philosophical Library, 1949)
Weiss, Frederick G., *Hegel: The Essential Writings* (New York: Harper & Row, 1974)
Westphal, Kenneth R., *Hegel's Epistemological Realism: A Study of the Aim and Method of Hegel's Phenomenology of Spirit* (Dordrecht: Kluwer Academic Publishers, 1989)
——— *A Philosophical Introduction to the Phenomenology of Spirit* (Indianapolis: Hackett Publishing, 2003)
Westphal, Merold, *Method and Speculation in Hegel's Phenomenology* (Atlantic Highlands, NJ: Humanities Press, 1982)
Williams, Robert R., *Hegel's Ethics of Recognition* (Berkeley: University of California Press, 1997)
——— *Recognition: Fichte and Hegel on the Other* (Albany: SUNY Press, 1992)
Winnicott, D.W., *Home is where we start from: Essays from a Psychoanalysis* (New York: Penguin Books, 1986)
——— *Human Nature* (London: Free Association Books, 1988)
——— *Playing and Reality* (London: Routledge, 2005)
Wollheim, Richard, *Freud* (London: Harper Collins, 1991)
——— *On the Emotions* (New Haven, CT: Yale University Press, 1999)
——— ed., *Philosophers on Freud* (New York: Jason Aronson, 1974)
Žižek, Slavoj, *For They Know Not What They Do: Enjoyment as a Political Factor* (London: Verso, 2002)
——— *The Indivisible Remainder: An Essay on Schelling and Related Matter* (London: Verso, 1996)

——— *Interrogating the Real*, ed. by Rex Butler, Scott Stephens (London: Continuum, 2005)

——— *Less Than Nothing: Hegel and the Shadow of Dialectical Materialism* (London: Verso, 2012).

——— *Organs without Bodies: Deleuze and Consequences* (London: Routledge, 2004)

——— *Tarrying with the Negative: Kant, Hegel and the Critique of Ideology* (Durham: Duke University Press. 1993)

Zupančič, Alenka, *Why Psychoanalysis?: Three Interventions* (Uppsala, Sweden: Aarhus University Press, 2008).

Index